This memoir is dedicated to my wife, Andi, the blind date who won me over instantly and who continues to inspire me.

Praise for *A SCHOOL OF THEIR OWN*

A School of Their Own is a vivid and important account of Mike Gross's remarkable half-century mission fighting for Navajo legal rights, especially the right to control their own schools. The book is full of fascinating and poignant stories, unforgettable portraits, and historic legal victories overcoming the dark legacy of boarding schools and forced assimilation. Anyone interested in the history of the Navajo Nation and its struggle for self-determination should read this extraordinary memoir.

> — **Douglas Preston**, #1 New York Times bestselling author and journalist

This is a must-read for anyone curious about how the national tragedy of Native American boarding schools and forced assimilation came to a screeching halt, thanks to the people who ushered in the Indian Self-Determination and Education Assistance Act of 1975.

> — **Bobbie Greene Kilberg**, former White House Fellow; CEO and President Emeritus and Strategic Advisor, Northern Virginia Technology Council

Finding himself in the hotbed of the Civil Rights Movement in 1966, Gross hoped to practice poverty law. But his first case to reopen a high school in a remote Navajo community convinced him to advocate for equally underserved American citizens. It was a journey that lasted more than five decades.

> — **John Echohawk** (Pawnee), Attorney and Co-Founder, Native American Rights Fund

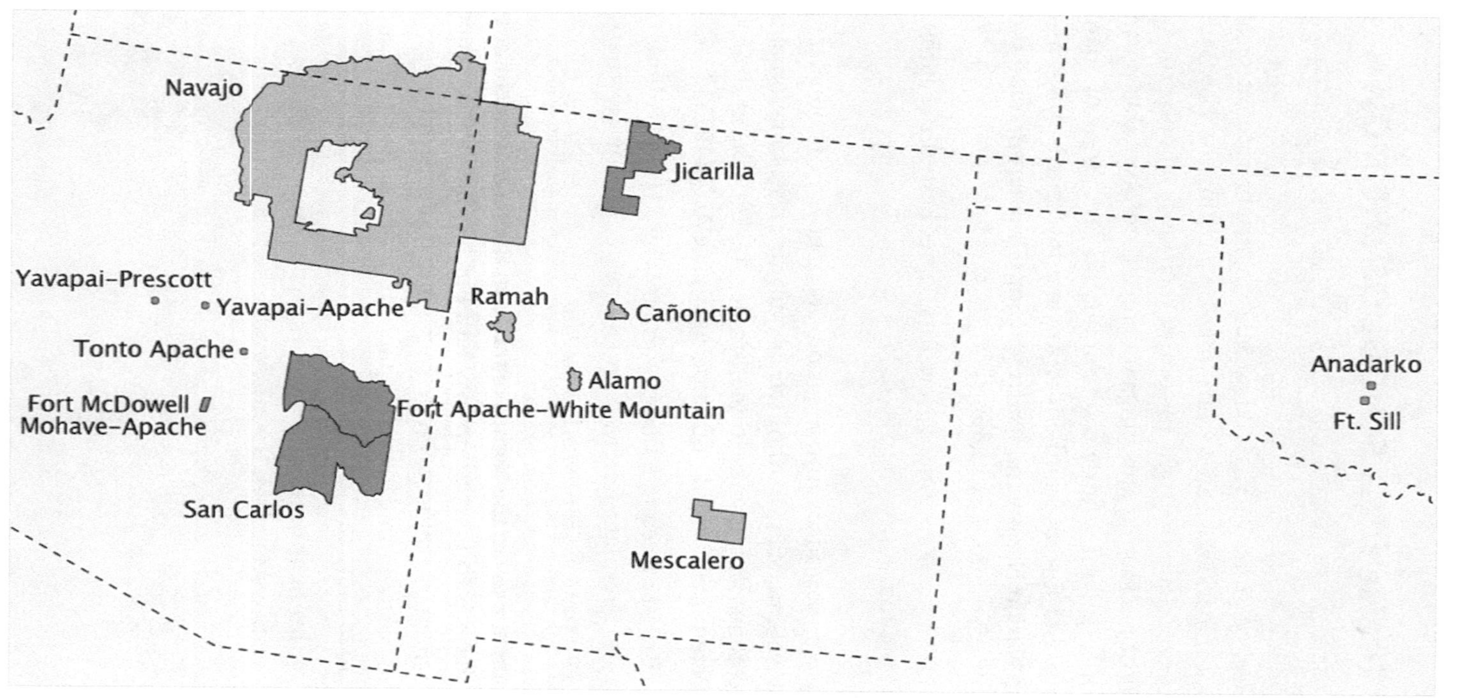

Map of the Navajo Nation and Apache Reservations

A SCHOOL OF THEIR OWN

Michael P. Gross

Cover art: Ramah Navajo weaving
Cover and page design by Anna Myers Sabatini

Paperback ISBN: 978-1-971030-02-9   Ebook ISBN: 978-1-971030-03-6

Green Fire Press
PO Box 377 Housatonic MA 01236

Publisher's Cataloging-in-Publication Data

Names: Gross, Michael P., 1942–, author.
Title: A school of their own : a tenacious lawyer and his Navajo clients' fight for Indian
self-determination, from remote New Mexico to the Supreme Court / Michael P. Gross.
Description: Includes bibliographical references. | Housatonic, MA: Green Fire Press, 2026.
Identifiers: LCCN: 2026901928 | ISBN: 978-1-971030-02-9 (paperback) |
978-1-971030-03-6 (ebook)
Subjects: LCSH Gross, Michael P. | Civil rights lawyers—United States—Biography.
| Navajo Indians—Education. | Education and state—Navajo Nation, Arizona, New
Mexico & Utah. | Navajo Indians—Government relations. | Education—New Mexico.
| Navajo Indians—Civil rights. | Navajo Indians—History | BISAC BIOGRAPHY &
AUTOBIOGRAPHY / Lawyers & Judges | LAW / Civil Rights | LAW / Indigenous Law &
Legal Systems | LAW / Legal History | LAW / Educational Law & Legislation

A SCHOOL OF THEIR OWN

A tenacious lawyer and his Navajo clients' fight
for Indian self-determination, from remote
New Mexico to the Supreme Court

Michael P. Gross

Green
Fire
Press

Housatonic
Massachusetts

CONTENTS

FOREWORD

BY ALFRED D. MATHEWSON

Emeritus Professor of Law and former Co-Dean,
University of New Mexico School of Law

Attorney Michael Gross came to visit me in my dean's office to discuss a donation he and his wife, Andi Gross, wished to make to the University of New Mexico Law School. We began our meeting by sharing our personal stories. It turns out that he too is a Yale Law School graduate, having finished ten years earlier than me. He expressed an interest in creating a forum for dialogue between Blacks and Native Americans, based on his participation in the Brown-Tougaloo Partnership as an undergraduate at Brown and later, in his Indian law practice in New Mexico.

Over the next four years, Mr. Gross led me on a journey, collaborating with Brown University and Tougaloo College to develop and stage a summer undergraduate research course on the shared histories of the descendants of involuntary Americans, with classes taking the form of dialogue circles on Zoom three hours a day for three weeks with students from Brown, Tougaloo, and the University of New Mexico. The course was dubbed "The Conversation." My collaboration with Mr. Gross on The Conversation led to a friendship inspired not only by our Yale connection, but also by our personal journeys in America. Mr. Gross's grandparents were Jewish immigrants who fled to the U.S. during the rise of the Nazis in Austria; my parents were HBCU graduates who raised seven children under Jim Crow segregation in North Carolina.

Mr. Gross has had an amazing life and career. He has been a witness to and an active participant in historic events. I remember seeing news coverage of James Meredith's entry into the University of Mississippi in 1962. When Meredith subsequently led his March Against Fear in 1966, Mr. Gross was there, deepening his commitment to pursue a more just society, which inspired his pathbreaking career practicing Indian law. This book about his life and career reminds me of Richard Kluger's *Simple Justice*, only this book, chronicling the fight to improve Indian-controlled

"

schools and advance legal self-determination for Indian tribes, is told by a lawyer deeply involved in that fight. It's a very personal story. Mr. Gross is quite modest in recounting his story with rich details that reflect a truly remarkable memory. He does not merely take the reader through important events—he is able to talk about interactions with people who played pivotal roles in these events.

Mr. Gross and I have had numerous conversations in the few years that I have known him. Quite frankly, I am embarrassed to say that I had not realized that I had been hanging out with a Civil Rights icon until I was offered the opportunity to read his manuscript. He takes the reader through his involvement in cases without any hint of their importance in the pantheon of Indian law. For example, I learned of the Indian Civil Rights Act in the course of my career. I was blown away when he mentions his encounter with it in its infancy, very early in his legal career. Mr. Gross was in the room or on the scene at the birth of the Indian Self-Determination Act, a major piece of legislation authorizing Indian tribes to run their own federally funded programs, instead of federal agencies. Mr. Gross played a significant role in its passage. He has twice taken cases to the United States Supreme Court and won: *Ramah Navajo School Board, Inc. v. Bureau of Revenue of New Mexico* (2003) on state imposition of gross receipts tax on a construction contract between a non-Indian company and a tribe; and *Salazar v. Ramah Navajo Chapter* (2016), perhaps the crowning accomplishment of his stellar career, in which the Supreme Court upheld a nearly billion-dollar judgment that he won for his tribal clients. Mr. Gross' involvement went well beyond the Supreme Court cases. He worked in the trenches with Indian tribes to open and operate their own schools.

True to his nature, Mr. Gross does not tell his story as though his achievements were accomplished alone, recounting the role of others who were significant players in his legal work. He expresses his deep admiration for his former law partner, C. Bryant Rogers, who worked with him to advance Indian self-determination in the Supreme Court cases. Hailing from Mississippi, Rogers shares a spirited interview that includes his own courageous activities during the Civil Rights movement. Their collaboration included *Omaha Tribe of Nebraska v. Swanson,* in which it mattered whether they could prove that Iowa was east of Nebraska. Among the highlights of the book are the transcripts of interviews with, in addition to Bryant Rogers, Anita Pfeiffer, Beverly Coho and Bessie

Randolph (formerly Begay), Mary Cohoe, Betty Gress, John Loehr, and John Amarant, all leaders in the Indian-led education movement.

I am indeed honored to have been asked to write the foreword to this autobiographical tome by such a highly accomplished American lawyer.

INTRODUCTION

BY KEVIN WASHBURN

Professor of Law at UC Berkeley School of Law and a citizen of the Chickasaw Nation, Kevin Washburn served as Assistant Secretary of Indian Affairs at the U.S. Department of Interior in President Barack Obama's Administration, from 2012 to 2016.

In 2011, the Supreme Court granted certiorari in *Salazar v. Ramah Navajo Chapter*. It was Michael Gross's case, and he had been Ramah Navajo School Board's attorney for more than 40 years. It was a very productive career in which he reached the U.S. Supreme Court not once, but twice for the same small client.

The case was about an important, but arcane area of the law governed by the Indian Self-Determination and Educational Assistance Act of 1975, usually shortened to "Indian Self-Determination Act," or "ISDA." This law allows tribes to take over the functions provided by federal agencies, initially the Bureau of Indian Affairs (BIA) and the Indian Health Service (IHS), but it has since been expanded to several other agencies, too.

In ISDA, Congress authorized tribes not only to take over federal functions but to receive the share of federal funding that the BIA or IHS would have spent to provide the same federal services. This meant that tribal employees would displace federal employees. The theory is that tribes can serve themselves better, and thus more successfully meet the treaty and trust responsibilities of the federal government to tribes, than federal agencies and employees can.

ISDA was slow to be implemented. One can imagine how federal employees felt about being displaced in this way. Many of them were lifelong public servants earnestly trying to help Native people. Even some of them who liked the idea in principle likely were not excited about being forced to give up their federal employment or move their families. Others viewed the law as a vote of no confidence in their work. Moreover, from a more cynical perspective, power is a zero-sum game, and this law very explicitly was designed to take power from federal officials and place that very same power in the hands of tribal officials.

Soon after the law began to be implemented, it became clear that funding for the direct services performed by the BIA and IHS was not sufficient. Tribes have needed to not only provide the direct services but manage the contracts, prepare budgets, hire and fire employees and provide benefits. The BIA and the IHS had offices and staffing to provide these services, but ISDA only required the federal government to contract with tribes for the direct costs of running the programs. To be successful, tribal governments also needed additional funding to cover all of the administrative costs that accompany this work. The costs are akin to the funding that research hospitals and universities receive when implementing federal grants, sometimes referred to as finance and administrative ("F&A") or "indirect" costs. For some universities, these indirect costs are more than 50 percent of the amount of the direct costs, and they are key to ensuring that a university can realistically provide the services which they are contracted to provide.

Congress eventually amended ISDA to allow tribes to recover such costs, called "contract support costs" in the ISDA context, but such costs, though real, were not politically popular. It was easy for a federal policymaker or legislator to understand the importance of providing funding for a tribal doctor or nurse or police officer, but not so much for appropriating millions of dollars for "administrative" costs. Contract support costs were, however, required by federal law.

Or were they? Though contract support costs were required explicitly by law, Congress also imposed an explicit limit each year on appropriations to cover the costs. In sum, Congress had enacted somewhat contradictory provisions. Thus, it was a live issue as to whether the law was enforceable.

Congress was not the only entity to blame for these circumstances. In the annual budget development process, which results in the Green Book that the President sends to Congress each year to request funding for the following year, the Executive Branch routinely failed to ask Congress for adequate funding

Enter Michael Gross.

The requirements of ISDA are technical, and this area of the law is considered somewhat arcane by most practicing lawyers, even those who regularly practice federal Indian law. For those reasons, the law and the cases interpreting it are not routinely taught in the law school course on federal Indian law.

Few crusaders for social justice have the willingness to do the hard work of parsing complex and perhaps uninteresting, bureaucratic rules of the ISDA. But Gross was unusual. He was tenacious, detail-oriented, and he had a passion for helping this particular client—Ramah Navajo was Gross's first client. He fought for the principles of Indian self-determination for more than 40 years.

Gross was fully committed to the idealistic aims of the ISDA, and he was practical enough to realize that those aims could never be fully realized without ensuring that the contract support costs provisions were properly implemented. With colleagues, he filed a class action, which ensured that not only his clients would benefit, but all tribes similarly situated. That action was originally filed in 1990, and it produced a win in the Tenth Circuit U.S. Court of Appeals in 1997[1] on what was initially the only claim pled in the case. That claim was settled for $76 million in 1999 for the initial years covered by that claim.[2] Later, after the class action complaint was amended to add two additional claims for recovery of contract support costs, a second partial settlement was reached for $29 million for one year on one of those claims,[3] and a third settlement agreement was approved granting equitable relief to the class on its claims in 2008.[4] The class later prevailed on its remaining money damages claims in the Tenth Circuit in 2011.[5]

The win was significant but was not a complete victory, however. The thorough majority opinion had drawn a lengthy dissent from the New Mexico judge on the panel, Harris Hartz.

Likely drawn to the financial significance of the case and the lengthy dissent by an able circuit court judge, the Supreme Court took certiorari in the case and agreed to hear the case in October Term 2012. After the narrow victory in the Tenth Circuit, it must have been demoralizing for Gross and his colleagues to know that they would have to continue fighting.

1. *Ramah Navajo Chapter v. Lujan*, 112 F. 3d 1455 (10th Cir. 1997)
2. *Ramah Navajo Chapter v. Babbitt*, 1999 WL 35794 068 (D.N.M.)
3. *Ramah Navajo Chapter v. Norton*, 250 F. Supp.2d 1303 (D.N.M.) 2002
4. *Ramah Navajo Chapter v. Kempthorne*, 2008 WL 11342943 (D.N.M.)
5. *Ramah Navajo Chapter v. Salazar*, 644 F.3d 1054 (10th Cir. 2011).

The challenge was significant. In Indian country, the United States has entered into hundreds of treaties with Indian tribes and failed to comply with most of them. American history is littered with "sacred" treaties ignored not long after the ink had dried. To prevail, Gross needed a more compelling argument than another broken promise to tribes.

Working with co-class counsel C. Bryant Rogers and Lloyd Miller, Gross and his colleagues realized at the Supreme Court phase that one of the keys to litigating the case would be to frame the issue as whether the federal government must meet its obligations not just to Indian tribes but to anyone who contracts with the federal government. While treaties have been made and broken for two centuries, government contracts are crucial to the workings of the United States government, including national security.

A stroke of brilliance was landing an amicus brief from the U.S. Chamber of Commerce. As a law school dean, I have often joked that I will take money from the devil himself if it would help me educate law students. I remember smiling when I learned that the National Defense Industrial Association had signed on to the Chamber of Commerce brief. I wonder if the young attorney who started serving the Ramah Navajo in 1970 would have imagined that he would someday jump into bed with the military industrial complex to help him preserve tribal self-determination.

The framing was perfect. Treated as a contracts issue, the case implicated the interests not just of Indian tribes, but many other government contractors. It was good lawyering, and it ultimately produced a close but significant victory.

When the decision was issued by the Supreme Court in late June of 2012, I was the dean of the law school at the University of New Mexico. On that day, I was in Washington, D.C., meeting in the offices of United States Senator Tom Udall in the Hart Senate Office Building. I walked across the street to the Supreme Court and asked the clerk for some copies of the slip opinion, which I distributed to the offices of Senator Udall and the state's then senior Senator, Jeff Bingaman. It was a glorious victory and, at the time, an unexpected one. The U.S. Supreme Court rarely granted cert in an Indian law case to rule in favor of a tribe when the tribes had won below. At 5-4, the win was also very close, and it was a very unusual lineup, with Scalia and Thomas joining Sotomayor's majority opinion, but Ginsburg and Breyer joining the dissent by Chief Justice Roberts. In sum, it was an odd but huge victory. After more than two decades of litigation, I recall being happy that the case was concluded.

A few months later, just a couple of months before the 2012 Presidential election, I was nominated by President Obama to become his Assistant Secretary for Indian Affairs at the U.S. Department of the Interior.

It was an unusual time to take such a nomination because of the risk President Obama might lose the election. In an election year, my nomination might not be taken up by the Senate, and even if it did and I was confirmed, Obama could have lost, and I would have had the shortest tenure of any Assistant Secretary in history.

However, the Senate took up the nomination quickly. Senator Jeff Bingaman's chief of staff, Trudy Vincent, made it her mission to ensure that my nomination moved forward. Presumably, Republicans did not want to be accused of harming Indian country in an election year by slow-walking Obama's nomination.

After a round of private meetings with Senators, my only opposition was Senator Dianne Feinstein, a Democrat. In my meeting with her, the Senator complained that Obama's previous Assistant Secretary nominee was dishonest with her. She said that he assured her that he did not like Indian gaming any more than she did, but then he recused from all Indian gaming matters and thus he never put his convictions into action. She said that she felt misled by him. I told her that I would not mislead her. I told her that I would hear her out on any issue, but that being opposed to Indian gaming was not an option. I firmly believed that Indian gaming was the most important tribal economic development initiative in American history, and it would be my duty to support and defend it. That was not the answer she wanted to hear. She initially refused to release her hold on my nomination, but a friend, Bob Shrum, succeeded in getting her to drop her opposition.

At my confirmation hearing, I made clear that my primary professional commitments were to tribal sovereignty and self-determination. I spent most of the time explaining how ISDA had changed the lives of members of my tribe, the Chickasaw Nation.

Throughout our childhood, my siblings and I had used hospitals and dental clinics run by the Indian Health Service in Talihina and Ada, Oklahoma. As a single mother of three children, my mother found that if one child had an appointment, it was best to take all three children because appointments were rarely on time. Consequently, we were familiar with the IHS system. Around the time I left for law school, the leader of my tribe, Governor Bill Anoatubby, decided to use ISDA to contract to take over the IHS healthcare operations for the Chickasaw Nation, including the Carl Albert Indian Hospital.

Though the decision to contract the IHS functions seems obvious in hindsight, it was a risky political action for a relatively new tribal leader. Members of my extended family were skeptical about the ability of the tribe to run a federal facility better than federal employees. I remember an aunt and uncle grumbling that Chickasaws could not run the healthcare facility better than the federal government, and they criticized Governor Anoatubby for taking a risk about something as important as healthcare. It did not take long, though, for things to change. After just a few months, it was clear that the delivery of healthcare in the Chickasaw Nation was improving, and tribal citizens were happy with tribal control.

All the handwringing about the Governor's decision demonstrates why ISDA works. By taking over the hospital, Governor Anoatubby made himself responsible for the success or failure of healthcare for the Chickasaw Nation, and he was directly accountable to the Chickasaw people. If it had not gone well, he likely would have been ousted in the next election. Governor Anoatubby showed great courage in taking on this responsibility, and it was ISDA that empowered him to exercise such bravery. It is clear now that Governor Anoatubby believed in the Chickasaw people before they fully believed in themselves. His loyalty and vision were rewarded by his voters. In 2026, Governor Anoatubby continues his decades of service as Governor.

Shortly after explaining my commitment to tribal self-determination by relating these events, my nomination moved out of the Senate Committee to the floor, and I was confirmed unanimously by the U.S. Senate.

Shortly after I took office, two things happened. First, President Obama won re-election. Second, I was summoned by White House staff to meet with the Office of Management and Budget (OMB) and the IHS to discuss the Ramah Navajo decision and contract support costs. OMB was preparing the Green Book to send to Congress to ask for appropriations for the operation of the federal government and wanted to discuss the issue.

It was a heady time, my first White House meeting, and I was very excited to be there. Given that the Supreme Court decision had been crystal clear that the law required the federal government to pay the full contract support costs required by the ISDA, I did not expect a difficult meeting.

When the meeting began, approximately twenty longtime career employees and political staff from across government were present, seated at tables that had been placed in a large square with an open center so that we could all face one another. As the discussion proceeded around the room, giving each representative an opportunity to explain their views, I was stunned to learn that the tenor of the meeting was *against* including contract support costs in the President's budget request. It appeared that the Department of Justice (DOJ), the IHS, and the OMB had been fighting the issue for years and were not inclined to let a mere Supreme Court opinion change their approach. As the conversation went around the room and people spoke, I began to fume. As a person who started his career as a DOJ lawyer, I have always believed strongly in the rule of law. I could not believe what I was hearing. As people kept talking as though the decision was still unsettled, I became angrier and angrier. By the time it was my turn to speak, I was livid. A tirade came forth. Emotions were high and I cannot recall exactly what I said, but my staff referred to the meeting forever thereafter as "the F-bomb meeting." In my first White House meeting, I had lost my cool and probably had embarrassed myself.

But it got results. I was the shiny new thing, the most recent recruit to the team, and I outranked everyone else in the room. The new guy threw a fit and it made a difference. The Greenbook for Fiscal Year 2014 included more than $230 million to cover tribal contract support costs at the Department of the Interior. The language explaining the request explicitly referenced the Ramah Navajo case in the justification, demonstrating the importance of Michael Gross's victory.[6]

After the victory, I had not followed the developments in the Ramah Navajo case. I had assumed that, though it was close, it was the end of the matter. I later learned that more work was needed to fully resolve the case. The case had been remanded to the federal district court in New Mexico where the parties continued to litigate. The Supreme Court had rejected

6. FY 2014 Greenbook for Indian Affairs, https://www.bia.gov/sites/default/files/dup/assets/as-ia/ocfo/ocfo/pdf/idc1-021730.pdf

the government's primary defense to liability, but there remained other serious questions about liability and jurisdiction[7] regarding the class claims and disputes about how damages for past amounts not paid should be calculated. The litigation was not over.

I learned that little progress toward settlement had been made because both sides had hired expert witnesses and were working on methodologies for determining damages. Both sides were steeling themselves and preparing for what could be several more years of litigation.

The Department of the Interior has very little role of leverage over a matter in litigation in the federal courts. While the attorney client relationship generally places the client in a position of control in most circumstances, that relationship is turned upside-down in the federal government. The Department of Justice has absolute primacy when a case reaches federal courts. In this case, the damages would be taken from the Judgment Fund (31 U.S.C. §1301), which is controlled by the U.S. Department of the Treasury but can be used by the Justice Department to pay judgments against the United States on contract claims. I cared about the issue, so I reached out to an old law school classmate who was in charge of the litigation, Assistant Attorney General Stuart Delery of the Civil Division at the Department of Justice. I offered my view of the importance of the case and encouraged resolution. Delery thanked me for the call but was non-committal.

Sometime later, in the fall of 2015, a settlement conference was set in Albuquerque. Though the Department of the Interior had little authority, Gross and his colleagues asked the Department of Justice to include me in the settlement negotiations. I gather that they told the DOJ lawyers that it would increase their trust in the process.

The case was a law school reunion of sorts. At the federal prep meeting at the Department of Justice, I learned that Stuart Delery had been elevated to Deputy Attorney General; the chief of the Federal Programs Section, John Griffiths, another law school classmate, was now in charge.

---

7. See *Menominee Tribe of Wisconsin v. U.S.*, 577 U.S. 250, 257-258 (2016) (reaffirming that a tribe seeking to recover damages under the Contract Disputes Act for the government's failure to pay contract support costs per an ISDA contract must present its own claim to a government contracting officer.

In light of the huge potential value of the case, Delery remained involved. Griffiths received settlement authority from Delery and an Acting Assistant Attorney General, and I traveled to Albuquerque with several DOJ lawyers.

The settlement negotiations began in the morning and continued through the afternoon. The judge was a senior U.S. District Court Judge known as "Gentleman Jim" Parker and we used his courtroom. I had been involved in many cases before Judge Parker as a federal prosecutor in New Mexico in the 1990s and, despite the fact that he was a graduate of the University of Texas, I had invited him to give the commencement speech when I was the dean at University of New Mexico (UNM) Law School. He had not disappointed. He assigned the Chief Magistrate Judge Karen Molzen, whom I had known a long time, to serve as the mediator.

As I recall, we met together to learn the ground rules and then Judge Molzen sent us out of the courtroom, separating the counsel for the tribes and the federal defendants in different rooms. She then began going back and forth between the two groups taking offers. After several rounds, in the middle of the afternoon, Judge Molzen came into the small room where the DOJ lawyers and I were huddled and said, "I have good news—you are only $100 million apart," and then she stopped herself, laughed, and said that she had never had a case in her entire career where a gap like that would be considered good news. Later that day, Judge Molzen helped us close the gap. By late afternoon, a tentative settlement was reached for $940 million, and the settlement was later approved by Judge Parker with no opposition from any class member.

We held a press conference at the U.S. Attorney's Office to announce the settlement. On a press call soon thereafter, I expressed great satisfaction, but still stinging from the White House meeting a few years back, I could not help myself from quoting the famous Winston Churchill aphorism: "the United States can always be trusted to do the right thing … once all other possibilities have been exhausted." Interior Secretary Sally Jewell, who was also on the call with me on the other side of a conference table, looked over at me wide-eyed, shook her head, and then grinned. Her look indicated acceptance of the idea that "you can take the man off the reservation, but you cannot take away rez humor!" To her relief, I think, the press did not print that quote.

I was quoted in the Department of Justice press release as follows:[8]

"Time and again, we have seen that when a tribal government runs a federal program, the program is more successful and more responsive to the tribal community," said Assistant Secretary Washburn. "Today's proposed settlement, together with President Obama's request for full, mandatory funding of tribal contract support costs in the future, removes one of the significant obstacles to tribal self-determination and self-governance. Tribes can now be confident that the federal government will pay sufficient costs to allow them to be successful in running federal programs."

The settlement was one of the largest in history with tribal nations. Michael Gross won a fight that had taken many years. The Department of Justice noted that the case had been pending through the administrations of four presidents, and the settlement occurred more than six and a half years into the Obama administration. During the time he litigated the case, he must have faced dozens and dozens of federal lawyers. Ramah Navajo had one persistent, committed attorney and they never wore him down.

Persistence and resilience have always been identified as Indian traits, but the person who started the Ramah Navajo case as a young Jewish lawyer from New Jersey proved that his well of resilience is as deep as any Native American's. To understand the continuing importance of Gross's victory, the Biden administration asked Congress for more than $420 million in contract support costs for tribes for Fiscal Year 2025. A lot of good people have fought over the decades for tribal sovereignty and self-determination, but no single person has been more important than Michael Gross in making this federal policy successful. It is remarkable that he accomplished this with his clients without

8. Press Release, Office of Public Affairs, Department of Justice, *Interior, Justice Departments Announce $940 Million Landmark Settlement with Nationwide Class of Tribes and Tribal Entities* (Sept. 17, 2015), https://www.justice.gov/archives/opa/pr/interior-justice-departments-announce-940-million-landmark-settlement-nationwide-class-tribes

serving in any federal office. That is not only a testament to Michael Gross; it is also a testament to a commitment to the rule of law, and a system that forces the United States government to obey the law even when Congress and the Executive Branch are reluctant.

Michael Gross, Kevin Washburn and C. Bryant Rogers

MY LUCKY BREAK

On a bright Saturday in late October 1966, I was throwing a football back and forth with my housemate Dave Brown on the beach outside our rented house on Connecticut's Long Island Sound. We had just started our second year of law school at Yale. Without warning, he suddenly changed our game from touch to tackle. At six foot three, Dave was a half foot taller than me. While most of me twisted to my left, my right ankle caught in the sand. We both heard my ankle snap like a piece of kindling.

Dave offered to drive me to the Yale Infirmary, but I declined. There was a dance at the law school that evening, and I was meeting a young lady from a nearby women's college on a blind date. Arriving a few minutes later, she took one look at me all crunched up with my leg bandaged, turned around and disappeared. I called Dave, and he promptly came back to pick me up.

At the beach house, Jane Kellogg, my law school friend Bob's wife, looked after me all night. They rented a house a few yards away from ours. Applying ice to my foot, neither of us slept a wink. The next morning, Dave kindly chauffeured me to the Yale infirmary. There my suspicion was confirmed: indeed, I had fractured my foot. After repositioning my ankle, the doctors at Yale-New Haven Hospital fitted me with a toe-to-hip cast.

Throughout that fall semester, Dave acted as my personal chauffeur, bringing me to and from classes every weekday. With my loaded backpack, I crutched my way around the large, neogothic campus to get to my classes and the numerous libraries. My professors were kind and did all they could to assure a modicum of law would find its way into my brain. Still, I had missed some classes, but perhaps more critically, I missed the fall hiring season for summer clerkships. Getting a summer job between second and third year is not required but recommended. Just after my injury, the law school bulletin boards had been crowded with announcements from fancy Wall Street law practices or other prestigious firms from around the country.

Once I returned in January after spending the holidays at home in New Jersey, the bulletin boards were bare. My chances of finding a summer clerkship had dimmed, and I was disconsolate as the empty boards silently screamed, "You lost out, buddy."

Then, in February, a lone business card appeared on the bulletin board. A law firm called Brown, Vlassis & Bain in Phoenix, Arizona, was seeking two summer clerks. A partner would arrive in a few days to interview. But Phoenix, Arizona, where daytime temperatures soar above 100 degrees in the shade and where right-wing politicians like loudmouth Senator Barry Goldwater were denouncing minorities on national TV? I wondered if Phoenix could possibly have prestigious law firms comparable to those on the coasts or in big cities like Chicago. With no other option, I signed up for an interview. Randy Bain was engaging and friendly. A few days later, the firm's founder, Jack Brown, offered me a summer clerkship and I grabbed it. That proved to be my lucky break.

Jack Brown, a Harvard-trained attorney, had begun his career several decades earlier with the Wall Street firm Cravath, Swain & Moore, serving an international clientele. When Jack's wife needed a dry climate for medical reasons, they moved to Phoenix where Jack opened his own practice and hired five spry young lawyers. With client referrals from Cravath, his new practice blossomed and quickly became a southwestern fixture. When I arrived in the summer of 1967, just two years after it had been established, Brown Vlassis & Bain had already become an exciting new flower on Phoenix's legal landscape. The work was challenging, my colleagues congenial, and the office magnificently air-conditioned. Jack's wife's health improved, and I adapted to searing daytime temperatures, which quickly moderated when the sun went down. But another problem still hovered: the Vietnam War was raging, and I received yet another draft summons.

I had been drafted for military service twice before arriving in Phoenix. I had signed up years earlier, feeling obliged to serve. I owed my existence to this country. In early 1939 my parents, their parents, and several other close relatives managed to escape from Nazi Austria to the United States, a story which I will tell.

As with the previous draft visits, I arrived at the Phoenix draft headquarters bright and early for a daylong battery of examinations to test my physical and mental competencies. And just as before, I was rejected for service because of the screw in my ankle. At that point I was relieved—I wanted to finish my legal studies, thinking I might not ever get a law degree if I interrupted my legal education.

That summer my mentor was Paul Eckstein, three years my elder. A Harvard Law graduate and one of Jack Brown's partners, he first asked me to help with a pro bono case he was handling for the ACLU. Without any due process or hearing, Phoenix police were routinely sweeping up drunken vagabonds from the streets at night and simply dumping them in jail cells until they sobered up. Days later, they would be deposited back to where they had been found, only to repeat the same drill over and over. This was merely a cosmetic effort to remove unsightly people from the downtown area without any attempt to rehabilitate them.

Paul and I worked to bring due process and real policy reform to the city's vagrancy problem. In short order he filed a lawsuit against the city and managed to end the abusive operation. The lesson for me was that practicing law to help society is a duty every licensed lawyer needs to perform, pay or no pay. Although Yale also taught that lawyers owe a duty to humankind as a whole, Paul demonstrated that the legal profession is more than a path to a lucrative career. I learned that sound, legal research and analysis are essential, along with excellent legal writing, skillful and honest presentation of cases and opinions to clients and courts, and courtesy toward everyone—especially opponents, judges and their staff. All people are entitled to representation by competent lawyers, and pro bono legal work is therefore required.

Nevertheless, I still felt guilty about not serving in the military. I thought that a stint practicing poverty law would be a good way to serve my country while getting practical training. That's when Jack Brown himself came into the picture as a mentor.

Every Friday that summer, Jack would fly off on a Frontier Airlines prop Douglas DC-6 or in a small, rented plane to the small city of Gallup, New Mexico, quite a distance northeast of Phoenix and just outside the Arizona border. When I asked what he was doing, he told me he was on the board of a War on Poverty legal services program, DNA Legal Services (DNA is an abbreviation for the Navajo phrase *Diné be'iiná Náhiiłna be Agha'diit'ahii*—Lawyers Who Work for the Economic Revitalization of the People) based in Window Rock, Arizona. He told me it was the government seat of the Navajo, the nation's most populous Indian tribe. Their reservation is the largest in the nation, occupying much of northeast Arizona, northwest New Mexico and a sliver of Utah, an area larger than

Rhode Island, Connecticut and New Jersey combined. Jack also explained that Arizona Senator Barry Goldwater was a militant foe of the War on Poverty and was especially incensed about DNA, which was staffed by hippie lawyers fresh out of law school. DNA Director Ted Mitchell, an ex-Mormon who grew up in Phoenix, was a Harvard-trained lawyer not much older than his neophyte colleagues.

Since their arrival in the "New World," the overlord European colonists had run roughshod over Native lands from coast to coast. Centuries later, Native Americans continue to be dispossessed, their treaties broken. Indian reservations, drawn up by the federal government, are but remnants of tribal ancestral homelands. The formal dispossession began in Georgia with the Cherokee Treaty of Hopewell in 1785. Entire tribes were relocated to strange lands, depending on how valuable their homelands were in the eyes of *bilagáanas* (white men in Navajo). Some tribes were forced to share a reservation with others.

By the 1960s the Navajos, like many if not most Native groups, were destitute. I learned from Jack Brown that exploitative pawn shops, crooked car dealers, and other non-Indian sleazes were still cheating Navajos routinely. Along with fat cats who had migrated to the sunny Southwest from colder, more populated parts of the U.S., these self-righteous Anglos were Goldwater's principal supporters. Jack told me that the DNA legal program needed lawyers to help fight the right-wing scourge led by Goldwater.

Little did I know that a broken ankle would determine my unlikely trajectory, propelling me away from the typical Ivy-league beeline to a prestigious and profitable profession in influential East Coast circles. Instead, I was launched on a tumultuous half-century's journey, fighting to improve Indian education and the idea of self-determination, the right of Indians to govern themselves without losing their federal protections, lands and services. But I also had help from connections made at my alma maters, Brown University and Yale Law School. And the natural symbiosis I felt in the Navajos' struggles were tied to my own family history.

This then, is the odyssey of a child of Holocaust refugees who wound up practicing Indian law in America and helped to bring about the promise for Native peoples made by those elegant but only partially successful international bodies, the League of Nations and the United Nations.

MY STORY

My parents came from Vienna. In March 1938, without significant opposition, Hitler took over Austria in what was called *der Anschluss* (the Annexation). The vast majority of Austrians welcomed Hitler. Antisemitism had been present in Austria and throughout central Europe since the Middle Ages. After the Anschluss, it became far worse.

Jews began migrating to Europe from the Middle East just before the rise of the Roman Empire (27 BCE). Growth of trade and commerce across the Mediterranean required contracts and ways to adjudicate disputes under them. As far back as two thousand years ago, Jews universally taught their children (albeit only boys) how to read and write. This religiously inspired custom created the first body of people trained in literacy in Europe, North Africa and the Middle East.[9] As ships became sturdier, commerce across the Mediterranean grew, and Jews were sought after for written legal agreements.

At first, Jews were welcomed. They helped grease the wheels of international commerce generally. They became indispensable, and their unique abilities helped grow international trade to unimagined dimensions. For that reason, kings and potentates welcomed them. But over time, prejudices arose as Jews became urbanized and wealthy without ties to the land.

At the time of the Anschluss, most Austrian as well as German Jews were completely assimilated. To this day my favorite meal remains the Austrian national meal—*Schnitzel* (breaded veal cutlets Viennese style). By outward appearance, most Austrian Jews were like other Austrians—they dressed alike and spoke the same heavily accented Austrian version of German.

My father, Karl, was the second of three sons, born to Josef and Malvina Grosz. He loved classical music and learned to play the piano at

9. Botticini, M. and Eckstein, V. *The Chosen Few: How Education Shaped Jewish History*, 70-1492, Princeton University Press (2012).

a young age. Late one evening in May 1938, when he was 27, he and his younger brother Robert were working late in their father's tailor shop when the Gestapo entered and arrested them. They were taken to Dachau concentration camp outside Munich where they were imprisoned for four months before being shipped to Buchenwald in what later became East Germany during the Cold War. That labor camp was near the city of Weimar, the historical home of Goethe, Schiller and the birthplace of the Weimar Republic where Hitler rose to power. Upon their arrest, their older brother Max immediately managed to escape Vienna through Switzerland and made it to the United States, where he joined the Army. The Army sent him to North Africa to translate for its German prisoners.

Karl and Robert spent five months in Buchenwald, where life was brutal. They were given just a piece of bread and a cup of watery soup a day and carried out forced labor. It was still before the war, and concentration camps had not yet become death camps, although prisoners were shot, and many of them died from mistreatment. While imprisoned, my father lost much of his hearing from illness due to freezing living conditions. He wore hearing aids for the rest of his life.

I grew up listening to Austrian-accented German—a softer, more musical version of the high German spoken in Germany. My parents, grandparents and their friends spoke Viennese German to my brother and me, but we replied in English. Austrian German is to high German as southern English in the United States is to English north of the Mason-Dixon line. Odd as it may seem, I still delight in hearing Austrian-accented German, the language of my upbringing, even though the police who arrested my father and uncle undoubtedly spoke the same dialect.

When my father and uncle were arrested, my parents and their parents realized that they and their families had to leave Europe. This wasn't easy. The visa quota for German and Austrian refugees at that time, set by the Johnson-Reed Act in 1924, remained at fewer than 30,000[10] per year after the Anschluss. My father had distant relatives in New York City, three sisters named Josephine, Gizella and Rose. They had emigrated to New York years earlier from what is now Slovakia. Gizella was married to a man named Armin Kohut, and they all lived together in an apartment on the Upper West Side of Manhattan.

---

10. https://encyclopedia.ushmm.org/content/en/article/immigration-to-the-united-states-1933-41

My paternal grandfather, who my brother and I called "Opapa," wrote to Gizella and Armin Kohut asking them to sign immigration papers. Not only did they do so for my father's immediate family but, despite the fact that my parents were not yet married, they did the same for virtually my entire family including my mother's side.

The Kohuts were my family's saviors. Such extraordinary magnanimity was uncommon. I never learned how they had come to America or how they had earned a living. I still remember their apartment on upper Broadway. I was fascinated by a piece of wooden furniture in their living room. It looked like an ordinary cabinet with a rounded top and wood paneling. Near the top it had a small glass aperture and two dials beneath it. When the knobs were turned in delicate ways, a fuzzy black and white image could be seen. It was called a television.

Most European Jews were not as lucky as my family. Facing the growing threat from Hitler and Nazi terror, many ensnared in Europe's tyranny begged those relatives already well-established in the United States (mostly in New York City and the Northeast) to sign required immigration papers for them. These earlier immigrants to the United States had prospered. An article I stumbled upon in the 1980s reproduced a number of responses to those letters. One after another, the replies contained pitiful excuses turning down their threatened relatives' pleas for asylum. Those denials undoubtedly resulted in the deaths of many, perhaps most, of their trapped kinfolk. The U.S. Holocaust Memorial Museum has published a number of letters detailing the desperation of Jews under Nazi control and the obstacles they faced.[11]

Armed with visas and financial affidavits from the Kohuts, my vivacious, attractive 22-year-old mother Lisl traveled by train to Gestapo Headquarters in Berlin and managed to get my father and uncle released on the condition that they depart Germany (then including Austria) within two weeks. They managed to get tickets on a Holland-America Line passenger ship to New York City. But first they had to get to Holland by train. The day of departure my uncle and father arrived at Vienna's *Westbahnhof* (west train station) an hour early. My mother hadn't arrived yet. My father and uncle waited and waited. Always nervous, my father fretted and paced. The train was leaving in 20 minutes, still no Lisl. Fifteen

11. https://perspectives.ushmm.org/collection/
jewish-refugees-and-the-holocaust

minutes, no Lisl. Ten minutes, no Lisl. Panic set in. With five minutes to spare, my father and uncle saw my mother running the length of the platform (which, last time I was there, seemed unchanged from the pre-war era). "Where were you? Where were you?!" my father screamed. "At the hairdresser," came her reply, as she showed off her new hairdo. The three made it to Rotterdam and caught the ship.[12] It was January 1939.

The entire three-week passage to the New World, my father was seasick. While he retched his way to New York, my future mother danced with my uncle, played the guitar, and sang folk songs. Thanks to the Kohuts, most of the rest of my father's and mother's immediate relatives were able to join them some weeks later.

But things weren't so easy in New York City. With the Depression still going strong, jobs were scarce. For a while, my mother waitressed at the New York World's Fair. Her English was not very good, so everyone was served carrots and peas no matter what vegetable they ordered.

Failing to find anything but temporary jobs, my parents were finally able to obtain steady work making army uniforms in Fall River, Massachusetts, where I was born in 1942. They saved their money, and in early 1944 my father bought a tiny cleaning and tailoring shop next to Lenox Hill Hospital on Manhattan's fashionable East Side. We moved to the not-so-fashionable Lower East Side.

With my mother needed to help my father get the new store up and running, my parents decided to send me to a sleepaway children's home in Connecticut, which was turbulent. When my mother finally came to take me home, I clung to my teacher. "Susie, Susie," I cried, reaching for her as my mother took me away. For the rest of her life, my mother regretted sending me to that facility.

Eventually, we moved to a fifth-floor walk-up apartment on West 96th Street in Manhattan. In our living room, wide windowsills formed

---

12. Decades later, my father moved to Santa Fe to be near my family. He was on vacation with us in Martha's Vineyard. On the day of departure from the Vineyard he was a nervous wreck. The first leg of the journey home to New Mexico was a ferry ride to Cape Cod. He insisted on leaving for the ferry well before its scheduled departure. At one point my wife Andi told him, "Pop, if we leave now, we'll be in time to take the earlier ferry!" He persisted, and sure enough we got to the ferry in time to make the earlier sailing.

ledges which little boys could sit on, perfect for gazing out at the street. One day when I was six, sitting on one of the sills, I suddenly saw a man jaywalking across the street. "Mommy, Mommy," I called. "Look at that man down there!" and I pointed. He was the first Black man I had ever seen. My mother told me that there are people of different races in the world, that man was one of them, and I must *always* treat Black people the same way I would treat anyone else—with courtesy, respect and consideration.

In 1950, only eleven years after coming to this country, my parents managed to buy a small suburban house in a New Jersey suburb, Bergenfield. I was seven. The night before we were to move, my parents loaded up our car, which was parked across West 96th Street from our apartment. The next morning, we found that our car had been broken into. Everything in it was gone. Undeterred, we moved to our new home, which was heaven: a lower middle-class neighborhood with one-family houses sitting on postage stamp lots along shaded streets. There were flowers, trees and grass everywhere and woods across the street, next to where two brothers our age lived. We played kickball in the street. On weekends, we played cowboys and Indians from morning until night in those woods. Little did I know then that I would be working with American Indians over the course of my adult career.

My mother was intensely interested in our education. She asked friends in Bergenfield about the elementary schools and was told that Lincoln was the best. Unfortunately, we lived one block outside its enrollment boundary, in the Franklin School District. Undaunted, my mother went to see the principal at Lincoln. Using her wit and charm once again, she persuaded him to sign a waiver so my younger brother Tom and I could attend Lincoln Elementary.

I made friends over the summer with future classmates at Lincoln Elementary School. In New York, my teachers had thought me a slow learner: at age 7, I still couldn't read. I had been going to "progressive" PS 93 on Columbus Avenue, where I wasn't making progress and was placed in the slow group. My mother took me to Columbia University for an IQ test but was never told the results. In second grade, all the kids in my class could read and write in cursive, while I was struggling with ordinary letters. At Lincoln, embarrassed, I taught myself how to read and write in two weeks. I must have known the basics already, but in first grade I had no incentive to read.

I had wonderful teachers, except in fourth grade. That lady was something of a tyrant. She insisted on a morning prayer each day. Okay, we used the Old Testament. But one day, she switched to the New Testament. I quietly continued reading a textbook. She called me aside and berated me—my first confrontation with authority. But then she stopped using the New Testament and went back to reading from the Old Testament. My first act of civil disobedience had succeeded.

Decades later, I feel the same way about that incident, but now recognize even more that religion has no place in public schools. Religion is a private matter, protected by the First Amendment no matter what belief system a person holds, so long as that person does not demand conformity from non-believers to that system in its religious aspect. That's why we have a First Amendment and a political and legal system that is not based on religion.

In sixth grade I had my favorite teacher ever, Miss Edna Roach. She was wonderful and took exceptional interest in every one of her students. She painstakingly taught each of us penmanship and ballroom dancing. She would sit with me, and later my brother, and have us carefully write each letter perfectly, which we did. Then she would ask us to copy a phrase or even a sentence by hand. Awful, pitiful, unreadable hieroglyphics[13] appeared on the paper. My brother and I were her only two penmanship failures, but we excelled in substantive subjects like history and arithmetic. We also had wonderful teachers in junior and senior high school. Mr. Kennedy managed student government, and as student body president I respected him.

On Saturdays in the summer, a friend and I biked around all day looking for available tennis courts. Until we showed up for dinner, our parents never knew where we were. We were given the freedom to explore and play as we wished, with no adult supervision. At age ten, another friend and I spent the whole day in New York, just wandering around the Bronx. No one knew where we were, yet we made it home unscathed.

My mother was attractive, charming and played the guitar. When I was a teenager, she worked as a salesperson for family friends in Manhattan who had also escaped Hitler. They designed and made costume jewelry, eventually building a prosperous business. Besides looking after us kids

---

13. My late colleague Dan MacMeekin confirmed that my penmanship remains as it was in 6th grade. Unreadable.

and household chores, my mother became our den mother in Cub Scouts. Late into the night she could be found in the living room reading books while eating an apple. Although she had never graduated from high school, she was one of the best-read people I ever knew. She always insisted that my brother and I do our homework.

My father took us on walks. He preached always doing everything you could do today, never leaving anything for the next day if at all possible. He also taught his sons to be frugal. He left the house every morning at 6 a.m. and commuted by car 45 to 60 minutes each way over the George Washington Bridge to his cleaning and tailoring shop on Manhattan's East Side. His little business catered to wealthy Park Avenue customers. One weekend a month, my mother would help him send out bills to customers. They would sit at the dining room table, write the bills by hand, and then stuff them into envelopes for mailing. This would take several hours. On Saturdays, I would sometimes help to deliver clothes. My father would come home at 7 p.m. every evening, eat supper, and go to bed. On Saturdays he gave himself an hour's more sleep.

My parents often entertained on Saturday evenings. My father would excuse himself at 8:30 p.m. and go to bed. My mother would continue to charm her guests. Once I tiptoed down the steps and eavesdropped as she told our family's story to our new friends in Bergenfield. She was funny, turning various parts of the rather frightening account into jokes, such as the hairdresser episode.

On Sundays my father gardened, growing beautiful flowers. Then our extended family often gathered in our suburban living room. My mother would cook a fabulous schnitzel dinner and then bridge tables would be set up. The living room quickly filled with cigarette smoke. All afternoon, my parents, grandparents and friends of the family from Vienna would argue about each other's bidding mistakes. I never learned how to play bridge. A few evenings a month my father played classical piano while my girlfriend's father, a gynecologist, played the violin. My father was a good chess player and taught me the game. I rarely beat him, and it still frustrates me mightily that I can't beat my brother.

Once, when I was 15, my father idly commented that he didn't want a Black family to move into our neighborhood because our home's value would drop. I yelled at him, and he never said anything like that again. But my father also taught us kids the virtue of hard work. Our parents lived for their kids.

Every year in August, our family took a vacation. All over the Northeast from Maine to the Adirondacks, we enjoyed lakes, boating and swimming. From the time I was five to eight years old, we would go with friends to Lake Hopatcong in northern New Jersey when it was still fairly remote, each family with their own cabin. One day that first summer, I flung a toy plane, and it landed in a tree. I tried to fetch it with a fishing rod with a hooked line. Instead of hooking the plane, I caught myself, burying the barb in my left forehead. I received no sympathy from my mother. She decided to teach me a lesson by walking me to the doctor's office with the hook still lodged in my scalp while following me and holding the fishing rod—a humiliating experience.

Years later, I broke my front tooth when I was riding on the handlebars of a friend's bike. My foot hit the spokes, ejecting me right onto my face on the asphalt. I walked home and mumbled through a bloody handkerchief, "Ma, I *boke* my *too*. The "r" and "th" were lost somewhere in my mouth. Once again, she hauled me off for medical care, a drive to the dentist's office some miles away. He cleaned up my stump and inserted a crown, which is still held by my original front tooth. I maintain the accident improved my looks.

I fought a lot with my brother, who is three years my junior. One day we got into a fight in our tiny new dining room. He took a giant swing at me with his fist. I ducked, and his momentum caused him to fall over, hitting his temple on the sharp edge of the dining room entry way. He fell over and didn't move. I started screaming, thinking I had killed him even though I hadn't touched him. A few minutes later he awoke, and a trip to the doctor's office ensued.

Our mother was fearless. One day, while I was in elementary school, I came home and told her that a schoolmate had called me a "dirty kike." My mother then invited the boy who made the slur to our living room for a chat whereby she explained how hurtful that kind of language was. The boy turned out to be good friends with me and my brother over the following years. He was also a super athlete in the great American trifecta—football, basketball, baseball—and admired by all.

In my early teens, our parents sent Tom and me to Camp Aquatic, a swimming camp in Massachusetts. The head swimming coach at Camp Aquatic also coached the Princeton swim team and taught me and my brother to swim expertly. Housed in small cabins with bunk beds, we also learned how to get along with a diverse group of new friends, and how to play baseball and basketball. I still remember the time I hit a home run. I also played tennis and beamed when at the culminating camp dinner in late August, I was awarded the most improved tennis player trophy.

Just a little over two decades after fleeing to America, our parents sent their two boys off to Ivy League colleges on scholarships. I went to Brown and Yale Law School, and my brother Tom attended Princeton, Yale and Harvard for undergraduate and graduate school in psychology. While I was at Brown, my parents adopted Nicky, a cousin by birth and the daughter of my mother's younger brother, our wayward Uncle Hans. Tom and I have always known Nicky as our little sister.

Uncle Hans was brilliant but crazy. Our mother often told us that his eccentricity was due to his having been accidently dropped on his head when he was four years old. He told funny stories. Every once in a while, he would lose it and start screaming, but never at my brother or me. Uncle Hans relied on our mother for assistance—moral, financial and otherwise. He was our favorite relative and treated us very well.

For a few years Uncle Hans was married to Erica, a wonderful Viennese woman and my mother's dear friend. One Sunday, we had a lovely dinner at Erica and Hans's apartment in the Bronx. I was sitting opposite Hans. In the middle of the table was a newfangled, pressurized whipped cream dispenser with a nozzle on top. I reached for the tube and pushed the nozzle to serve myself some whipped cream. Out sprang a frothy jet, which leapt over the table and landed smack on the left shoulder of Hans's dark blue turtleneck sweater. Without a word he meticulously lifted half of the dollop off his left shoulder and dabbed it onto his right shoulder, creating matching epaulets of sorts. We howled in laughter.

In summary, I grew up idealizing this country. My family was saved by this country, and growing up, I believed it generally treated all of its citizens equally or was making strides toward doing so. It took many decades for me to realize that my family story is different. Everything the Statue of Liberty stands for came true for us. We were your apple-pie version of immigrant success: America as savior, America as land of milk and honey, America as protector of civil rights, of minorities, of decency. My adult experiences have revealed deep flaws and fissures in our basic systems that prevent many citizens from experiencing America as my family has. It has taken me since my college days to learn that America's promise has not been kept.

My journey has taught me how complicated and difficult life has been and still is for many, many Americans, especially those of color. And real threats to our democratic system continue today.

HOW THE JUNIOR YEAR ABROAD DERAILED MY PLANS

I loved my new school in Bergenfield, New Jersey, and I quickly made new friends. In high school, I played sports and discovered a small talent in public speaking, getting elected as student body president. I graduated in 1960, and a scholarship made it possible for me to go to Brown University.

I majored in International Relations and spent my junior year in Vienna. My year abroad in 1962-1963 was informative and productive. While there, I retraced my parents' childhood and their escape from Nazi Austria. I signed up for courses at the University of Vienna on the *Ringstrasse*, a few blocks from a garret I rented for $25 a month. My father's cousin Paul Grosz and his lovely wife Hennie provided a connection with family away from home. I had not as yet realized how truly blessed my family and I had been. Only years later, when I encountered the despair, fright and hopelessness on many Indian reservations, did I come to realize that the American Dream did not encompass all Americans, especially many of those whose ancestors were here first.

To this day my favorite movie is "The Third Man," which fascinated me with the same Viennese dialect my parents spoke as well as quaint medieval streets and buildings. Every so often I watch it again, and it never bores me, even though by now I know almost every line. In Vienna that year, I went to a showing of it at a downtown Viennese theater not far from the streets on which the drama was filmed. The movie deals with post-World War II Vienna under control of the four allies. The Russians and Americans were, of course, the dominant powers, and I became acutely aware of that during the Cuban Missile Crisis. During the Cold War, Vienna continued to be a place of international intrigue and post-war corruption between Americans and Russians, complicated by illegal smuggling and crime, which infected the city like a tropical disease.

In the fall of 1963, after returning to Brown University from Vienna, I had to take oral exams to receive credit for the courses I had taken in

Europe. European universities do not give grades for individual courses, as is the practice at Brown and most American colleges. Later, when applying for a degree, that's when European students would take rigorous oral exams. When I had arrived in Vienna, I had simply enrolled at the University of Vienna where tuition was something like $20 a course, and there were no entrance requirements. After looking through the University's course offerings that year, I chose several classes corresponding roughly to courses I would have taken at Brown. I stuck to history, political science and economics.

To graduate with my class at Brown I needed eight credits from Vienna, one for each subject. While walking around the Brown campus with individual professors (all uniformly kind and helpful) I was quizzed on the various subjects I had studied abroad. I was planning to go to law school right after graduation. All went well with the first seven oral exams. Then came International Economics, which did not go so well. I wound up with seven credits instead of eight, and so could not graduate with my class in June.

Missing one credit, my plans to start law school in the fall were derailed. Therefore, I had to take a summer course at Columbia University. It didn't matter what the subject was, so I took the most convenient course I could find, a class in poetry. I had to drive to an evening class twice a week from my home in northern New Jersey. I managed to get a part-time summer postman gig in my hometown walking various routes, substituting for regular postmen on summer vacation. Most circuits took about five hours to complete.

I can't remember a single poem I read in that summer course at Columbia. On the bright side, working as a part-time postman helped me build my savings for the first year of law school. It also kept me in great shape, but that was small consolation for losing the whole academic year. A related problem appeared. How would I support myself for the next year? That one missing credit was the first in a series of mishaps that derailed my ambitions.

I had to work, of course, but at what? I had no idea. Then my luck changed. I told a friend at Brown about my dilemma, and she put me in touch with a man who needed to find someone to replace him as a field representative for something called People to People (PTP), as he was going off to medical school. PTP was a nonprofit do-gooder organization founded and supported by Hallmark Cards in Kansas City, Missouri. Its mission was to promote academic and cultural relationships and activities between American college students and foreign students, achieved through PTP clubs on American campuses.

My friend gave me a name and number to call, and amazingly, I was hired over the phone to be a field representative for a year, organizing and servicing PTP clubs at East Coast college campuses from South Carolina to New Jersey.

PTP was right up my alley. By luck I had just the right mix of real-life experiences, having studied abroad and having pretty good college credentials. In high school I had organized a chapter of the American Friends Service Committee, whose aim was identical to PTP's. As a field representative I was based in Washington, D.C. Along with other related issues and interests, PTP spawned a lifelong curiosity in the history of the South and civil rights.

Once organized, PTP clubs would contact international students on campus, socialize with them, help them get settled, and arrange social and academic events to help introduce them to Americans and vice versa. The activities included guest speakers and excursions to interesting historical sites around their campuses, aimed at promoting better understanding of world affairs. A summer travel program featuring homestays with families in Europe was also available if one could pay, which proved very popular.

At a student ambassador orientation, I was able to take part in the August annual meeting with PTP staff at Hallmark's impressive headquarters in Kansas City, Missouri. There I got acquainted with their advisory board, headquarters' staff and fellow field representatives during a day and a half of group conferences and private sessions. I was awed by the attendance of one particular board member and advisor, Rafer Johnson, the 1960 Olympic decathlon champion. He boosted their prestige considerably. To say he was impressive is like saying the Empire State building is tall—it does not adequately convey his remarkable presence. Friendly, thoughtful and helpful, Rafer was down-to-earth, funny and concerned. He sparked a feeling in me that I had lucked out.

Rafer participated energetically with us through the entire first day. We worked through lunch, which was brought down to us from Hallmark's cafeteria. Everything seemed perfect. I liked the people, the atmosphere, the agenda and the thrill of getting immersed in foreign affairs. The day went by quickly and smoothly. The other field reps were delightful and interesting, too. One was Bill Cloherty, a Harvard graduate from Back Bay, Boston. His accent was so thick it was difficult even for me—having been born in Massachusetts but not raised there—to understand. He spent much of the day quipping in his "r-less" Boston brogue ("kaah" for car, etc.). He was a font of arcane knowledge and fascinating experiences, including door-to-door campaigning for John F. Kennedy in Appalachian West Virginia. He was overwhelmed by the poverty he encountered when he visited with a family living not too far from a well-traveled, hilly road. He described how he was talking with them when suddenly the entire family disappeared up to the road, ran a piece down it and past a curve, which had some loose gravel on it. They then hid behind some trees. After the grinding gears of a truck began laboring up the hill, it picked up some speed on the straightaway. As the truck jolted, a quantity of black coal leapt from the truck bed and onto the road, and the family all ran out with their bags, scooped up the coal and skedaddled back to their cabin.

The other half-dozen or so field reps and several central office people were also impressive, personable, smart and committed to fostering peace and international understanding. In short, it was a joy working with this congenial, convivial organization. I was therefore totally floored by what happened next.

At the end of the day, our crew, including Rafer, stood outside the Hallmark building entrance for an important discussion: where to have dinner. And an unexpected, awkward verbal bombshell exploded in our midst.

In the 1960s in America, the subject of getting a meal was not simple, especially if racism reared its ugly head. Hateful prejudice still sucks the lifeblood from American democracy, egalitarianism and freedom. For me it has been the central social and political problem plaguing the United States in one form or another for hundreds of years, but never before had I been personally confronted by it. There had been only one Black family in my hometown in New Jersey, and their children appeared to have no problem in our school system. I became familiar with the U.S. Supreme Court case, *Brown v. Board of Education*, from reading the *New York Times*, but aside from that had only a bookish, mostly one or two-dimensional view.

Now, the Great American Dilemma created a mushroom cloud over us, as we stood on the street in Kansas City. What I had thought was a cosmopolitan, modern part of the United States suddenly turned into an instantaneous lifting-of-the-tent-flap of the racist backdrop all around us.

We were all affected the same way—with despair and agony. In the presence of no less than a world-renowned hero, we were confronted by what on the surface had appeared to be such a mundane question—where to eat—which was precisely why the issue was so frightening.

Trying to decide where to eat, I wondered, would freedom and the Bill of Rights extend to all races including those who were brown-skinned, or was the freedom to choose any restaurant confined to only the light-skinned among us? If the latter, how could we go forth onto college campuses preaching democracy, equality and fraternity?

I was informed that Missouri law forbade an Olympic champion, Rafer Johnson, who had brought immense honor and prestige to our country, from eating with us at a restaurant or staying at the same hotel in this worldly city. Kansas City was segregated, something I learned only when Rafer mentioned it standing outside the building chatting, as a kind of aside. He would now have to depart for somewhere in the "colored section" of town as it was then called, to grab a meal and stay in a hotel there as well.

All at once, for me, the whole premise and promise of People to People was cast into a cauldron of hot doubt. How could we build greater international understanding on college campuses when our sponsoring institution, Hallmark Cards, an American icon, was a contradiction. The city screamed segregation. Or so it appeared to me at that moment.

I immediately thought of my parents and their family who had luckily escaped from Nazi Austria just before World War II started. They too were the victims of similar human prejudices. My father and uncle's incarceration in Nazi concentration camps always hovered in the background of my upbringing, a constant lesson to me about ethnic and religious intolerance. I couldn't believe I was now seeing a "fear of the other" that my own forbears and other minorities have experienced over the history of humanity.

Various thoughts started racing through my head: Should I quit PTP? Should I eat separately from the main group? Should I go home that night? I was overwhelmingly and unwillingly cast in the role of oppressor—I would be allowed (in fact commanded by law) to eat with my privileged group of fair-skinned non-Blacks, while possibly the best person among us, our Olympic hero, would have to eat somewhere else in Kansas City. Things suddenly didn't compute.

In a flash, the two-dimensional "White" and "Black" restroom signs along the bus ride to Atlanta three years earlier merged into this real-time agony. The horror of racial prejudice hit me upside my head like nothing I had learned from all those news stories of Blacks marching in Mississippi or Atlanta or Washington, D.C. I was appalled, ashamed, stupefied. Someone I had admired was made into a de facto totem of the Other America—the imperialist, racist, cruel, superior-minded, nose-in-the-air America that had bullied its way to world power.

America's fundamental dilemma had now trespassed into my personal life. I thought of fleeing.

Rafer Johnson

SUMMER AT TOUGALOO

My journeys with People to People took me to Historically Black Colleges and Universities (HBCU) as well as bastions of southern gentility such as Duke and UVA. That year put me up against the harsh realities of race discrimination in other places as well. The South was in turmoil. The rising tide of civil rights reforms had triggered mass resistance throughout the South and racial politics dominated the news. One way or the other, the whole country was engaged in the struggle.

During my senior year at Brown in 1963-64, I had heard lectures by Martin Luther King Jr., Malcolm X, and George Wallace. At the same time, the Vietnam war was escalating. Though I was not involved in the Civil Rights Movement, the People to People job brought me into direct contact with both sides as I visited staid white colleges as well as mostly Black colleges such as Howard University, Morgan State College and Morehouse College. I became intensely interested in the South and the movement towards reform of race relations. I read every book I could get my hands on about the history of the American South, by authors such as C. Vann Woodward, author of *The Strange Career of Jim Crow* (Oxford University Press, 1955).

In April 1965, I attended the 100th anniversary of General Robert E. Lee's surrender to Lt. General Ulysses S. Grant at Appomattox Courthouse, Virginia. Bruce Catton, the author and Civil War historian, gave the keynote address. Senator Harry Byrd Sr. spoke to the crowd. I noted the absence of Black people. The speeches were sober and reflective. The country was changing. Congress had passed major civil rights legislation. The Civil War was finally ending—or so we thought. The historians and politicians at Appomattox that day seemed to recognize that the era of Jim Crow was fading. Yet broad southern white hostility to civil rights raged at a fever pitch and indeed continues today in the form of racial profiling by police and the shooting of unarmed Blacks, voter suppression, and attempts to end women's reproductive rights. President Lyndon Johnson famously remarked that his support for the civil rights laws passed on his watch would cause a political sea change, changing the Democratic South to the mostly (white) Republican South it is to this day. In the 1950s and 60s, Republicans used the Southern Strategy to build political support among southern white voters by fomenting racism against Blacks.

The year off from school enabled me to experience this profound social and political conflict firsthand. At places like Howard, I sat with Black students and began to feel their pain and fervor for reform. I noticed that even at the mostly white colleges, student opinion seemed generally to favor civil rights reforms. Many more such experiences were to come. Meanwhile, I needed to think of my future.

Having now received my college diploma, I applied to several law schools and one graduate school, Columbia, in history. I was fortunate to get accepted by every one of them, including Harvard and Yale. I was already leaning towards Yale. It had a smaller enrollment and a reputation as a socially conscious place interested in applying legal principles to societal issues. But I couldn't simply dismiss Harvard. I decided to visit both schools, neither of which I had seen before.

On a cold January evening, I arrived in Cambridge, Massachusetts, to look up a friend from Brown who was then a first-year law student at Harvard. When I knew him at Brown, he was a jolly fellow—open, friendly and socially active. He had been student body president during our senior year. I looked him up at his law school dormitory. This turned out to be a huge, ultra-modern, antiseptic, impersonal structure. Designed by the famous Bauhaus architect Walter Gropius, it featured tile throughout. Endless corridors and bright fluorescent ceiling lights lit up the place like a hospital. I found my friend's room and knocked on the door. "Who is it?" a strained voice cried out. "Mike Gross," I replied. I heard footsteps. The door opened and there stood a wraith. Pencil behind the ear, in a t-shirt, holding a stack of books in one hand, with bloodshot eyes, stood the ghost of my friend. In a disembodied voice he said curtly, "Oh, hi. I haven't got much time. Why are you here?" I murmured something about getting in and wanted a recommendation for a class to attend the next day. He quickly suggested a class in property law at eight o'clock the next morning and gave me the room number. He dismissed me, apologizing somewhat for his abrupt manner. It was obvious he was under great strain. I quickly thanked him and went off into the night.

The next morning, I showed up early at the lecture hall he had given me. It was a cavernous, semicircular amphitheater of tiered desks and chairs, all centered on the podium at the well of the room with a big blackboard behind it. Students poured in, most as bleary-eyed as my friend had been the night before. At two minutes past the hour, the professor, wearing a dark three-piece suit, marched in, holding several large books under his arm. Without acknowledging anyone, he strode to his command center. Making a great show of arranging his books and the day's outline on the podium, he looked at the class list in front of him and pointed to a student midway up the amphitheater to my right. "Mr. Smith (not his real name). What happened in case such-and-such?" he intoned. Mr. Smith rose slowly and said, "Professor ___, I am sorry. I am unprepared." An ominous gasp permeated the chamber followed by a few moments of inescapable silence. Then, Mt. Vesuvius erupted. A tirade such as I had experienced never before spewed from the professor's mouth. He was scathing, brutal, imperious and totally dismissive. It was obviously his intent to humiliate and embarrass the unfortunate soul who had uttered the sinful words, "I am unprepared." The professor's tirade seared itself into my brain. I had never in my life heard such language employed in a public place in what I thought was supposed to be a refined academic setting. The poor student stood silently hanging his head in shame. I felt sick. The episode left me with the indelible impression that law as taught at Harvard was nothing more than a boot camp for waging legal wars against all opponents. The scene in the film "The Paper Chase," actually filmed at Harvard several years later, graphically preserves that memory.

The next day, I went to New Haven, Connecticut, to see what Yale Law School was like. At Brown for one semester as a sophomore, I had escaped the bedlam of my new fraternity by living in the college's quiet dormitory. There I met Howie, reputed to be the smartest student ever to attend Brown. He lived in a garret by himself. The room had bare walls, a Spartan desk, a chair, a pull-down plastic window shade, a small bookshelf filled to the gills, and a bed. Howie was always sitting at the desk with a pile of books stacked in front of him and a typewriter. He had graduated from Brown with highest honors in three years and was now a third-year law student at Yale.

Howie met me at the dean's office. He had grown a visible paunch. He was wearing a mohair sweater, had a well-groomed beard and was smoking a pipe. We walked to his room in Yale Law School's massive gothic, largely wood-paneled stone building that housed the school's classrooms, library, offices, dining hall, recreation areas, two squash courts and the dormitory. Howie opened the door to his small L-shaped suite. African masks decorated a bamboo screen divider. There was a rug on the floor. The short leg of the room contained a closet and shelves for books. The bed was covered with a fancy bedspread, and the walls were decorated with art. Howie reclined on his bed, lit the pipe, and put his hands behind his head. "Yup," he said. "There sure are a lot of smart people around here, but they don't work you hard enough."

When I didn't accept Harvard's invitation to join its next class, they sent me a short questionnaire asking me why I had turned it down. I did not send it back.

Not once in the three years I spent at Yale Law School did I ever experience anything resembling the treatment of students I had witnessed at Harvard. Everyone was treated with respect and courtesy. I found the work rigorous and challenging. But the idea that law should be practiced as war by other means was never presented. Instead, studying Law at Yale was an intellectual exercise, a logical and psychological technique to win arguments with words, not tirades. The idea was to protect clients from lawsuits, if possible, not foment them. Social consciousness infused the very idea of law. Law school at Yale was a training ground for clear thinking and expression, not a coliseum pitting spears against knives. While bringing and defending lawsuits was part of the curriculum, these skills were never regarded as shouting matches or fights to the death.

Note: While the above is all true, I would be remiss if I didn't make clear that throughout my entire career I have worked with Harvard-trained lawyers, none of whom ever behaved as rudely as that one professor had. For most of my career, I worked closely with a Harvard alum, C. Bryant Rogers, who will later figure prominently in this story. He is a brilliant, dedicated, and abundantly talented person. While his approach to the law differs markedly from my own, the differences are intellectual, not gladiatorial. In fact, Bryant and I both believe that the dynamic tension between us has benefited our clients. I also single out my mentor at the summer clerkship in Phoenix in 1967, Paul Eckstein.

After my first year of law school, I needed a summer job. Traditionally, law students seek summer work at law firms after their second year, not the first year. In college during my Brown years, I worked summers as a postman. I enjoyed that work but wanted to do something else that summer after the first year of law school. A friend from Brown told me that Brown University had formed a new partnership with a southern HBCU and needed summer tutors in 1966 to prepare incoming freshmen for college. Founded shortly after the Civil War, Tougaloo College, ten miles north of Jackson, Mississippi, was one of several storied southern Black colleges, providing college educations for the children of former slaves. Together with such schools as Morehouse, Tuskegee and many others, Tougaloo has played a decisive role in educating Black professionals in the South. Their graduates have provided a steady stream of teachers, doctors and lawyers who have provided the core of the Black middle class in the South. Unlike most of the other similar partnerships between northern colleges and southern HBCUs formed in the 1960s, the Brown-Tougaloo Partnership has endured for more than fifty years. The program allows Tougaloo and Brown students to spend a semester or more at the other partner's school.

In 1966 the partnership was only two years old. I applied as a tutor and was hired. In preparation for a summer in the heart of Dixie only two years after the horrendous Chaney, Goodman and Schwerner assassinations, I wanted to take precautions. During my year with People to People, one of my favorite destinations was Chapel Hill, North Carolina, home of the University of North Carolina. The editor of *The Daily Tar Heel* was a personable North Carolinian from Raleigh. His name was Neal Jackson, and he became a longtime friend. Preparing for my summer in Mississippi, it occurred to me that it might be a good idea not to drive around in a car with New Jersey license plates. Neal instantly agreed to let me use his home address in Raleigh to get a North Carolina plate for my car. I believe I had the only Volvo P-544 with North Carolina license plates in Mississippi that summer.

Weeks before leaving for Mississippi in June 1966, the evening news was filled with stories about James Meredith. He had applied to law school at Ole Miss, the University of Mississippi, and was denied admission because he was Black. To protest, he began marching from Memphis, Tennessee, to Jackson, the state capital, calling it the March Against Fear. Just past the Mississippi border, a Ku Klux Klansman pelted him with birdshot from behind a bush. After spending a few days recovering in the hospital in Memphis, Meredith continued marching. Wearing a pith helmet to protect his head, he attracted workers in the fields along the way who joined his march. Soon, folks from other parts of the country and the press from all over the world began to accompany him. The *New York Times* reported their progress every day. For the three weeks or so of its duration, this spontaneous march became the center of the Civil Rights Movement. Meredith's pith helmet became a symbol. Every day, national headlines and the evening TV news reported his and the marchers' progress. Constitutional equality was their goal. My parents were worried. "You're going *where* for the summer? Mississippi? Into the middle of that mess?"

"Don't worry, Ma," I replied. "I'm going to a quiet, rural college campus. I'm not joining the march." And indeed, at least technically, I kept my promise. I didn't join the march; the march joined me.

Two days after my arrival at Tougaloo, Meredith and thousands of fellow marchers showed up on the campus, located on their path down U.S. Interstate 55. The night before, there was a confrontation with state troopers at a place called Greenwood, north of Canton, only a few miles up I-55 from the campus. Exhausted marchers descended on the oak-shaded, moss-covered Tougaloo campus. For the next four days, the pastoral college served as an island of tranquility in a sea of hostility. Thousands of marchers camped out on the grounds, including civil rights and labor movement leaders. Inevitably, I got caught up in their fervor. During the days, groups of marchers and civil rights leaders gathered under the Spanish moss to debate the issues of their movement. The biggest was Black Power. In his overalls, Stokely Carmichael, who had recently come to prominence as an advocate favoring a more confrontational approach to civil rights, and James Meredith huddled under an oak while other groups of marchers, Black and white, stood in circles debating nonviolence versus Black Power.

Stokely Carmichael speaks with James Meredith,
Tougaloo, MS, summer 1966. Photo by Michael P. Gross

One evening, a group of us tutors from Brown decided to go down
the dark dirt pathway behind the college to Mama T's, the local speakeasy.
They had the best hamburgers I ever tasted. The place was packed. There
seemed to be no room. Someone yelled that there were a few spots in a
back room. We elbowed our way there. Through the dim lights I could
see people seated on benches, but there were still some empty spaces. I
squeezed into a seat at one table. A guy across from me was telling hilarious jokes, one after the other. At first, in the dim light, I couldn't make
out his face. One of his jokes featured a Black man in WW II who had
been painted with white face and parachuted into China. I can't remember the punchline, but it was hilarious. The guy next to him was offering
scatological side comments every few seconds. After my eyes adjusted, I
realized the jokester was comedian Dick Gregory and the commentator

was Claude Brown, author of *Manchild in the Promised Land*. Others at the table included the nonviolence activist James Farmer and Whitney Young, executive director of the National Urban League.

Newspapers were trumpeting the growing philosophical split in the civil rights community over Black Power. Martin Luther King Jr.'s stance of nonviolence was being attacked for being too slow. Would the Movement become violent? Many wore T-shirts emblazoned with a pouncing black panther. On the Saturday evening before the march to Jackson, politics stopped as people gathered outside on the campus. King wandered all over, smiling, contented, unafraid, but not in charge. Entertainers and prominent celebrities took over. On a makeshift stage on the ballfield, James Brown strutted, Sammy Davis Jr. crooned, and national leaders, including Dick Gregory, Burt Lancaster and Marlon Brando, entertained the marchers.

Michael Gross with James Meredith in background. Tougaloo, Mississippi, 1966. Photo by Joel Pasternack

Michael Gross with fellow marchers, Tougaloo, Mississippi, 1966.
Photo by Joel Pasternack

Staying true to my promise back home, I did not march. Instead, with Joel Pasternack, my buddy from Brown who had accompanied me on my journey to Mississippi, I drove into Jackson that Sunday to get good places at the state capitol where the march was to culminate several hours later after their 14-mile walk from Tougaloo. I took dozens of photos. Twenty-five years later, after I became chair of the Brown-Tougaloo Partnership Committee of the Brown Corporation, the best photos were featured in the Brown Alumni Monthly to accompany an article I wrote about the experience.

Martin Luther King Jr., Tougaloo, Mississippi, 1966.
Photo by Michael P. Gross

Martin Luther King Jr. at podium, March Against Fear Rally,
Jackson, Mississippi, 1966

ANDREA HUGHES

While I attended Yale University, two of my law school friends promised to fix me up with a date if I would drive them the ninety minutes from New Haven to Mount Holyoke, a women's college in South Hadley, Massachusetts. I had the only car in my circle of friends, a Volvo P-544, the upside-down bathtub model with a stick shift on the floor between the driver and passenger seats. I agreed. We took our dates to a pub in nearby Northampton, home of Smith College. My date's name was Andrea Hughes. It was April 1968; she was a senior and I was in my last semester of law school. Neither of my two buddies ever saw their dates again. Mine married me, even though she was forced to straddle the gear shift as I drove that evening, and she tore her mesh stockings on something protruding from my car door.

Andi comes from an old New England family. Her parents lived in Concord, New Hampshire, where her father was a weatherman while her mother ran a nursery school. It didn't hurt that Andi's father was also a Brown alum, while her mother was an alumna of Mount Holyoke. Her grandparents were rock-ribbed New England Republicans. They lived near Litchfield, Connecticut, on a 150-acre property called Wildwood Farm, which bucolically featured a few cows and chickens, a little pond, an old barn, and a main house built in the Revolutionary War era. Migrating geese flew overhead in bomber formations honking mightily. It was heaven.

Her well-read grandmother, Ruth Rodenbach, nicknamed "Gaga," was a liberal Republican who had sat on a United Nations committee with Eleanor Roosevelt. She and Andi's whole family, including a southern wing, welcomed me with open arms, and Gaga invited me to read whatever books I wanted from the vast library in her capacious living room. Andi's Uncle Bill had made a career in the Air Force, starting in World War II. I didn't find out until after he died that he had won the Distinguished Flying Cross in Vietnam and later served as a U2 pilot over the Soviet Union.

In my last year of law school in late April 1968, Professor Fred Rodell arranged for the students in his seminar on legal writing to meet with members of the United States Supreme Court, including his close friend, Justice William O. Douglas. The professor had once shown us a six-page handwritten letter from Justice Douglas to him. The last sentence of the letter said: "This letter would have been shorter if I had had more time."[14] Justice Douglas had given Rodell the exclusive privilege of bringing his classes for these annual encounters. Each of us was allowed to bring one guest. I invited Andi. It was our first date after the original blind date. So it was just two weeks after we met that she and I flew to Washington, D.C., her first ride on a jet.

The Monday morning of our class's interviews with justices at the Supreme Court, we all met outside the imposing Supreme Court building. Fred, as he liked to be called, always dressed in baggy pants, a well-worn sweatshirt and his usual crumpled cowboy hat perched on his head. Visiting the Supreme Court was no exception. The rest of us wore formal business attire. We sat in the main Supreme Court chamber listening to the Court's announcement of new decisions. Justice William Brennan had written one of them. The case concerned a Long Island druggist who had been convicted of selling a *Playboy* magazine to a 15-year-old boy in violation of a local ordinance.[15] Contrary to his liberal reputation, Brennan's opinion was strangely conservative, upholding the conviction. At lunch we ate in the Supreme Court's cafeteria. Several justices ambled in and out while we were there, taking their food to nearby tables or back to their offices.

In the afternoon, we were led into an ornate chamber: plush carpet, chandeliers, fancy upholstered chairs in neat rows, a massive carved wooden conference table, and behind it a stately chair for each of the justices. We interviewed six of the nine justices. Most sat facing us with hands neatly folded on the table while my classmates posed pedantic questions to them about this or that case or that rule of law. Each answered graciously, no matter how jejune the question. I had not opened my mouth.

---

14. This expression was originated by French philosopher and mathematician (in French) in Pascal, Blaise. *Lettres Provinciales ou Les Lettres Ecrites par Louis de Montalte*, Gallica, 1657, and was subsequently used by John Locke, Benjamin Franklin, Henry David Thoreau, Mark Twain among others.

15. *Ginsberg v. New York*, 390 U.S. 629 (1968)

This was the Vietnam War era. One day, well before our Supreme Court visit, the Reverend William Sloan Coffin, Chaplain of Yale University and a vocal opponent of the Vietnam War, had come to Rodell's class. Coffin stood in front of us and reamed us out for not asking hard questions about the war. Existential questions were indeed looming. Yet now when we had the opportunity, my classmates and I were similarly reluctant to ask tough questions of the justices. This changed when Justice Black appeared.

Justice Hugo Black departed from the routine; instead of sitting in front of us in the ornate chamber, he led us to his chambers. We sat on his carpeted floor while he made himself comfortable in a big easy chair. He was one of the most congenial people I had ever encountered. He remained so even when one from our group asked the only hot-button question of the day: How would he rule if the World War II era Japanese Exclusion Case, *Korematsu v. United States*,[16] had come up today?

Without hesitation and without taking any offense, Justice Black replied that he would rule exactly the same way now as he did then. He said that the decision protected the Japanese American U.S. citizens from the fury of enraged mobs following the Japanese sneak attack on Pearl Harbor, an argument flatly rejected by scholars since the war.[17]

The last of the justices to submit to our questions was the Court's most liberal justice, William O. Douglas. As had Justice Black, Justice Douglas

---

16. *Korematsu*, 323 U.S. 214 (1944), was infamous. In his opinion for the Court, Justice Black had upheld the constitutionality of the post-Pearl Harbor round-up of Americans of Japanese ancestry, most of whom were born in the United States. They were placed in concentration camps for the duration of the war, echoing the incarceration of American Indians defeated in the wars of the nineteenth century. For me, of course, I could not help but be reminded of the Jews under Hitler.

17. Forty-seven years later, President Reagan signed the Civil Liberties Act of 1988, Publ. L. 100-383, 102 Stat. 904, to compensate the more than 100,000 people of Japanese descent incarcerated in federal internment camps during World War II. The legislation offered a formal apology and paid $20,000 in compensation to each surviving victim or his or her family. The law won congressional approval only after a decades-long campaign by the Japanese American community.

departed from the norm. He did address us in the ornate chamber, but he refused to sit down. He paced. My fellow law students reverted back to pedantic questions. He was plainly irritated. It was now 4 p.m. and for the next half hour he kept looking at his watch, saying he had a dental appointment. His answers to our questions were curt and humorless.

So far, I had not opened my mouth. All afternoon I had been strangely frozen. Chandeliers always cow me. But at 25 minutes past the hour, maybe because I thought it would be the last chance that I would ever have to pose a question to a Supreme Court justice, I raised my hand. I don't know what compelled me but, when he called on me at almost 4:29 p.m., I rose and asked, "Mr. Justice Douglas, why is the Supreme Court so hung up on sex?" Heads turned around and mouths opened in shock. But Justice Douglas, looking at his watch while back-peddling out the door, curtly responded, "I don't know about that; Justice Brennan wrote a book a few years ago called "An Affair with State."[18] Whereupon he vanished.

Not long after this memorable day visiting the Supreme Court, I set off to the first job of my legal career in Window Rock, Arizona. A couple of months later, Andi, by then my fiancée, traveled 2,000 miles from her New England roots to join me on the Navajo reservation, a world apart from East Coast establishment.

---

18.   Brennan, W.J. and Friedman, S.J., ed. *An Affair with Freedom: A Collection of His Opinions and Speeches Drawn from His First Decade as a United States Supreme Court Justice.* Atheneum (1967). This reference might be to Brennan's First Amendment opinion in *Roth v. United States*, 354 U.S. 476, 487 (1957): "Sex, a great and mysterious motive force in human life, has indisputably been a subject of absorbing intrest to mankind through the ages; it is one of the vital problems of human interest and public concern."

Andrea Hughes outside DNA legal headquarters,
Window Rock, Arizona, 1968. Photo by Michael Gross

ARRIVAL AND FIRST ASSIGNMENT

My formal legal career began on the cracked faux-leather couch at a two-bay foreign car garage on West Maloney Street in Gallup, New Mexico. It was late July 1968 and at age 26, I had just graduated from law school and arrived for my first legal job at DNA's headquarters in Window Rock, Arizona, capital of the Navajo Nation.

In early July, I had set off from northern New Jersey in my 1961 Volvo on a meandering journey west through Montana and then south to Window Rock, Arizona. Due to start work on August 1, my plan was to do a War-on-Poverty legal service stint for a couple of years before moving on to a regular, business-oriented law firm, perhaps even Brown, Vlassis & Bain.

I purposely arrived a few days early in Window Rock, intending to get settled and deal with my vehicle before my job was to start. My ancient Volvo's water pump had failed outside Chicago, and a makeshift fix got me to my destination, but now a real repair was needed. The nearest garages were in Gallup, 26 miles southeast of Window Rock. Only one advertised expertise with foreign cars. It turned out to be a hole-in-the-wall establishment hard by the Santa Fe railroad tracks. Slow-moving, 50-car freight trains rumbled by every few minutes. Years later, the endlessly long trains would blow their shrill whistles at the same intervals during board meetings of the Navajo Code Talkers organization, for which I eventually became legal counsel. Its headquarters were at the Gallup train station. In that era, the trains were still coming through every ten minutes. Route 66 (now largely replaced by an interstate road, I-40) still runs parallel to those same railroad tracks. The vast Navajo Nation, the largest Indian reservation in population and land mass in the United States, occupies a vast stretch of desert and forest in the Four Corners region that includes portions of New Mexico, Arizona and a smaller area of southeastern Utah. Ramah and two other small satellite Navajo communities lie to the south and east of the main reservation, all three in New Mexico.

While waiting for my beat-up Volvo to be repaired, I was leafing through some old car magazines when the phone rang. Easing out from underneath my car while wiping grease from his hands, the mechanic picked up the phone. Slightly annoyed, he looked at me and said, "It's for you." I was startled. I didn't remember telling anyone where I was going but later became aware of the social osmosis characteristic of small towns. I put down my magazine and took the receiver. The voice on the other end belonged to Vard Johnson, our deputy director and my supervisor. A lanky Midwesterner from Nebraska and just two years out of Harvard Law School, he had the most court experience in our organization and was in charge of litigation. "We need your help on a new case," he said. "When are you getting back?" He mentioned something about a remote Navajo community, a hundred miles from our offices and south of Gallup, called Ramah (pronounced RAY-muh). I learned later that "Ramah" comes from the Book of Mormon, meaning a high or lofty place.

Vard told me the State Education Department had just shut down the only high school in the Ramah area serving this remote Navajo community. Without access to the Ramah public school, students would effectively have to travel hours, possibly a full day's drive from home, to attend school. I would learn more when I got to the meeting.

"The Navajos want the local school reopened, and we need to file suit fast because school is due to start in less than a month. Mitchell promised we'd do this. When can you get here?" Vard asked.

"The car's almost ready. I'll be back in an hour," I responded.

A few minutes later, the mechanic triumphantly handed the keys to me. I paid, hopped in the car, and drove off. Within 200 yards the car stopped dead. I ran back to the garage. The mechanic came back with me and opened the hood. After he correctly repositioned the distributor cap, the car started right up, and I started off for Window Rock to receive my first legal assignment.

I passed the outskirts of Gallup, an already fading coal mining town and now a staging area for much of the Navajo Reservation's modern services, especially pickup trucks and groceries. A Public Health Service hospital occupied a prominent hill near the business district. A BIA warehouse loomed near Ya-ta-hey junction where I turned west onto Arizona State Route 264 towards the Arizona-New Mexico state line. The two-lane highway meandered over and around treeless hills, an endless landscape unlike anything in New Jersey. Cattle and sheep appeared as specks on the mostly bare, high desert countryside. At one point, a turnoff led to a Peabody coal mine on Black Mesa. Here and there stood a few mission churches. Dotting the landscape were hogans—traditional one-room housing often made of mud or logs housing Navajo families. Every so often, trailers with giant roof antennas appeared. These were revivalist radio stations blaring "Jesus" messages in Navajo and English all day and much of the night. Just before the New Mexico state line and still off the reservation, I passed an infamous bar called the Navajo Inn. Yearlong, but especially now under the summer sun, in the open spaces out front at least a dozen drunken men were passed out in the dirt, a scene of desperation and hopelessness, which the War on Poverty had not yet alleviated.[19]

During the 30-minute drive back to Window Rock, I mused about how I had come to be on the Navajo Reservation.

I was assigned to a small, two-bedroom house about a mile from the DNA headquarters, which I shared with a former Yale classmate, Dan Press. My first week on the job, Ted Mitchell had sent me to Phoenix to get a legal brief printed and filed in the 9th Circuit Court of Appeals, this, of course, being decades before online electronic filing. When I returned that Monday evening, I went over to Ted's house to give him a report. Because of the trip, I had missed a meeting in the Navajo Council Chamber of the tribe's Advisory Committee, conducted earlier that day. Mitchell proceeded to tell me of an incident at the meeting involving Annie Wauneka. My memory of his account and the startling event we experienced the next day echoed throughout my legal practice in ways that my formal education or summer clerkship never could have prepared me for.

---

19. DNA mounted a massive effort to get rid of this and other bars defining Gallup. Although the Navajo Inn disappeared, the overall effort failed. By the mid-1970s, Gallup had the highest alcohol-related fatalities in the nation.

ANNIE WAUNEKA:
MATRIARCH V. PATRIARCH

A nnie Wauneka was formidable. Standing six feet tall or more on a large frame, she was always dressed in colorful Navajo skirts, blouses and jewelry, her jet-black hair neatly pulled back into a *tsiiyéél* or Navajo bun. She was, however, more than just physically imposing; she was a revered icon and political leader with a storied Navajo lineage.

The daughter of Henry Chee Dodge, the Navajo Tribal Council's legendary founder and first chairman, Mrs. Wauneka, as she was generally addressed, had an honored position among Navajos. Her work in healthcare had benefited her people greatly and added to her reputation. In 1963, she received a Presidential Medal of Freedom from President Lyndon B. Johnson for her efforts. She was thus one of the most respected and admired members of the Navajo Tribal Council.

It was therefore, shall we say, *dramatic*, that the first time I saw Mrs. Wauneka, she displayed all the raw emotion and frustration that Navajos and American Indians must feel daily, a side that reflects a human need more critical in some ways than food, clothing and shelter—a quality which over the next fifty years I have seen displayed numerous times in many ways: a need for respect, dignity, and recognition beyond Presidential medals or material wealth. Her manner of displaying this universal need in the Council Chamber, however, was unique.

The year 1968, when I arrived for my first job as staff attorney at DNA Legal Services, was perhaps one of the most contentious years in modern American politics. The year began with the Tet Offensive in Vietnam, which caught Americans by surprise. They had been told repeatedly that the "police action" in Vietnam would soon be over. It wasn't. Instead, the war escalated. Americans' fear of a protracted colonial war in a far-off country most Americans had never heard of was unfolding seemingly without end. In late March, President Johnson, a different kind of victim of the War in Vietnam, surprisingly announced he would not run for office again. In April, the Reverend Martin Luther King Jr. was assassinated, and in June, so was Senator Robert Kennedy. The anti-Vietnam War riot outside the Democratic Convention in Chicago in August nearly ignited a civil war. The world was coming apart just as my career was beginning.

Mitchell, DNA Legal Services' director, had a great sense of humor and a magnetic, though mercurial personality. After graduating from law school, he quickly focused on reforming life for Indians on the Navajo reservation. Given his tenacity, it was not surprising that in my absence another confrontation with a Navajo political leader had occurred. Only this time, it was with a leading icon of the tribe—Annie Wauneka.

Upon returning to Window Rock that Monday evening, Mitchell told me that the tribe's Advisory Committee, along with most of the Navajo councilmen, officials, dignitaries and observers, had been listening to a presentation by a Department of the Interior lawyer on a controversial new law enacted by Congress called the Indian Civil Rights Act of 1968. Previous civil rights laws were aimed at controlling anti-Black discrimination. Persons acting under state or federal law who deprived anyone of his or her basic civil rights could now be punished. But Indian tribes occupy a unique place in America. They are neither a state nor an instrument of the federal government, but are recognized as "domestic dependent nations."

Thus, they were not subject to the Civil Rights Act of 1964. Growing numbers of abuses of basic civil rights by Indian tribal governments were coming to Congress's attention. The new Indian Civil Rights Act of 1968—ICRA 25 U.S.C.§§ 1301-1304—was designed to fill this gap.

Inevitably, there was resistance to it from tribal governments, none more so than the Navajo government in Window Rock. Largely because of the upheaval caused by Ted Mitchell's brazen activities suing Navajo officials, the new law became an especially hot topic for the Navajo Nation. Tribal leaders of all political persuasions, including Annie Wauneka, thought the new law deprived them of their sovereignty. Though not a friend of the current tribal leadership, she was outraged by Ted Mitchell. This echoed among the tribe's leaders as a whole. How would the new law affect the raging battle between DNA's flamboyant, messianic Anglo director and the Navajo tribal leadership? Would precious tribal sovereignty over non-Indians on the reservation as provided for in the Navajo Treaty now be void? The basic fear was that the Indian Civil Rights Act would deprive them of their Navajo way of life and self-governance.

Mitchell had been urging and filing lawsuits against corrupt Navajo officials, and talk of his expulsion from the reservation had already started. During our last semester at Yale Law School, Mitchell had been sending his recruits news articles about the increasing tensions on Navajo Nation that chronicled growing concern over his actions against its leaders. Indeed, he had been busily confronting massive tribal corruption and misuse of governmental power, especially by Navajo Council Chairman Raymond Nakai, the tribe's Chief Executive and highest official. Mitchell believed correctly that flagrant political corruption by Nakai and other high Navajo officials aided and abetted by BIA officials of the Interior Department directly harmed tribal members, and Mitchell was backed by DNA's board, which included two revered and respected Navajo medicine men. For the first time, a systematic engine of reform was at work attacking these cozy sinecures, and Navajos needed DNA's assistance. The board also included the deans of the two Arizona law schools and several prominent Arizona trial lawyers including Jack Brown, for whom I had clerked the previous summer of 1967 in Phoenix. The new civil rights law seemed to give Mitchell broad avenues to fight Navajo tribal leaders' corruption. His brash personality and unconventional methods had, however, incensed those officials and others, which as noted included many of Nakai's political opponents, chief among whom was Annie Wauneka.

In effect, DNA's board of directors saw Mitchell as a champion of reform trying to expose and eliminate old, harmful tribal and federal governmental practices of the sort mimicked by the classic Hollywood western movie trope of corrupt federal government officials teaming up with corrupt tribal leaders for mutual benefit—the classic "I'll scratch your back, you scratch mine" system undergirding colonialism all over the world. Increasingly, the War on Poverty was exposing this phenomenon countrywide, but at Navajo Nation the effects seemed even more volatile. Meanwhile we, his new legal shock troops, were divided, and I was part of the group that staunchly defended him while others were opposed to him and formed a loose cabal against him. I thought this was dastardly. Why take a job in a remote area when you had already formed the opinion that the director of your program was no good?

Mitchell told me that an acting associate solicitor for the Interior Department had been explaining the controversial new Indian Civil Rights Act to the Navajo Council. At one point, Mrs. Wauneka rose to ask a question. In the formal manner employed by Navajos in settings like this, she asked the assistant solicitor whether the legislation would take away the Navajo Tribe's treaty right to kick bad white people off the reservation.[20] Clearly aware of the growing controversy over Mitchell, the assistant solicitor, obviously wise to the situation, dodged the question and instead of answering her, he asked, "Do you have anyone particular in mind?"

As Mitchell described it to me that evening, and as he and others later testified in court, Mrs. Wauneka instantly replied, "No"—an obvious lie that drew broad laughter from the audience including Mitchell, except that Mitchell's laugh was much louder, a real guffaw. He did not deny that he laughed more exuberantly than anyone else but claimed he did so out of embarrassment since everyone was aware that he was the immediate target of Mrs. Wauneka's reaction. After the laughter, she glowered at him, and the meeting resumed without further disruption. Ted seemed satisfied the episode was over and done with. It wasn't.

The next morning just before eight o'clock, I reported for work. Mitchell was already at the office. When he saw me, he suggested we go to the Council Chamber a mile away. He wanted me to hear the rest of the assistant solicitor's explanation of the new law. In view of what happened the day before, I asked whether that would be wise. He assured me it would be fine. So, we hopped into his pickup and drove to the Council Chamber in the Navajo capital of Window Rock, named for the massive natural sandstone wall with a huge hole in the middle carved by wind over eons that rises majestically just a few hundred yards away. The sky was a brilliant blue. Summer flowers dotted the grassy expanses leading to the dark blue ribbon of forest in the distance to the west. It was another typically beautiful summer day in the high desert of the Navajo Reservation.

We were early. The session was to start in about 45 minutes. We were thus able to park right outside the main entrance. (That turned out to be fortunate.) The main doors were still shut. We opened one and walked in. We immediately sat down, just inside the entrance on two folding chairs

---

20. Navajo Treaty of 1868, Art. II (15 Stat. 667): "[N]o persons except those herein so authorized to do, and except such officers, soldiers, agents and employees of the government, or of the Indians, as may be authorized to enter upon Indian Reservations in discharge of duties imposed by law, or the order of the President, shall ever be permitted to pass over, settle upon, or reside in the territory described in this article."

near the center aisle in the back row behind more rows of seats facing the stage. (That turned out to be unfortunate.) A center aisle divided the seats for members of the Council into two sections. On the stage dignitaries were already assembling. Between ours and the delegates' seats was an open space several yards wide stretching around the back and sides of the chamber.

Soon the place was packed. No one seemed to notice us. Mitchell began pointing out key personages on the stage: the principal target of Mitchell's ire, tribal chairman Raymond Nakai, was greeting others on the stage; Graham Holmes, the Interior Department's Navajo Area Director, whom Mitchell also disparaged, was doing likewise; Harold Mott, tribal attorney, was in deep conversation with someone; various other dignitaries roamed on or near the stage. Mitchell pointed out Annie Wauneka, who was already seated with her back to us in the first row of seats reserved for Council members. She had not noticed us. Off to the side on the stage facing the audience were several Navajo women who would later speak into what appeared to be megaphones. Mitchell explained they were interpreters. Everything was to be translated from English to Navajo and vice versa but only for the benefit of Council members, not spectators.

Shortly after nine o'clock, the meeting was called to order, and everyone rose for a Navajo blessing. Announcements came next, and then the assistant solicitor resumed his explanation of the new Indian Civil Rights Act of 1968. He explained how the new law granted Indians full access to the U.S. Bill of Rights on or off Indian reservations. The first thirty minutes were mundane and boring. The tensions of the previous day seemed to have dissipated.

I was ready to leave and was about to nudge Mitchell to suggest we go back to the office. Just then, an unnamed council delegate rose from his seat on the far right side of the chamber. The meeting droned on as he slowly walked towards the rear. I assumed he was headed for the restroom. Nobody paid any attention to him. He continued walking to the back of the chamber, turned to his right along the back in our general direction, then without looking at us, turned right again and began walking down the center aisle finally stopping beside the first row where Mrs. Wauneka was sitting. Her back was to us. He bent down and whispered something in her ear. Slowly, she stood up, turned around, and looked straight back towards us, a distance of perhaps 20 or 30 yards. Again, no one seemed to notice as she rose and started marching up the aisle towards the doors and us. The speaker droned on, and the audience continued somnolently listening to his presentation. Clomp, clomp, clomp, she drew nearer. Still, no one paid any attention as the revered matriarch of the Navajos, winner of the Presidential Medal of Freedom, marched steadily to the rear of the chamber. That is, until she was midway up the aisle, when Mitchell whispered ominously in my ear, "She's coming for me."

We needed to depart immediately. But now, terrifyingly, we discovered we were trapped. Without our noticing it, someone had opened the double front doors that had been closed when we arrived. The nearest door was now latched to a chain at the foot of our row, blocking us from exiting the way we had entered. Nor could we escape over the unoccupied row of chairs in front of us which Mrs. Wauneka was now fast approaching. Instantly, the picture grew menacing. When she was within just one empty chair away, a Kilauea of hot lava spitting from her eyes and spilling over us, as she glowered down at Mitchell.

At that, everything happened at once. Ignoring me, Mrs. Wauneka confronted Mitchell. Her steaming presence towering directly above us, she shouted, "YOU GONNA LAUGH AT ME AGAIN, TED MITCHELL?", raising her right arm horizontally palm-side up and simultaneously swinging as hard as she could directly at Mitchell's head while he was still facing her. As he started to rise, the first blow met his left cheek. He turned away, but not in time. The next landed near his left eye. Now standing, he turned his back toward her. She continued to pound him several more times with the same fury, striking his back. The place erupted. Bedlam reigned. It seemed everyone was screaming, yelling, running towards us. It was the first and only time in many years, thankfully, that I felt like I was in a riot. Mitchell continued to try to apologize, saying, "I think we'll go now." But where?

I moved to my left, the only direction which might offer a way out. Later, Mitchell jokingly accused me of cowardice for opening a path for him. He followed me. Somehow, we managed to wind our way through the berserk crowd now rushing towards us. The meeting dissolved into a melee. We managed to exit through the now open doors unscathed, except for the blows Mitchell received from Mrs. Wauneka. Fortunately, Ted's truck was nearby. We jumped right in and sped off just as the crowd was emerging from the chamber. A few minutes later back at the office, we nervously laughed our heads off. That's when I realized practicing law on the Navajo Reservation was not going to be anything like the staid Phoenix business-oriented law firm where I had worked the summer before.

Two days later, the Navajo Advisory Council met in special session. Citing Article II of the Navajo Treaty, it formally expelled Mitchell from the reservation, charging him with causing the disturbance in the Council chamber. Without delay, armed Navajo police escorted him off the reservation. DNA subsequently sued the tribe for illegally removing him from the reservation.

For the next few months until the lawsuit ended in Mitchell's favor, he lived in the storied El Rancho Motel in Gallup, famous for the many Hollywood idols who stayed there while filming westerns near Gallup. He parked a red trailer just off the reservation at the Arizona-New Mexico state line, the eastern boundary of the reservation two miles from DNA's headquarters and used it as his office, continuing to direct DNA. Later, he told me he would sneak back home at night to be with his family. A few months later, I was a witness at the federal court hearing in the lawsuit spawned by his exclusion under the new Indian Civil Rights law. I recounted Mrs. Wauneka's assault on Mitchell.

Within a few months, Mrs. Wauneka finally got the answer to her question. The federal judge in Phoenix held that under the facts of the case, the Indian Civil Rights Act gave Mitchell and DNA the right to sue for relief because Mitchell's right to due process had been violated.[21] Under the new law, a boorish guffaw in a packed Council chamber was not grounds for excluding an offensive white man from the reservation. Mitchell returned home and resumed running DNA from its headquarters.

And I started working on my first case.

---

21. The only hearing in the lawsuit spawned by Mitchell's exclusion led to a reported ruling in *Dodge v. Nakai*, 298 F. Supp. 26, at 29 (D., Az. 1969). The court vacated the expulsion order against Mitchell holding that the Indian Civil Rights Act amended the Navajo Treaty clause by limiting its exercise to expulsions conforming to the procedural requirements and protections of the Indian Civil Rights Act. A few years later the U.S. Supreme Court construed the Act narrowly, eliminating most civil remedies thus confining the Act mostly to criminal convictions which might trigger incarcerations violating civil rights. Abuses of civil rights continue to plague Indian reservations, although lately courts have been paying renewed attention to the problem of civil rights on Indian reservations, especially focusing on women's rights.

ON COERCIVE ASSIMILATION

first encountered Mormon missionaries that summer of 1968, en route to Window Rock. I had heard about them before but had never spoken with one. I had taken a meandering journey from New Jersey via Bozeman, Montana, where a law school buddy lived, and was headed for Window Rock, Arizona by way of Utah near Lake Powell, which borders the Navajo Reservation. I had stopped at an overlook in Bryce Canyon National Park. As I was gazing at the spectacular scenery, a woman and her gorgeous, twenty-something daughter drove up beside me and, with purpose in their eyes, immediately walked up to me. For twenty minutes first the mother and then the daughter tried to convince me to join the Mormon Church. I endured it as long as I could. Finally, after they had repeated their spiel ten different ways, I said, "If you can show me why everything you told me is not rank superstition, I'll join." Upon hearing that, they turned in unison and hopped back into their car. At that point, I had not known that Navajos and other tribes were particular targets of the Mormons. The beginning of my education was not far off, however. Exactly two weeks.

The lesson began in the company of Abe Plummer. Abe had been assigned to work with me as a Navajo-speaking counselor/interpreter. We would soon become lifelong friends. On my first visit to Ramah, he and I had driven in his Chevy pickup toting a bright blue camper to interview some of the Ramah Navajo people who might serve as plaintiffs in the lawsuit against the Gallup-McKinley County School Board to reopen Ramah High School. We had a list of people to speak with but no addresses, phone numbers or directions to their hogans. For a very good reason: they did not reside in numbered houses on named streets; they used post office boxes to receive mail. All we knew was that they lived somewhere on the other side of Ramah village within the vast checkerboard area partly owned by their tribe, their chapter, the state and private interests as allotments—an area of some 900 square miles with only one paved road. From Window Rock, we drove south through Gallup and proceeded farther south towards the junction of

New Mexico state road NM 53, a highway that extends from Grants, New Mexico, on the east end and travels west through the Ramah Navajo lands before reaching the Zuni Reservation, which lies west of Ramah village and near the Arizona border.

The scenery along the twisting road south of Gallup was impressive: forest-covered land with exotic rock outcroppings, and summertime wildflowers dotting the spaces between trees, everything looking fresh and untrammeled. Arriving at NM 53, we turned east for about ten miles until Ramah village, a Mormon settlement, came into view. It resembled a transplanted New England town with tree-lined dirt streets straight out of the late 19th century. There were no traffic signs, lights or signals. We arrived at what looked like the center of town. On one corner stood the Daisy Malt Shop, on the opposite corner the Bond Trading Post. We planned to stop there to ask for directions to peoples' hogans.

Edgar Bond, the original owner, was still alive, standing behind the counter, a grizzled figure with a smile, wearing overalls and a checkered shirt. While waiting for him to be free, we roamed around the store. All manner of horse gear and farm equipment was for sale, along with tools, clothes, groceries, knickknacks, candy bars, ice cream, rifles, ammunition and old pawn—Navajo-made jewelry used as collateral for loans which, if not paid off, was put up for sale, the trading post owner pocketing any profit.[22]

Mr. Bond was friendly. He was not being sued by DNA and seemed welcoming as we told him who we were and that we were looking for certain Navajos to testify for our lawsuit. The townsfolk were upset about the closing of the high school, too. We told him we needed directions to some Navajo homes, and Edgar Bond proved to be a font of knowledge. He gave us detailed directions to each of our target Navajo names given us by the Chapter leaders. After a few more minutes looking over the store

---

22. Trading posts became one of DNA's prime targets. They routinely set high interest rates on impossibly short terms, which perhaps most Navajos could never pay back. Hence, they were continuously in debt to the trader. This practice, along with crooked car dealers preying on Indians, became the central foci of our caseload. The Bond Trading post, however, did not attract DNA's attention, perhaps because it catered to a non-Indian clientele as well as the Navajos, and the town of Ramah was a community with shared interests in reopening the school.

and purchasing sandwiches and a few trinkets, we set off. Unfortunately, Edgar Bond's directions did not conform to any I was used to. They consisted of descriptions of features of the land, prominent landmarks such as big trees or strategically placed large stones, or outcroppings instead of street names. This was not suburban New Jersey.

Soon, we were well off NM 53, traveling over barely single-lane dirt trails. Gears grinding, we tumbled over rocks poking up from the rugged road, trying to follow the directions Edgar Bond had given us. For what seemed like miles and miles, up and down and around we went, looking for Ben Jose's hogan. He was first on our list. We had been told he had a daughter at the Albuquerque Indian School who had previously attended the now-shuttered Ramah High School. Hopelessly lost, we were about to retreat when we crested another rock-strewn stretch and popped over the top. There before us was not a hogan but a stock tank. The windmill was turning, and the tank was filled with water, it now being the rainy season. Around the tank a dozen or more sheep were taking their fill. And around the sheep were about ten or so Navajo children tending them. Seeing the truck, the kids took a quick look at us but resumed their activities— playing with each other and watching the sheep. But, as we got nearer and nearer, they suddenly swooshed off in all directions. In a flash, they simply disappeared, the sheep with them. In a matter of seconds, we were alone. No sheep, no children, only a windmill turning slowly in the breeze. I was puzzled. I turned to Abe and asked him what had just happened.

Carefully, Abe looked me up and down, taking in my dark pants, white shirt and narrow tie. After what seemed like an eternity, he said laconically, "They think you… Mormon… missionary… come to take them… to Utah!"

I never again wore dark pants, a white shirt and a tie in Navajo country. Eventually we did find the Jose hogan, and Mr. Jose became our lead plaintiff.

Although that all was amusing, the sinister side of the missionizing of Indians by whites soon became clear. To be sure, I already had an aversion towards missionizing acquired while still in high school, as my encounter at Bryce Canyon showed. Something about the practice smelled of condescension, arrogance, exploitation and superiority.

I admit it. I am biased, prejudiced, one-sided. I hate proselytizing. I make no bones about it. I can't stand somebody telling me or anyone else how to think or how to get to heaven. Reasoned debate is one thing. But cajoling another to change his fundamental beliefs—especially someone perceived to be on a lower social scale or poor—is a sin. It is abhorrent to me. Reasoned theological debate among equals is one thing. But the Christian practice of exploiting other people's poverty or lack of education to get converts is detestable to me. When I learned that European colonialism rested on the twin peaks of converting Natives to Christianity and exploiting their resources, I realized that what makes the practice so obnoxious is that it is targeted mostly at people who are materially weaker than the proselytizers. Yes, many Christians believe exactly the opposite. To them, bringing the word of Christ to heathens is a virtue, indeed a duty. Let me tell you—it is not. Many wars have started because of this practice. Case in point: the Crusades.

No group in history has been the victim of aggressive missionizing more than American Indians from coast to coast and from the tip of South America to the Arctic. Ever since the white man appeared in the New World, Natives have been the target of aggressive proselytizing and, of course, even worse—genocide. As I learned at the Bryce Canyon National Park overlook, aggressive missionizing still goes on—a lingering curse of the European conquest of the Americas since Columbus. Europeans started with military invasions such as the Crusades, followed by genocide, followed by the sins of the clergy in scaring people with warnings of hell if they did not convert, often accompanied by mass sexual assaults. All of which, of course, was and is aimed at economic exploitation, for along with converting Native peoples to alien beliefs went slavery and the seizing of land. Indeed, slavery and land theft produced America's wealth. But along with slavery, to me, nothing is as evil as forcing weaker human beings into accepting someone else's religion when they have not asked to be converted or have any real means of warding off an aggressive Elmer Gantry. Undeniably, indentured labor by Natives, a form of slavery, extended into recent times right here in New Mexico[23] and still exists in the 21st century in the form of human trafficking.

---

23. Reséndez, A. *The Other Slavery: The Uncovered Story of Indian Enslavement in America*. Houghton Mifflin Harcourt, 2016, 314. Reséndez cites the Albuquerque Journal, April 26, 1967: "The War on Poverty administrator in New Mexico, Alex Mercure, estimated the number of agricultural workers living in 'economic peonage' to be about 120,000 in the entire state."

Sometime after my first trip to Ramah with Abe, I was watching a local rodeo on a dirt field near the high school. Two Mormon missionaries, dressed as I had been that day with Abe, were sitting in front of me. In between watching bareback bronco riding and roping, they compared notes of the numbers of Navajo children they had successfully recruited for this modern-day system of cultural genocide.

Persuasion is just one means of producing conversions. Among Navajos, conversion by missionaries handing out desperately needed baskets of food was said to be common. I have seen the effects of this "benign" form of discrimination: losing one's children by allowing them to be raised far from home in "Christian" surroundings, often forbidding contact with parents, all aimed at erasing the Navajo in them. To me, this is as cruel and exploitative as physical assaults. Mental sickness, despair, aimlessness, self-delusion, and inability to function as independent, self-reliant human beings are the result of such assaults by wealthier outsiders with guns. Missionizing among Native Americans has produced joblessness, family breakups, suicides and dependency.

To be sure, there are benign forms of missionizing. Not all religions use threats of damnation or grotesque offers of food to entice desperate Indians to convert. Later in my career, I befriended an Episcopalian priest on the Wind River Reservation in western Wyoming, the Reverend David Duncombe. He and his family respected Indians' own beliefs and customs. I just want to make it clear that I am aware of the kindness and humanity of many white people, whether acting as representatives of their religions or simply as do-gooders who have worked tirelessly, often under difficult circumstances, to help Indians get through life. Father Duncombe was one of these. He believed in education and, yes, opened the church doors to Native people. But he did not force anyone to attend. He was a humanitarian through and through who sacrificed his life doing good deeds. Answering a late-night call to drive home a drunken 15-year-old in April 1976, the young man immediately hopped into his car. On the way to the teenager's home, the youth suddenly pulled out a knife and stabbed the 55-year-old Episcopalian priest to death. The tragedy drew hundreds of folks from the entire reservation to his elaborate Indian-Christian-style funeral. High Episcopalian bishops conducted a service in the picturesque church beneath the snow-covered Wind River Mountains, while traditional Indian songs and ceremonies also took place. I remained friends with his children, who return periodically to visit their father's grave in the small graveyard next to the church at Ethete, Wyoming, and renew friendships with the kindly Northern Arapahos and Shoshones who live there. Folks like this kind preacher respect Indian cultures and skillfully weave their personal religious beliefs into their worldview and customs without overbearing threats and bribes as some denominations do.

So, to be clear, I am not talking about legitimate arguments between two equally matched persons concerning philosophy or religion or politics. Honest debate is the lifeblood of democracy, the law and legal process. Nor am I talking about truly charitable activity to help desperately poor people get through life on Indian reservations. But there is a fundamental difference between honest, fair disputation accompanied by kindly assistance not in conflict with ancient tribal customs and beliefs and that of psychological subjugation. The former is central to the Academy, to science, to the evolution of culture, to simple decency. These private activities are the essence of an enlightened polity and a democratic society. Coercive assimilation, on the other hand, rests on a foundation of inequality. The conqueror verbally assaults the vanquished Native in his dirt-floored dwelling with six hungry kids by promising gifts of food and an afterlife if he (a) gives up his land, (b) converts to the conqueror's religion, and (c) allows his children to be taken from their mothers' skirts and hauled off to distant boarding schools to be forcibly converted to a foreign religion.

Coercive assimilation is neither charitable nor benevolent. It is a psychological and sometimes even physical assault—behavior initiated by a conqueror to force conquered subjects to change their customs and beliefs and to adopt those of the conqueror, often accompanied by stealing valuable resources from their land. In the late 1800s some people thought that taking Indian children from their homes at age five and educating them in distant boarding schools was benign. It was certainly better than physical genocide. But psychological genocide is still genocide. In the late 19th century, white men who thought they were enlightened began realizing that killing Indians was no longer tolerable. Instead, they thought it acceptable to transport Native children hundreds and even thousands of miles away to white men's boarding schools. There, they would be clothed in formal white man's clothing—little plaid skirts for girls and neat shirts and trousers for boys, their heads shaven. They were required to speak only English with mouths washed out with soap for transgressions and forced to attend church on Sundays.[24] Deprived of the companionship and love of their relatives sometimes for years, they were deemed barbaric, and their Indian religions and other customs were forbidden.

The practice had the full backing and underwriting of the U.S. government and numerous churches. President Ulysses S. Grant adopted it as official federal policy. Reservations were divided up among church denominations, much as economic franchises akin to how the Dutch East Indian Company or English mercantile companies divided their colonies amongst shipping companies for colonizing exploitation. Military force hovered in the background in case of resistance.

In the late 1800s, the U.S. government felt that Native American traditions were at odds with assimilating them into European American society. In 1883, Secretary of the Interior Henry Moore Teller, a Colorado lawyer and militia leader, instructed Hiram Price, his Commissioner of Indian Affairs, to create the "Code of Indian Offenses," which prohibited practices like ceremonial dances and medicine men, essentially criminalizing Indian culture.[25]

When I got to the Navajo Reservation in late 1968 and was assigned to the Ramah Navajo case, I needed to do research. I found a monograph on Indians in New Mexico focused on their education and standard of living, written by a Ph.D. anthropologist named Anne M. Smith, who lived in Santa Fe. She viewed these colonizing practices with disdain. Noting that Indians comprise only six percent of the State's population, Dr. Smith wrote:

> ...[S]ince of all groups in the State they rank lowest in years of education and in health, and highest in the percentage of unemployment, they present a formidable problem.... [T]he solving of their problems and the development of their

24. A government psychiatrist working at the Albuquerque Indian School told me in the summer of 1968 that the practice at that BIA school was to require all children to attend church on Sundays. Those who refused were forced to stand outside regardless of weather, until the others returned.

25. Price, Hiram. *Rules Governing The Court of Indian Offenses*. March 30, 1883. https://commons.und.edu/indigenous-gov-docs/131/.

potential must be the concern of all New Mexicans.... How we help them solve their problems of education will have direct bearing on freeing their human potential and the ultimate contribution that potential can make to the State in countless ways.[26]

The psychological and physical effects of more than a century of coordinated coercive assimilation is incalculable. We don't even need to get into the numerous sexual abuse cases recently coming to light. It is enough to record the massive number of suicides, deaths from sickness, runaways, and mentally impaired human beings who came and still come out of these hellhole "Christian" institutions.

The Indian Student Placement Program, originally called the Lamanite Indian Student Placement Program, was operated by the Church of Jesus Christ of Latter-day Saints between 1947 and 2000, and for more than five decades, they placed an estimated 40,000 children[27] in Mormon foster homes. Most people referred to it as "Mormon Placement." Many Navajo children were taken from their homes in Arizona and New Mexico and placed with Mormon families hundreds of miles away to be raised as semi-white children. When I arrived at Ramah in the late 1960s, the LDS Church did not recognize Indians or any people of color as "delightsome" and thus deemed them unfit for the highest rank of immortality after death. The incident with Abe at the well is explained by the children's own fear of being taken from their homes and shipped off to foster families in Utah.

I have in my possession a letter written in 1969 by the Church of Jesus Christ of Latter-day Saints to Navajo parents, warning them of the dangers of bringing their children home during the Christmas holidays from Mormon Indian Student Placement Program.

26. Smith, A. M. *New Mexico Indians*. Museum of New Mexico Research Records (1966), No. 1, p. 2.

27. Landry, Alysa. "How Mormons Assimilated Native Children." *ICT News*, Oct. 7, 2017. https://ictnews.org/archive/how-mormons-assimilated-native-children/

of
The Church of Jesus Christ of Latter-day Saints

10 East South Temple, Suite 1250
Salt Lake City, Utah 84111

Phone (801) 364-2511
Ext. 2045

December 10, 1969

Dear Parents:

The Holiday Season is approaching and you will probably be missing your children who are away from home. I know it will be hard for you and you are to be complimented for your strength in doing what is good for your children.

Many of you may be thinking of visiting your child and his foster family sometime during the Holidays. I hope you will not do this. Most of the time it is not good for you or your child. It makes you both homesick and your child must adjust again after you leave. It is also dangerous for you to be on the highway during the winter months.

If you feel you must visit, it is better to come later in the spring. Christmas is not a good time to visit. In any event, children should not be away from their foster family on Christmas day. May I also suggest that when you do visit, you plan ahead and make sure you have enough money for motels, meals and other expenses.

As you know, no student is allowed to go home for any reason during the school year and children should not be kept away from their foster families for more than a few hours and definitely not overnight.

Your children are generally doing very well on Placement this year. By the time you get this letter, one of the caseworkers should have already talked to you about your child. If you could not make it to the meeting, I hope to see you when I visit again next spring.

May the Lord bless you in your efforts to provide an education for your children. I wish you a happy Holiday Season!

Sincerely,

Tamara Holdrey
District Social Worker

Mormon Placement holiday letter to parents, 1969.

My friend Tom Luebben, in the early 70s, was working as staff attorney and director of litigation at the Native American Legal Defense and Education Fund. At the time, his boss, Richard L. Young, was litigating to close the Intermountain Indian Boarding School in Brigham City, Utah. The school had a student body consisting entirely of Navajos recruited on the main reservation in Arizona and bussed to Brigham City. The facility had previously served as the Bushnell Army Hospital during World War II, which at its peak had grown to roughly 6,000 inhabitants, including patients, military personnel and civilian employees. After it was closed, the almost all white Mormon citizens of Brigham City sought a new payroll source from the federal government.

In 1949 President Truman authorized funds to remodel the facility to accommodate over 2,000 Navajo students, grades 1-12, with the explicit aim to assimilate them into white society. In 1971, the National Indian Youth Council, represented by the Native American Legal Defense and Education Fund brought a class action lawsuit against the Bureau of Indian Affairs on behalf of the Navajo students, who alleged they were sedated with Thorazine, illegally racially segregated, provided an inferior education, and proselytized to abandon their native religion, including the Native American Church, in favor of Mormonism. The case, *National Indian Youth Council et al., Plaintiffs, v. Louis R. Bruce et al., Defendants*, was dismissed in 1973. Enrollment of Navajos dwindled, and by 1975, the boarding school had become the Intermountain Inter-Tribal School and enrolled students from nearly 100 tribes. Fortunately, the school was shut down in 1984.

While that school was open, the overall effect of proselytization on children was devastating. Self-hatred and hatred of their families became the norm. The psychological damage was and still is immeasurable. In the ranks of human predation this so-called Christian practice amounts to church-sanctioned kidnapping and brainwashing.[28] In every way it deserves condemnation and recognition that such practices are no longer in conformity with international law under the United Nations Universal Declaration of Human Rights—the right to be free from coercive assimilation. Some, such as Janine Pease, a MacArthur Fellow and a research historian and Board Chairman of the Crow Language Consortium, have been seeking a Truth and Reconciliation Commission to begin the healing from these horrors.[29] Some states, such as Colorado, tasked by its state legislature in 2022,

---

28. Garrett, Matthew. *Making Lamanites: Mormons, Native Americans, and the Indian Student Placement Program, 1947-2000* (University of Utah Press, 2016)

29. https://www.wbur.org/hereandnow/2022/05/20/indigenous-boarding-schools

have undertaken investigations into their history of boarding schools in consultation with tribes.

In June 2021, U.S. Interior Secretary Deb Haaland announced the creation of the Federal Indian Boarding School Initiative, aimed at investigating and documenting the deaths and lasting consequences from the cruel treatment of Native American students at these schools. The same year, a U.S. Representative from Kansas, Sharice Davids, introduced H.R. 5444, the Truth and Healing Commission on Indian Boarding School Policies Act, which as of this writing has not yet become law.

On October 25, 2024, President Joe Biden was the first U.S. President to make an apology for the U.S. Indian Boarding Schools program, which traumatized generations of Native Americans. The initiative found that at least 18,000 children were sent to boarding schools, some as young as 4, between 1819 through the 1970s. The investigative report documented nearly 1,000 student deaths and 74 gravesites at more than 500 federal boarding schools.

The Federal Boarding School Initiative made policy recommendations to Congress and the Executive Branch to continue a path to healing and redress for Indigenous communities and the nation, but now in 2026, progress is unlikely on that front in the coming four years. Nevertheless, the grave injustices of the boarding school era show just how important it was to return control of education to the tribes.

MY ACCIDENTAL CAREER IN INDIAN LAW

I thought of my new job as a fledgling lawyer for Navajo Indians as a Peace Corps-type gig to be of service to my country, since the metal screw in my ankle resulted in me flunking the physical after receiving my third draft notice. My stint at DNA Legal Services was supposed to be temporary, something worthwhile to do for a year or two before settling down to a real job.

I never planned a career in Indian law, but that's the thing about it. It is captivating. Only rarely is anything cut-and-dried. Culture clashes often underlie, inform and define real problems. That both interests and baffles me. Issues involving cultural, linguistic and spiritual conflicts are embedded even in situations that appear simple, at least to a non-Indian. Yet many issues are often intractable and only superficially resolved. Navajo culture and religion remain extremely active and undergird most legal fights; Anglo law overlays a complex, centuries-old tradition of problem-solving through endless talking. In most cases, a resolution requires compromise.

For many in Navajo Nation, livelihoods are still based on a centuries-old barter economy. The Navajos weave exquisite rugs with the wool from their churro sheep, a breed first brought to America from León Spain, in 1493 on Columbus's second voyage, and again in 1519 by Hernán Cortés. They craft jewelry from Southwest sources of silver and turquoise, "heishi" shell beads and coral traded since pre-Columbian times from Mesoamerica, and even the berry seeds from the ubiquitous juniper trees. They learned agricultural practices from the Puebloan peoples and bring meats from their livestock to local trading posts. When I arrived in the late sixties, it was not unusual for a Navajo to trade a magnificently crafted weaving—the patterns made with hand-dyed plant and mineral pigments that took many months to produce—for a pickup truck. A matriarchal society, Navajo women control the purse strings.

Life in Indian country is fraught with uncertainty. Most disputes involve existential issues involving psychology, language, economics, lifestyles, tradition and philosophical disagreements, all complicated by the never-ending ominous hand of what I have heard Navajos refer to as the "Great White Father in Wash-in-done." During the 19th century Presidents took a paternalistic stance in negotiating treaties with American Indians, and from the 1860s to early1900s Western adventure dime novels may have popularized the term "Great White Father."

Control of land is often at the center of disputes. Anglo lawyers do best by fighting the federal or state governments, as well as merchants, on behalf of Navajos. Ted Mitchell was on their side, and he understood who was exploiting the Navajos, like the Anglo car dealers and traders. This still goes on half a century later.[30] The American capitalist system allows for those practices by businessmen.

Published estimates of the Indigenous population in the Americas when Columbus arrived in what he first thought was India are around sixty million people. Some historians argue for at least a hundred million. They comprised thousands of bands, tribes, cultures and languages. Myriad tribes in this part of the world managed to survive despite the mass slaughter, genocide and infectious disease, which took place after 1492 at the hands of Europeans. Not that life was peaceful before their arrival. Raids or "mourning wars" to avenge the death of kin or tribesmen raged constantly but often did not involve existential disputes. Most were territorial. Hunting grounds often overlapped. When one tribe prevailed, the loser simply found new ground to inhabit.

The amazing book by Charles C. Mann, titled *1491: New Revelations of the Americas Before Columbus* (Knopf, 2005), captures the scene just before Europeans arrived. Mann describes the first meeting between Spanish conquistador Francisco Pizarro and the Inca leader, Atahualpa, in Peru in 1532. The Inca numbered in the thousands while the Spaniards numbered around two hundred. Pizarro's soldiers showed up mostly on foot and some on horses, encumbered by steel armor and a few blunder-busses, which the Inca people had never seen before. Upon meeting with Pizarro's interpreter Valverde, Atahualpa was handed the Roman Rite of

---

30. Office of Navajo Nation Human Rights Commission Press Release, July 29, 2021: $450,000 Settlement agreement between the Federal Trade Commission and Tate's Auto Group

(https://www.navajo-nsn.gov/News%20Releases/NNHRC/2021/PR_07292021_FTCPressRelease.pdf)

the Catholic Church which he threw to the ground, so Pizzaro promptly had his armed men execute scores of Inca soldiers and placed Atahualpa under capture, demanding that the room in which he was held be filled with silver and gold as ransom. Despite having received the ransom, Pizarro had Atahualpa tried and executed the following year, effectively ending the Inca Empire, the largest in pre-Columbian America. Events such as this marked a major turning point in world history. American Indian tribes on both continents would never be the same again.[31]

Later, African slaves were brought over on perilous voyages from a distant continent, transforming agriculture in the Americas and altering the demographics of the New World forever. Forced, brutal, unpaid labor by both Native Americans and Africans has caused five centuries of earth-shattering tragedy. The legacy of cultural theft and enslavement continues to dominate and undermine society on both continents and indeed the world. Human lives changed everywhere because these two newly discovered continents offered Europeans pathways to power and wealth.

My appearance in this foreign, Indian-inhabited territory of the largest reservation-based tribe in the country—the Navajos, occupying a strikingly beautiful but often desolate landscape in northern New Mexico—was not driven by any messianic impulse. I stumbled into this unfamiliar world with its mysterious natural splendor and hearty, dignified people more by accident than by design. I did not plan to settle on an Indian reservation or anywhere near one. But my initial assignment never seemed to reach a decisive end. Looking back over the decades, I realize there was never a distinct plateau from which I could reflect and say, "Okay, now I'm done; I've concluded this phase of my life, and now it's off to do other things…." What turned out to be my life's work just evolved in stages. A new wrinkle, a new concern, a partial victory—all prevented me from moving on. For years I assumed I would eventually move into a corporate-style law practice. While working in Indian law, problems would get resolved, but new ones would emerge. Until they were handled and set right, I could not break away. Each "case" or "project" led inexorably to a new one related to the old.

---

31. Except for remote groups of indigenous peoples in voluntary isolation, mainly in the Amazon Basin, which were largely left alone until the 20th century. Their existence has been imperiled ever since.

After my first lawsuit at DNA—an attempt to prevent the closing of a remote public high school serving the isolated Ramah Navajos in northwestern New Mexico—fizzled, Mitchell wanted me to quit the case and move on to the next lawsuit. He was ready to concede defeat; I was not. He thought I was wasting my time, so we had a falling-out. Mitchell eventually migrated to the Far Pacific to establish a remote islands legal service program, and we never saw each other again.

It was impossible for me to just abandon my first clients, the Ramah Navajo Chapter. Indeed, their problems seemed intractable, especially to lawsuits, yet their situation was dire and compelling. What most people take for granted in America—free access to a public education—was being denied to this community, and the remedy that the Gallup-McKinley School District proposed was reprehensible. There *had* to be a solution.

Things morphed into new phases, just as challenging and risky. The same central problem permeated all struggles for the Ramah Navajo: how to achieve a decent standard of living without abandoning their native identity, and in this fight, how to educate their children close to home. After a couple of years of presiding over failed litigation, I finally suggested that the community try to start their own school from scratch. No Indian community had done that since the 19th century. All such attempts had triggered swift pushback from non-Indians, especially church groups who were not going to allow Indians to run their own schools in their own fashion. Luck played a major role, but so did my sense of purpose and temperament. I was not going to abandon the Ramah Navajos until either they fired me, or we reached a truly impossible impasse. So, we slogged along.

One showcase, Indian-controlled school did exist: the Rough Rock Demonstration School (RRDS). Also located on the Navajo Nation, it had been conceived in Washington, D.C., by the Bureau of Indian Affairs and Office of Economic Opportunity as a part of the War on Poverty in the early 1960s, opening its doors in 1966. Indeed, Rough Rock is still a model of Navajo-centered learning. The BIA had built a new school at Rough Rock, which sits on top of a mesa east of Chinle in the valley. In the early 1960s, Senator Robert Kennedy had launched a nationwide examination of Indian education. He and his committee journeyed from the most remote parts of Alaska to the southernmost tip of Florida in their quest for information and first-hand accounts of education at BIA-funded schools, state public schools and religious schools run by various versions of Christianity. The results were contained in a two-part summary report, "Indian Education: A National Tragedy—A National Challenge," the tragedy referring to an account of heartrending records and investigations, and the challenge being the subcommittee's recommendations for fixing the crisis. A preprint was released in the summer of 1968, a month or two after I arrived in Window Rock to start my gig as a DNA lawyer. I sent away for a copy of the report. It changed my life.

The Rough Rock story was exciting and provided the model for the Ramah Navajos. Its curriculum was developed by teachers committees that created detailed plans for the subjects of English, Math, Social Studies, Navajo Language and Science. The Navajo community still operates it and has changed its name to Rough Rock Community School, having gone through the incorporation process in 1994.

To illustrate a striking contrast between the centuries-old federal boarding school model aimed at assimilation and a curriculum that centers a child's self-worth, cultural appreciation and sense of belonging, here is an excerpt from Rough Rock's 1969 Compilation of Curriculum Guidelines[32]:

STUDENT ORIENTATION

Suggestions for student orientation in all classes where English is used as the language of instruction for two weeks at the beginning of the year.

Student situation:

1. Lacks self-confidence.

2. Comes from an environment without English language stimulation.

3. English language skills have in all likelihood regressed.

4. May be physically below par.

32. https://files.eric.ed.gov/fulltext/ED036389.pdf

Student needs:

1. Feeling of personal worth and confidence in his ability to succeed.

2. Recognition of school and learning as pleasurable experiences.

3. Physically and emotionally strengthening environment.

4. Language skills: thinking in, listening to, and speaking English in an experiential framework.

Teacher musts:

1. Make a tactics plan which encompasses all needs as outlined for his group.

2. Vary activities to eliminate restlessness.

3. Take time for each child as an individual each day, even if it is only saying goodbye to each child at the end of the day.

4. Use some informal evaluation (sociometric and linguistic) for measuring growth during orientation period.

5. Forget desire for a quiet classroom.

6. Work with small groups at some time during each day to reduce tension in using the second language.

7. Remember that planning should concentrate on providing a climate of warmth, acceptance, and stimulation that emphasizes a high percentage of classroom time devoted to oral English.

8. Be willing to make "a fool of himself."

9. Let the textbooks wait.

10. Praise liberally and sincerely, avoiding any negative criticism except that which comes from the group concerning a group activity, or from an individual concerning his own performance.

Here is an excerpt from the Navajo Language (Diné) Curriculum:

Diné

A guideline and a suggested sequence for a course of study on Navajo culture (including the encoding and decoding of the language) whose purpose is making explicit that which has been implicit)

Preschool levels:

niilyáii (that which has been placed)

hot'aah niilyáii (in the sky)

identification of jihonáa'éí (the sun),

t1éhonáa'a (the moon), and so' (the stars)

nahasdzaan bikáá niilyáii (on the earth)

nihokáá (on land)

nahokáá, hináanii (creatures that live on land)

naagháii (walkers)

naaldlooshii (four legged) identification

and care of animals

dine' (mankind)

concept of different cultures

diné

health and safety, beauty, physical fitness.

language for structuring of thought

exercise

sensory perception

bááhádzidii (harmful creatures)

identification

naat'a'ii (flyers)

observation and identification

naana'ii (crawlers)

observation and identification

na'atii (small animals)

observation and identification

ch'osh (insects)

observation and identification

nanitse' (plants)

identification and use of beneficial and harmful plants

nahasd záán bighi' niilyáii (in the earth)

collecting of łeezh (soil), tsé (rock), and beesh (metals)

diné baniilyáii (given to the Navajos)

diné yikéhgo yigáałii (way of life, fun songs, listening to squaw dance songs, experiencing rhythm, listening to and discussing Grandfather, Coyote, and Wolf stories

ya'át'eehgo (childhood role in ʻiináago na'adá—the good way of life)

respecting elders

caring for younger children

respectful of guests

carrying wood and water

care of hogan

simple food preparation

family relationships

doo yá'át'eegóó na'adá (bad ways)

thinking bad thoughts i.e., taboos

The Kennedy Report had one major flaw: it provided no instructions and no manual for a replication of Rough Rock Demonstration School. It did tell their story from before the community was chosen for a contract to operate a local Indian school funded by the federal government. It had a powerful impact on me, and it occurred to me that here was the perfect example of what should be done at Ramah: give the keys to the family car to Indian tribes and communities. They could do a better job at educating their own children than anyone else would. I tried to persuade them to start a branch at Ramah, but Dillon Platero, Rough Rock's headmaster, a Navajo educator and superb orator, turned down the request on the grounds that RRDS was a handful already, and they could not spare the time or personnel to take on another project, especially one 250 miles away.

So, my first client, the Ramah Navajos of western New Mexico, would simply have to start its own school from scratch.

ROUGH ROCK DEMONSTRATION SCHOOL: AN INTERVIEW WITH ANITA PFEIFFER

In August 2018, I visited Anita Pfeiffer at her home in Albuquerque. Anita Pfeiffer is a legendary educator because of her role in helping to develop the innovative curriculum at the Rough Rock Demonstration School, the first culturally centered Indian School. Kip Bobroff, her son-in-law and a professor at the University of New Mexico School of Law, listened in.
This interview has been edited for brevity and clarity.

Mike: What is your Navajo clan?

Anita: *Totach'eeni*—Bitter Water.

Mike: And I know when you introduce yourself, there's more to it.

Anita: My dad's clan was *Tsendikinne* (Beneath the Cliff House), and then my grandfather on my mother's side, *Tsuka'anehe* (Reed Clan). Then on my father's side is the Mexican clan.

Mike: Where were these clans located, or were they all over?

Anita: Well, the Bitter Water Clan, there's a whole bunch around the Kanton area, and then there are pockets in different areas.

Mike: So, Rough Rock was not one of them, I take it.

Anita: No. My dad was from between Round Rock and Rough Rock.

Mike: So, where did you start to school?

Anita: Kayenta, in a one-room schoolhouse. That building is still there. It was run by Arizona Public Schools. I think it went up to 10th grade, first through tenth in one room.

Mike: And after 10th grade?

Anita: I only went to Kayenta until 2nd grade. My family moved to Bellemont, so first they put me in the Tuba City boarding school. My parents came to visit me and they saw me under a large cottonwood tree with a box and my beautiful ribbons and a doll—with no friends around me. They felt so sorry that they took me out of school. I finished 2nd grade at the public school. But then we were moving to Phoenix and my teacher said, "I want you to skip 3rd grade. So, when you go to Phoenix, I'll write a letter that you should be in 4th grade." That's what happened. After that and through 7th grade, I went to Tucson. It was another boarding school run by the Presbyterian mission, much like the Menaul School (in Albuquerque), the same sponsors. I was there for two years. Then my dad got sick, so I went home to Klagetoh where my family lived. So, we were there and we had some friends from California, a Methodist minister and his wife. They were talking with my parents while I was outside doing some chores. After a while, they came out and my dad says, "Our friend here would like to suggest you go back with them and that you go to public school." Dr. Werbach was the Methodist minister. I thought about it and said, "OK." I flew to California and was there as a 9th grader. I missed all my friends in Tucson, so I only spent one year there and went back to Tucson.

Mike: Did you have brothers and sisters?

Anita: I'm the oldest of 13.

Mike: So, after high school, what happened? Where did you go to college?

Anita: I had a four-year scholarship to the University of Arizona in Tucson, and my teacher said, "You know, you're a budding pianist. There's a really fine college at Hastings, Nebraska." So that's where I went. She talked me into it and said, "I'm getting married in August and I'd like you to be my bridesmaid." Her family lived in Omaha, which is where she was going to get married. So, I was her bridesmaid, and then they took me to Hastings College.

Mike: How much contact did you have with your family in those years?

Anita: By letter, and then I went home as much as I could, depending on expenses. I always thought it was a good thing that my teacher suggested Hastings College because I was a freshman, and Cam came from Oberlin College to Hastings, and that's where we met.

Mike: Oh, a side benefit! So, you got married while still at Hastings?

Anita: I was a freshman, and he was a sophomore. During my sophomore year, I applied to study abroad, and I was selected, so I went to Madras, India, to study for a year. Before I left, we became engaged.

Mike: Who paid for the India expedition?

Anita: The same people who sponsored the school that I went to in Tucson, the Presbyterian Mission. After Madras, I still had one more year to finish my BA, and that was the year Cam was graduating from Hastings. I went to see my family and then went to Cam's graduation. Then we drove to Arizona to see my parents, and we decided that I should finish my senior year in Tucson where he was enrolled in their master's program. So that's what we did.

Mike: What was his field when he went to graduate school?

Anita: Cultural anthropology. My degree was in elementary education.

Mike: Did you go to work after you graduated?

Anita: There was a school in a rural area outside Tucson that hired me. It was a very nice school. There were no minorities there, just Anglos. I hadn't visited the school or asked if I could teach there. I was interviewed in the education department in downtown Tucson. With a name like Pfeiffer, the school thought, oh! So, I went there, and they were surprised to see me. "Are you Anita Pfeiffer?"

I said, "Yes, and my husband is Cam Pfeiffer." I taught there until I got tenured, and Cam also taught at the high school level at a different school. After that, while I was working on my masters, we thought we should really go to the Navajo reservation and see if there was a school that served elementary up to high school students. We drove up and visited the different districts, talked to the superintendents, and they were very nice except the one in Chinle. We decided that was where we would sign our contracts.

Then we went back to Tucson, thinking about packing and so forth, when a nice man came to visit us. I guess he had heard that there was this couple looking for jobs. Anyway, he said, "We're starting a new school at a community called Rough Rock." He asked if we would be interested in it. It was going to be controlled by the community. That was 1966. So, we broke our contract in Chinle. We wrote a letter to the board members, and then we told the superintendent that we would accept their offer to teach at the new Rough Rock school.

Mike: Was Rough Rock Demonstration School already functioning when you first got there?

Anita: They were putting things together. Everything was being developed.

Mike: Do you know the story that was told in the special senate sub-committee report—I think it was there—about how the BIA and Office of Economic Opportunity (OEO) got together? I guess they only looked at the Navajo reservation because they had the biggest boarding school problem and the largest tribe. So, some people at OEO and BIA were building a school at Lukachukai, right?

Anita: The buildings were already there, and they had apportioned other buildings for the community school, but the people didn't really work well together, as I understand it.

Bob Roessel Jr.[33] was at that time trying to work on this idea of community control, and then it really flourished. The elementary school at Rough Rock had already been built. Dr. Roessel and others, the BIA, and funders at Navajo Nation decided that they would set it up as a community-controlled school.

Mike: Having a school operated by an Indian tribe was a novel thing. That hadn't happened before as far as I know, at least since the 19th century Cherokee schools were closed.

Anita: It was an idea that Bob really wanted to initiate. Because this was a brand-new building, there were no board members, no individuals that were hired yet, so it seemed like a perfect place to try this idea.

When Cam and I went there, I was supposed to teach 1st grade in Navajo. There were no books available. No furniture. We all had to help order books and furniture for the school. We wanted to start school in August.

Mike: What kind of housing was there?

Anita: BIA usually structured the schools then with homes for the staff. Before the new school was built there was an old, one-room schoolhouse constructed of rocks near the trading post. Chava Watson taught elementary kids 1st through 3rd grade. After that, the children went down to Many Farms to the BIA school for 4th grade on up.

---

33. A leader in Indian education: https://center-for-indian-education. asu.edu/content/dr-robert-roessel-jr-founding-director-1959-1966

Mike: And they had a dormitory there too?

Anita: I think it was a day school.

Mike: When you got to the new Rough Rock Demonstration School, was it a boarding school at all, or was it always a day school?

Anita: Because we recruited students from different areas around the Rough Rock area, some of the roads were very rough. There were no paved roads, so the kids who lived the farthest from the school could stay in the dorm. The others who lived nearby were day students. So, we had quite a few boys and girls who stayed in the dorms, and then they went home on the weekends.

Mike: How was the Rough Rock Demonstration School Board formed?

Anita: Soon after we arrived, the whole community was brought together in the school gym, and there were presentations by Bob Roessel and some of the community people about this new school, that it would be run by the community and be very different from the BIA. Dr. Platero interpreted for Bob because he didn't speak Navajo. They explained that at least seven people would be selected to form a school board and make decisions on everything that went on in the school.

Mike: How were these seven people chosen?

Anita: They were mainly community leaders, and there was one woman. Some of them volunteered and others were nominated.

Mike: This was going to be a BIA-funded school, though.

Anita: Yes. At that time Ned Hatathli, Sam Billison, Ellen Yahzee, and there seemed to be a fourth one, proposed managing the funds. Ned Hatathli was director of the Navajo Nation's department of resources, so they had a role in the Navajo government. These four people incorporated Diné Bi' Oltá. They brought the idea of this board to the community at Rough Rock, and then asked them to elect a school board in order to formulate policies.

Mike: Did the Rough Rock community itself decide to vote to do this project to take over the school?

Anita: In the initial meeting that I went to they asked, "How do you feel about being part of this new idea, that you as parents would be really involved in your children's education?" They said it was a new idea. Nobody had ever asked them that question. People who spoke at that meeting indicated that it was a fine idea that they would have a part in their children's education. One person said, "You know that our children, the ones that would just be starting school don't speak English. So, you can't teach them in English because they don't understand it. You have to teach them in Navajo until they learn English. We want them to learn English, but it has to be done in a way that will help them learn the second language. But teach them in Navajo."

Mike: Who got the seven-member board incorporated?

Anita: Well, Bob Roessel was there the first two years, and then he hired Dillon Platero, who was working at Arizona State University. He came on board as director of the curriculum center, where Navajo books were to be written for the school. The following year he was made executive director.

Bob Roessel started the idea of the Navajo Community College, so that was his next role. Many Farms had some buildings available, so that's when they first started the college. Then, he went to Tsaile to talk with the people there about this college, and the Navajo Nation and Tsaile community decided where the site would be for the Navajo Community College.

Mike: How long were you at Rough Rock?

Anita: The first year I taught the first-year students, so I taught them in Navajo. Then they decided I should become principal, so I did that for two years. The fourth year they asked me to be the assistant executive director. And then the fifth year, I went out to Harvard for my graduate work.

Mike: You got a degree from Harvard too?

Anita: I went there to get my doctorate and only did my qualifying paper. I never finished my dissertation. Then I came over to UNM as a professor.

Mike: I remember a trip that the Ramah Navajo School Board made to Rough Rock in the spring or late winter of 1970. And I think that's where I first met you and Cam. Do you remember that at all?

Anita: Yes. And I remember going with Cam to Ramah. You wanted us to talk about Rough Rock, which we did. You were there. And as we finished, you said, "Let's do it. Let's do it for the Ramah Navajo too." That's how they started.

Mike: Well, Rough Rock was the prototype for Ramah, of course. The first time I was at Window Rock was 1968, and Robert Kennedy had just been assassinated the previous June. But he had initiated this study committee on Indian education and went for two and a half years around the country, from Alaska to Florida and all in-between, to do that amazing study. That led to the Indian Education Senate Report that came out under Ted Kennedy's name. Do you remember that? Ted Kennedy visited Rough Rock, by the way.

Anita: Ted Kennedy—he was our first graduation speaker.

Mike: Yes, Ted Mitchell and I met him for five minutes at the airport in Chinle, which is the nearest airport.

Anita: Yes. Because there's no hotel in Rough Rock my family moved out to another friend's place, and Ted Kennedy and his two assistants slept in our beds!

Mike: How do you see Indian education, the developments, since the days of Rough Rock and the beginning of Ramah? Can you summarize any views about where Indian education stands now?

Anita: Well, there are 32 contract schools on Navajo Nation and one grant school, and that is Rock Point. And then because of all the visitors that came to Rough Rock, other tribes initiated taking some of the ideas they observed at Rough Rock back to their communities. I haven't kept up to date on how the other Indian groups have continued with the new ideas, but today we have the BIE (Bureau of Indian Education). They are trying to include more of the Navajo curriculum, but still the majority of the schools are run by the Arizona public school system.

Mike: But there are school districts on the Navajo Reservation like Window Rock School District where the school board members are all Navajo because of the electorate on the Navajo Nation. Correct?

Anita: Right. That has changed. It used to be that just the *bilagáanas* [white people] would be board members. But now, as you say, there are Navajo boards.

Mike: I remember Pete Zah[34] was on the Window Rock School Board, so it was clear that that was a form of Navajo control of public schools.

Anita: Right. But I was executive director of the Navajo Division of Education at that time, and we wanted to make it a Department of Navajo

---

34. Chairman of the Navajo Nation from 1983-1987.

Education. When I left, it was the Department of Diné Education. We hired someone to start working on Navajo language and culture and to incorporate it into the schools.

Also, because the Arizona statistics on how our children were doing wasn't coming to the Navajo Nation, we started a research office so that we could collect our own data to see how the kids were doing. When Pete Zah asked me to do the work that would be the Department of Diné Education, he wanted a thousand teachers who would go to college and get BA degrees in elementary education, so we set up an office to do that. Those were the main new offices that we established. The data from the schools came to the education office, and people could see how badly our children were doing in the public schools. They weren't reading very well, they weren't doing math very well, they were doing very little in science.

They're still not doing well. We have a lot of kids who graduate from those schools who really are ill-equipped to go to college. They have to go to a remedial place in order to gear up their skills to get into other colleges. The Navajo Community College offers an associate of arts degree, and in the last two years, now offers a bachelor's degree in elementary education. The technical university at Crownpoint now is also offering degrees.

Mike: Was Rough Rock a participant in the Coalition of Indian-Controlled School Boards (CICSB)?

Anita: Yes.

Mike: If you look back now, where do you think Indian education is today compared with 1966?

Anita: A lot of things have changed. When we started at Rough Rock, like I said, the kids who started school didn't speak English.

Mike: Do you have any contact with Rough Rock now?

Anita: No. The last contact was when I was teaching at UNM. I had a project at Rough Rock. We wanted more people to get BA degrees in elementary education. I would go out there and talk with the students and teach a course. It was my first year as a professor at UNM. I had my courses all worked out and my trips to Rough Rock worked out. And somebody changed the schedule so that the days I was going out to Rough Rock, I was also teaching in the evenings. So, I would leave from here at four in the morning, get to Rough

Rock, do my thing, and come back and teach. I would get back ten minutes before my class started.

Mike: That was an eight-hour journey or more! Do you have any final thoughts about your career and the whole subject of Indian education?

Anita: I think that during my career, Rough Rock was the most exciting to me because we were trying a lot of different things. UNM was okay, but Rough Rock was the big thing for me.

BACKGROUND ON RAMAH

Sagebrush, piñon, juniper, howling coyotes, elk, buttes and eons-dormant volcanoes dominate the vast sweep of high desert in northwestern New Mexico that is occupied by the Ramah Navajo. To their north, the Zuni Mountains run along NM 53, which extends from Grants—situated at the base of Mount Taylor, *Tsoodzil*, the southernmost of the Four Sacred Mountains of the Navajo—to the Arizona border. While the Zuni Mountains are a Precambrian uplift, Mt. Taylor is an ancient volcano that last erupted over a million years ago.

Going south from Grants and then west on NM 53 as it heads toward Arizona, part of what is known as the Ancients Scenic Byway, some of my favorite scenery in the Southwest opens up—first through a pass in the extinct Zuni-Bandera volcanic field, which had eruptions as recently as 3,000 years ago. This landscape of basalt cinder cones bedecked with juniper serves witness to the violent geological upheavals that took place there. The lower slopes are dotted with piñon trees that produce rich nuts, an important traditional food, and taller ponderosa pines. Deer and occasional elk can often be seen from the road.

Crossing the Continental Divide, atop which the Zuni Mountains sit, produces a sharp temperature drop. The mountains hem in the prevailing westerly winds and accompanying moisture, which keeps the western side cooler and wetter than the area to the east. Coming from Albuquerque at 5,000 feet altitude, the terrain rises to nearly 8,000 feet through a high pass. This is more than a thousand feet higher than the highest peak in New England, Mt. Washington, at 6,288 feet. Just before the sign for the Continental Divide, a privately owned tourist attraction called the Ice Cave invites travelers to descend into caverns that maintain a steady 40-degree temperature year-round. Continuing west, the vegetation transforms a few miles later from pine forest to a high-desert plain dominated by the historic butte that is now El Morro National Monument, which appears like a massive ship moored in the surrounding high desert sea. In the late 1500s at the base of El Morro, the Spanish conquistadors etched their names into the solid rock wall. (Carving anything on the rock walls today risks jail time.) In 1540, Coronado had marched through the area in search of the rumored mythic lands of gold called the Seven Cities of Cíbola.[35]

Standing on El Morro's flat summit amidst the ancient, abandoned pueblo ruins, a 360-degree panorama unfolds, to the northeast the verdant Zuni Mountains, to the northwest a series of buttes, one of which features wind-carved pinnacles sticking up as though they were guardians of the world, and to the south and west a sea of grassland eventually gives way to a high-desert piñon forest. The view from the top freezes time. Except for portions of the road, not a single human structure is visible. One stands on the shoulders of history, imagining the people who once lived in these empty, roofless ruins. One can imagine the conquistadors, hot, tired and hungry from their lengthy trip north from Mexico, finding at the base of this natural landmark a perpetual water supply percolating up from the aquifer underneath the butte, filling a small year-round pool.

From El Morro the two-lane highway heads due northwest for about ten miles. The traveler has now entered the Ramah Navajo Reservation, although no marker or sign heralds this news. The Ramah Navajo reservation exists more on paper than in real life, although it has legal status. Normally, most reservations are owned by the United States in trust for an Indian tribe. Their lands cannot be mortgaged or confiscated by anyone without tribal and BIA permission. This is not true for the Ramah Navajo Reservation. This is checker-boarded territory. Great swaths of privately owned land, railroad land, and state and federal lands exist within its boundaries. That circumstance makes development and life in general quite complicated and precarious at times for the Ramah Navajo Band.

Three decades after the Mormon Battalion, a U.S. Army infantry comprised exclusively of soldiers from The Church of Latter-day Saints, traversed New Mexico from its northeast to southwest corner, in 1876 the missionaries were successful in converting among the Zuni in western New Mexico. The missionaries settled in the valley they called Ramah, a name from the Book of Mormon meaning a high or lofty place, shortly after the Navajos had returned from their incarceration and attempted ethnic cleansing by the U.S. military courtesy of U.S. Army Officer Kit Carson at Fort Sumner, one of the world's first concentration camps, on

---

35. Preston, D. *Cities of Gold: A Journey Across the American Southwest.* (Simon & Schuster, 1992)

the Pecos River in eastern New Mexico at Bosque Redondo. Between 1864 and 1866 the Navajo had been rounded up in multiple raids, first at Canyon de Chelly in what is now eastern Arizona, then in other areas, and forced to march nearly 300 miles east across most of what is now the State of New Mexico, in what came to be known as the Long Walk. Women, the aged, children and the infirm died along the way.

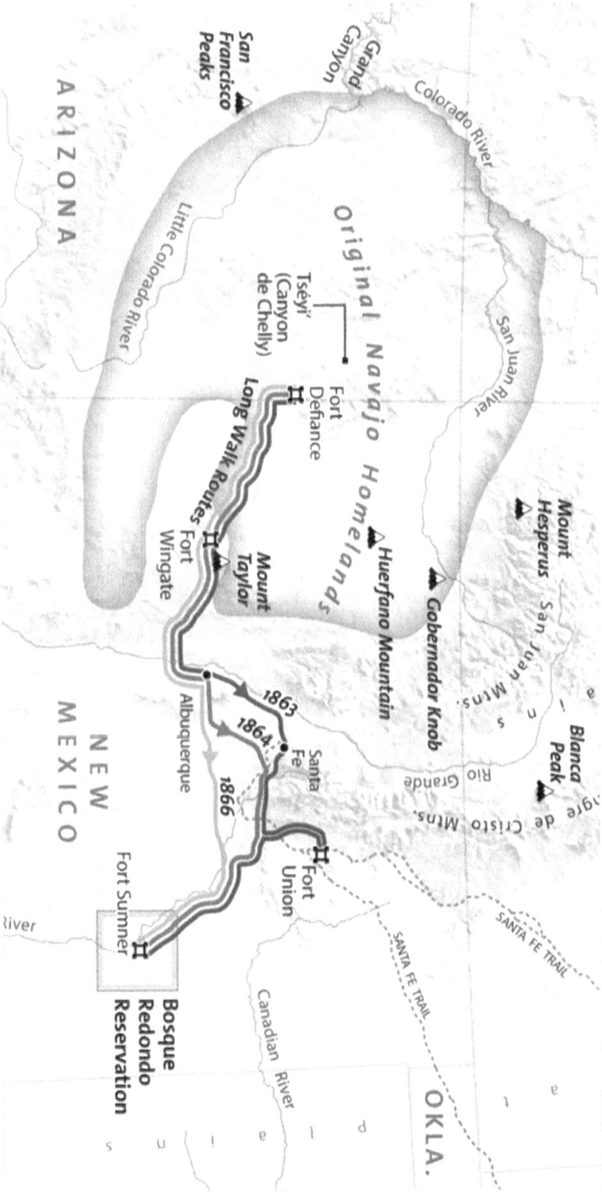

Traditional Navajo Homelands with path of The Long Walk, Smithsonian Institution, 2019

Although there were economic bumps in the road, the period after the Navajo Treaty of 1868 restored most of their traditional homeland to the tribe, except for the Ramah, Alamo and To'hajiilee / Cañoncito Bands, which are geographically separated in communities elsewhere in New Mexico. From a population of 10,000 or so in 1868 at the end of their incarceration, the Navajos slowly and then more rapidly began to multiply. Sheepherding, cattle-ranching and Navajo crafts and jewelry making were profitable, and that allowed their numbers to swell. By the mid-twentieth century, the population grew such that the Navajo people became the largest reservation-based tribe in the country. When I arrived in 1968, the Navajo people numbered around 105,000. As of the 2020 census, the figure was close to 170,000 tribal members living on the reservation and approximately 160,000 tribal members living off the reservation.

The Ramah Band, as they were known, had walked back 200 miles to their ancestral homeland in western New Mexico—land they had occupied for centuries before the United States was founded. Unfortunately, this territory was not included in the formal Navajo Reservation, which General William Tecumseh Sherman negotiated with the 8,500-member tribe in 1868, after the Navajos were released from Bosque Redondo. When the Ramah Navajo Band returned in the 1870s, Mormons armed with land patents from Santa Fe kicked them out of the best-watered areas and built their own town in a typical Anglo architectural style—a collection of New England or Midwestern-style pitched roof houses shaded by cottonwoods and other deciduous trees adapted to the high desert environment, making it seem like Anyplace, U.S.A, circa 1930. The largely non-Indian Mormon village of Ramah is nestled between two bluffs, one north and one south, which help create a channel through which runoff from the Zuni Mountains flows.

At the time the Navajos lived here, I was told that this channel was called Little Onion Grass because of the small wild onions growing on the stream banks. When the Mormons took control of this land, they improved the Navajo-built dam between the two buttes, creating a small lake. For most of the 20th century, a trading post operated on the corner of NM 53 and the town's Main Street. After the Mormons built what is now the unincorporated village of Ramah and settled near the picturesque twin buttes and the Navajos' precious stream, the Ramah Band resettled in the drier parts of the area in what is now Cibola County (previously

Valencia County). They were ignorant of the white man's customs of land ownership and so couldn't fight back.

Although the Treaty of 1868 between the Navajo and the U.S. did not include the Ramah Navajos, the U.S. recognized the community as part of what became known as "Big Navajo."[36] But the Ramah Navajos never quite fit into the Navajo political world. The reason probably lies in the peculiar checkerboarded land ownership in their area. Because of this situation the Bureau of Indian Affairs placed the Ramah Navajos under the control of the Southern Pueblos Agency, setting it apart jurisdictionally from the other 100-plus Navajo Chapters, which were placed under the Navajo Area Office.

In the 1930s, however, two Mormons seeking to expand their land holdings persuaded lower-level officials in the BIA to switch jurisdiction of the Ramah Navajos to the Navajo administrative capital in Window Rock, Arizona. That change would remove an important, if only bureaucratic, protection for them. As quasi-outcasts, the Ramah Navajo people would be submerged in the politics of the Navajo Nation. They feared this constraint would rob them of their independence. At the Ramah Navajos' request and contrary to his staff's recommendation, Commissioner of Indian Affairs John Collier reversed the lower-level decision of the BIA to put the Ramah Navajo Chapter under the Navajo Area Office and ordered the Southern Pueblos Agency to retake jurisdiction over them. To this day the Ramah Navajos revere John Collier, who had earned the enmity of the Navajo Nation as a whole because of a program in the late 1940s and 50s to reduce Navajo sheep herds to control diseases among them. This caused considerable economic harm to Navajo families across the reservation.

This arbitrary border reflected how impractically the lines were drawn in this entire region by the U.S. government from the start. The Ramah Navajo Reservation follows the county line separating the former Valencia County[37] (now Cibola County) to the south from McKinley County to the north, which also serves as the boundary between the two school districts. In setting up these boundaries, *no geographic, demographic,*

36. Tapahonso, L. Photographs by Daniella Zalcman. "For More Than 100 Years, the U.S. Forced Navajo Students Into Western Schools. The Damage Is Still Felt Today." *Smithsonian Magazine*, July 2016.

37. Cibola County was created out of the westernmost area of Valencia County in 1981.

cultural or linguistic circumstances were ever considered. The nearest public elementary school and high school serving the Ramah Navajo Chapter sits just north of their county line in the McKinley County School District. Therefore, the bulk of Ramah Navajo children attending public schools actually come from the south side of this arbitrary boundary, from the Grants-Cibola County School District.

Following the Mexican-American War, the Treaty of Guadalupe Hidalgo was signed in 1848 when the United States had acquired the Southwest from Mexico. The new territory of New Mexico included what is now Arizona. Later, for cultural and linguistic reasons, Arizona was split off from New Mexico to form a new state. The Language Policy Archives by the U.S. Commission on Civil Rights[38] explain:

"Arizonans' fears were summarized in a Protest Against Union of Arizona with New Mexico presented to Congress on February 12, 1906, which stated: '... the decided racial difference between the people of New Mexico, who are not only different in race and largely in language, but have entirely different customs, laws and ideals and would have but little prospect of successful amalgamation ... [and] the objection of the people of Arizona, 95 percent of whom are Americans, to the probability of the control of public affairs by people of a different race, many of whom do not speak the English language, and who outnumber the people of Arizona two to one.'"

What became today's New Mexico was simply divided into mostly right-angled counties by drawing arbitrary lines on a map.

Years later, the problem was compounded when school districts were created using these same arbitrary county lines. Not just at Ramah but throughout the state, school districts were formed ignoring demography, geography, existing population centers (especially Indian communities) and most every other kind of sensible, fact-based, pragmatic arrangement. These arbitrary school-district boundaries have contributed to immense (and largely unnecessary) problems for the Ramah Navajos and still plague them today.

---

38. U.S. Commission on Civil Rights: Language Rights and New Mexico Statehood http://www.languagepolicy.net/archives/nm-con.htm

Grazing sheep at Ramah, NM. Photo by Andrea Gross

Los Gigantes "hoodoo" sandstone formations near Ramah, NM.
Photo by Andrea Gross

NAVAJOS AS PAWNS

When I reached the Navajo Reservation in 1968, the immediate problem facing the Ramah Navajo, our client, was the fact that a couple of decades earlier, the Mormons in the town of Ramah had wanted their own public school, yet did not have enough high school-aged children to qualify for one. In 1952, without the expertise of an architect or possibly even a building permit, the Mormon village of Ramah residents gathered $15,000 to build a new school. To fill the enrollment gap, the townspeople turned to the Ramah Navajos, suggesting that they enroll their children in the new Ramah public school as well, despite the fact that the Ramah Navajos lived over their school district boundary line to the south. Because the Navajo children lived miles away without reliable transportation, they would need a dormitory. So, the unincorporated town of Ramah persuaded the BIA to build and operate a dormitory for the Navajo children on their land, right next to the new school. In 1952, the Ramah Navajo voted for the dormitory, and the U.S. government agreed to pay the state of New Mexico to allow students to stay there. The dormitory opened in 1954 with some one hundred Navajo boarders.[39]

The Gallup-McKinley County School District had convinced the New Mexico Department of Education that the dormitory students should be considered residents of Ramah village and thus be part of the population for public school purposes. This, in turn, enabled Ramah village and the Gallup-McKinley County School District to count the Indian students living in the dormitory for public school funding purposes in Gallup-McKinley County Schools. In other words, the town borrowed Navajo children from a neighboring school district (Grants-Cibola) to qualify for state funds to operate a public school for the Mormon children in the village of Ramah. Grants-Cibola School District presumably did not

---

39. Blanchard, Kendall. ERIC ED064017: The Ramah Navajos: A Growing Sense of Community In Historical Perspective. Navajo Historical Publications Historical Series No. 1.

object because it saved it the burden of building and operating a school on the western side of the Zuni Mountains.

But pretty soon, a big problem began to develop. The Navajo tribal rolls mushroomed—from under 10,000 of those who straggled back in 1868 to their homeland after the Long Walk—to around 105,000[40] in 1970, with the majority living on the reservation, making it the largest tribe in the country.[41]

Consequently, the state built an elementary school near the original community-built school structure in Ramah. In the 1950s up until the early 1960s, this arrangement seems to have pleased everyone. The Navajo students would be driven to the high school on Monday mornings, usually in their parents' dilapidated pickups, sleep in the dormitory during the week, where they were fed and received medical attention, and attended the school next door to the dorm. Their enrollment sufficiently satisfied state standards. The Navajos did not seem to mind that they could not vote in Gallup-McKinley school district elections. Indians hardly ever voted in Anglo elections anyway.

When the dormitory began running out of beds, no meaningful consultation between the school district, the BIA or the Navajos seems to have taken place. I have found no record of any consultations with them about these developments. Having their children live in the nearby dormitory and coming home on the weekends—or at least giving parents a chance to visit them on their way to Gallup—was far better than having the BIA haul them off to distant federal Indian boarding schools, often a hundred miles or more away from their homes. Despite the construction of an elementary school on the other side of the BIA dormitory and a surge in Navajo enrollment, apparently no one had thought about how all these Navajo kids could attend school if the dormitory ran out of room.

Each year for several years, the state Department of Education would send warnings to the Gallup-McKinley School District that enrollment in Ramah High School had dropped below state standards. It seems no consideration was given to providing small buses to gather up the Navajo

---

40. Barber, C.E., Cook, A. S. and Ackerman, A. The Influence of Acculturation on Attitudes of Filial Responsibility among Navajo Youth. *American Indian Quarterly*, Vol. 9, No. 4 (1985), pp. 421-432.

41. *The Navajo Times*, April 20, 2020. 50 Years Ago: Census raises questions about true Diné count

kids and bring them to school in Ramah.[42] Once the dormitory reached its capacity, it seems the BIA dormitory superintendent simply decided on his own to make room for the younger Navajos first, limiting the space available to accommodate middle and high school students.

According to Edgar Bond, in 1967 the Gallup-McKinley superintendent asked the BIA to expand the dormitory from 150 beds to 200. The limited beds forced some high school-aged Navajos to drop out of school entirely. Parents who could not read or write and did not have phones lost touch with their children. In what amounted to complete indifference, the New Mexico Public Education Department failed to make any documented effort to understand what was happening at Ramah. It simply closed Ramah High School. In short, a public high school serving Navajo children was closed because the school system could not handle the increased Navajo population, and no one in authority cared. Such was the condition of Indian education in the late 1960s.

A month before I showed up on the Navajo Reservation, Senator Robert Kennedy, campaigning to succeed his brother to be president, was assassinated in Los Angeles. Luckily, his draft report on Indian education was in its final stages of completion. I got hold of a copy in August, less than one month after arriving on the reservation, and it changed my life. In searing language Kennedy's report excoriated Indian boarding schools for their brutality and forced proselytization of Indian children. Kennedy's report called the practice of removing children from their families *coercive assimilation*.[43] Indian children who spoke their native languages had their mouths washed out with soap or were subjected to corporal punishment. Some Indian children, attempting to run away from boarding schools in winter, froze to death.[44]

Had someone, including us Ivy League lawyers, ever asked how school enrollment could fall when the population was rising, the ensuing closure of the school requiring a lawsuit might have been avoided. But that question was not asked when the lawsuit started, and its answer made

---

42. One reason for this neglect might have been a state rule forbidding cross-district school busing without special permission. But there is no evidence that busing the Navajos from their homes was even considered.

43. Indian Education: A National Tragedy - A National Challenge (Kennedy Report)

44. Donavan, B. 50 Years Ago: Boys freeze after running away from boarding school. *Navajo Times*, Jan. 11, 2018.

itself plain only later: the problem was the bottleneck of the dormitory. Faced with a rising number of younger and younger Navajo school children, the dormitory became overcrowded. Without consulting the Ramah Navajo Chapter, the Gallup-McKinley School District, the Navajo Tribe or even the BIA's own headquarters, the local BIA's dormitory superintendent unilaterally decreed that preference in the dormitory would be given to the youngest children first.

Year by year the number of beds thus available for high schoolers declined, and the surplus of them were simply unable to get to Ramah High School. Naturally, when capacity of the two schools in Ramah village was increased due to a rising Navajo birth rate, more Navajos were attracted to the dormitory. The overlapping jurisdictions made comprehensive community planning impossible, producing a steep decline in the high school enrollment. So, by closing the high school, the Navajo high schoolers were stranded. Nobody cared but the Navajo parents who didn't speak English well and couldn't navigate the bureaucracies.

The short of it is this: The Interior Department, the Bureau of Indian Affairs, the Navajo Nation, the State of New Mexico Department of Education, The Gallup-McKinley School District and the Grants-Cibola School District were all complicit in denying the Ramah Navajo children's basic human right of access to education. The Ramah Navajo Chapter officers were compelled to write this letter to Washington sent three and a half years before I arrived, discovered by Honor Keeler, who briefly interned for me in the summer of 2004 and gathered information at the Ramah Navajo Chapter offices:

Ramah Navajo Chapter
Ramah, New Mexico
December 9, 1964

TO: Whom It May Concerned:

SUBJECT: Ramah High School

References: People of the Ramah Navajo Tribe and its children.

        Since the establishment of our Old Day School in 1943, by the BIA
at the present Old Day School site, which provided educational opportunity
for our children from kindergarten and had to be transferred to different
off reservation schools to further their schooling, if no serious problem
affected their family status to prevent them from going further with their
educations, and also to make room for those coming of school age. As time
past by our children were beginning to be over crowded, we began to look
forward to find a way to have our children keep up with their schooling, so
numerous requests were being made to have our Day School to expanded and its
dormitory accomodations. At that time many attempts were been made to have
our school and its facilities be established at its present site, but were
been neglected of its intended site. So it was transferred from its site
to the village of Ramah, whereby, quaranteeing that our children have the
same type of educations been granted them at the Old Day School and to let
them finish and graduate from High School locally, and not to let go off to
different High School to finish their High School. It was confirmed at that
time that this will be their permanent school, where our future prosperity
will meet their educational opportunity. Up to the present we had encountered
a problem which will deprive our children of their education and to finish
High School locally as it was been quaranteed before transferring of its site.
We, the Ramah Navajo people are disapproving of our local High School been
discontinued, and be demoted to Junior High School, and are requesting for the
continuous of the existing High School standard. We also request for morely
qualified teachers with higher degree of educations, which in turn will help
our children get a good education, which they need to meet their challenges
that our changing society has to meet, and to meet the challenges when they go
for further educations.

                          Concurred by:

                          THE RAMAH NAVAHO CHAPTER OFFICERS,

                          ____
                          Bertha Lorenzo, President

                          ____
                          Lee Pino, Vice-President

                          ____
                          Curley Biggs, Secretary

Letter from Ramah Navajo Chapter Officers to the BIA, 1964.

The order to close the school came down a month before I arrived. Though Ramah students were citizens of the state and by state law entitled to a public education just as every other resident of New Mexico was, the bureaucrats in Santa Fe did not consider them at all; the BIA failed to consult the Ramah Navajo leaders; and DNA failed to sue all the right parties to obtain relief.

The New Mexico Department of Education's only response to its own order to close Ramah High School was to provide students a single school bus to operate daily to Zuni High School and back, a one-way distance of 26 miles. Except for the one school bus, they made no accommodation for the 120 Navajo high school-aged children living outside the boundaries of the Gallup-McKinley Public School District. Beyond that, the Navajos and Zunis were ethnically, culturally, and linguistically different from one another. The Navajos would not have sent their children to a school in Zuni even if adequate transportation to and from their individual homes were made available, which, for logistical reasons, would have been impossible. The Navajos didn't live in the village of Ramah but in a nearly 900 square-mile swath of territory to the south and west of the town of Ramah. The Navajos had only been able to attend Ramah High School by living in the BIA dormitory next to the school during the week and going home to their parents' hogans on weekends. For them, the single bus from Ramah to Zuni was entirely inadequate since most of the Navajos lived an average of 50 miles from Zuni. It was positively Kafkaesque.

THE JOB OF A LAWYER

Just out of law school and knowing next to nothing about Indians during my first lawsuit over the school closing at Ramah, I failed to realize that the case was loaded with language issues. That was why DNA hired skilled Navajos to act as counselors/interpreters. Even with them, I was absolutely unequipped to engage in a thorough analysis of a Navajo client's problem, especially one as complex as Ramah's. Time pressure was also enormous. Avoiding the closure of the tiny Ramah High School before the start of the next school year would require fast action, so our initial urge to file a quick lawsuit may have been justified, but our ignorance of the complexities still plagued our case. Although I was oblivious to the language problem, the presence of Abe Plummer alleviated that circumstance.

Mitchell had told us what the problem was and directed us to file a lawsuit to keep the school open. The state had closed a school and not made proper arrangements for the education of more than half the enrollment before closure. To him, this seemed to be the be-all and end-all of the problem, an open-and-shut case. A school serving Indian students near their homes had been closed suddenly, leaving dozens of Indian children without a local school, and the emergency required immediate action. As cub lawyers, we rushed into state court in Gallup.

I suggested we add a segregation count to our complaint: the Ramah Navajo students would be leaving a school that was 50 percent white and 50 percent Indian and were expected to attend a new school, which already was more than 90 percent Indian. It seemed a violation of *Brown v. Board of Education*. Adding a few dozen Navajos to Zuni High School would increase the already lopsided Indian enrollment in the Zuni school. This idea—my first attempt at analyzing a legal problem in a real case—never made it to Mitchell's decision level. As lawyers, we should have explored the entire situation and not just focused on the way the State had interfered in local school matters. Nor did we evaluate the BIA role in creating the under-enrollment in the first place—its unilateral decision to cut off dormitory access to high school-aged Navajos when the younger student population began to spike. Mitchell and the rest of us were oblivious to this issue. More seriously, we did not realize how complex the problem really was. It literally took me years to fully understand the enormity of the wrong committed against the Navajos.

Nor were the Mormons entirely innocent. The Navajos had been made pawns by the Mormons, who wanted a public high school built and operated for their tiny unincorporated village. Bringing Navajo students from another school district to the town public school in Ramah enabled the Mormons to keep their children in a local high school. It was the Navajos' crossing the Cibola County line into the Gallup-McKinley School District that made it possible for a public school to operate in Ramah village in the first place.

As if that were not enough, no one thought to ask the voting rights question: how was it that the State and BIA authorities allowed a sizeable Navajo population to send its children into a school district in which the parents could not vote? To be sure, they might not have voted even if their territory had been part of the Gallup-McKinley County School District. But they were New Mexico citizens, and as parents they had a right to send their children to a public school district in which they could vote. Most Ramah Navajos could not vote in McKinley County and were thus disenfranchised.

In hindsight several federal causes of action were available. Had we sued in federal court we could have joined other state entities including the State Board of Education in one lawsuit and had a much stronger case. We could have raised due process and equal protection issues and joined the state as well as the local school district. At the time, New Mexico required suits against any state official or agency to be filed in Santa Fe County, but this law would not have prevented us from suing the state and the BIA in federal court. Ted Mitchell was fixated on reopening the school immediately, believing we could walk in and out of state court the same day with an order that it be kept open.

Due to our inexperience, we lost in state court. My first effort to win a legal victory for clients in court failed.

Years later, I learned why and what we should have done. I also learned that even if legal advice is followed, results may not meet clients' expectations. Although not affecting DNA at the time, legal fees may be difficult to estimate. Moreover, culture clashes heighten when clients' problems are novel. Cynics say the law is whatever the last judge to rule says it is. But if it were so black and white, there would be much less need for lawyers. In the case at Ramah, our clients meekly accepted whatever we told them, including advice from me—a 27-year-old, not-yet-licensed Anglo lawyer.

A few weeks into my DNA sojourn, Jane Fonda showed up at our offices in Window Rock. I was introduced to her as a resident expert on Indian education. For about five minutes we sat alongside each other on my wooden office chairs discussing Ramah. Considering how that case had developed, I should have contacted her a few years later to show her how lawyers can help Indians solve their own problems by organizing, voting and petitioning in Washington for redress of grievances.

A lawyer must understand a client's problem before recommending a solution. This seems obvious, but I have often witnessed the mistake of leaping to a conclusion about the client's problem before learning what it is and how it developed. Facts are often complex, and so is the analysis of them. The determination of whether or not a law requires changes in behavior often involves lengthy litigation, or adjustments that the client resists. Dealing in a cross-cultural, cross-language arena, the lawyer has an increased responsibility to make sure there is an understanding of both the client's problem and the lawyer's explanations.

Law is not a monolith hanging in the sky like a star; it is malleable, often flexible. Conflict resolution through the courts depends on argument and persuasion. Both sides may be right and wrong at the same time. Solutions may depend on skills quite different from those of doctors. Persuasion is often needed; psychology is always a factor. The law may change. Or indeed, as here, the law *must be* changed. Most especially, lawyers must not be wedded to a single remedy to a client's problem. As my first Ramah Navajo case graphically demonstrated, the solution may lie outside the courtroom, in the legislature or the halls of Congress.

So now, fifty-plus years after I first heard of Ramah, what does the score card show? What has been accomplished both for the Ramah Navajo and more generally for Indian country? As objectively as possible I want to assess the impact on the national scene, and on me, of my career representing and working with this one isolated Indian community and many others like it around the country. Without false modesty, I am aware that my career has been unusual and has given me a unique perspective. Whether readers will agree or not with my conclusions, they should remember the complicated circumstances that produced them. But when you're a player it is often difficult to see what the spectators in the bleachers see.

When in 1968 Ramah's Navajo leaders first met me at DNA's office in Window Rock, I must have looked like a teenager: an ignorant, wet-behind-the-ears, mid-20-something, not-yet-licensed law clerk. I sat protected by the enormous barricade of my scholarly-looking desk, while the elders of the Ramah Navajo community, mostly in their 60s, sat on stiff office chairs in front of me as I expounded on what we lawyers were going to do, namely file a lawsuit. They didn't know that I had never heard of Ramah, never been in court, never filed a brief or even written one, except in moot court in law school. Nor did they know that I was entirely ignorant of Navajo history, which stretches back about 1,000 years[45], and their culture or experiences. I was unaware that I was playing the stereotypical role often represented by Hollywood, of the officious, white bureaucrat lecturing to Indians.

Just six weeks out of law school, I was being asked to take a lead role in diagnosing the Ramah Navajo Chapter's school crisis. When I started working at DNA, I had asked Ted Mitchell whether there were any courses in Navajo language available. In fact, I had heard there was a course running in Gallup, but Mitchell told me the Navajo language was too hard and that I'd be better off reading a bunch of Indian law cases he had compiled for us new lawyers. So, confronted with my first client's situation and having been asked to help prepare a lawsuit to reopen the closed Ramah High School, I literally did not know what to do. Meeting the clients was one thing I did think to do. Hence the first trip to Ramah with Abe Plummer and the little kids running away from my truck as they saw what looked like a Mormon missionary come to take them to Utah. The immediate task was to work up our case for trial. For this I needed to do some studying about Indian education.

Through one of DNA's Navajo counselor/interpreters, I lectured more than I listened. I told them I was assigned to Mitchell's team to prepare and file a lawsuit as quickly as possible. I mentioned Mitchell's promise to them to file a suit before the beginning of the next school year. I told them our goal was to ensure the school would reopen in late

---

45. Doering, Briana N, Julie A Esdale, Joshua D Reuther, and Senna D Catenacci. 2020. "A Multiscalar Consideration of the Athabascan Migration." *American Antiquity* 85 (3). New York, U.S.A: Cambridge University Press: 470–91. doi:10.1017/aaq.2020.34.

August. Of course, at that point I had only a rudimentary understanding of the circumstances at Ramah and no experience addressing or conversing with clients, let alone with Indians barely able to speak English. It wasn't until after we lost the case that anyone thought to ask why the enrollment in the Ramah public high school had dropped. Until we lost our lawsuit, no one had examined the role the BIA dormitory played in the closing of the high school. It took a while for me to gain perspective and start asking questions.

Until the late 1960s, law schools were strictly academic. Broad-scale training in how to practice law began during my last year at Yale. They had not yet adopted hands-on, supervised internships as a requirement for graduation. But before the 20th century and even into it, legal training was exclusively conducted through apprenticeships with practicing lawyers, and on-the-job training was the norm. Somewhere along the way, the Bar started to consider that teaching anyone how to apply the law to real-life situations was insufficient, so law schools became more like graduate schools. Practical application gave way to a more academic curriculum. Apprenticeships invited nepotism, and in the late 1800s, bar associations were akin to social groups, with little attention paid to members' performance. As commerce spread west with the Gold Rush, the legal system was in disarray and citizens formed vigilante tribunals, taking justice into their own hands. This necessitated higher standards and gave rise to formal bar associations with more rigid educational requirements.

Of course, law is not science. The practice of law depends on skills that most academics rarely even think of, let alone display: verbal acuity, close reasoning, charm—yes charm—a skill needed in many situations requiring persuasion. Legal principles were to be gleaned from studying legal opinions written by judges. Law was something discoverable, like a gold mine under a pile of rocks and dirt. Brush away the distractions and there was the mother lode. It was late in my first year that I discovered that some smarter-than-me classmates had figured it all out.

When analyzing a legal issue, search for cases that back up your desired outcome and use them as your musket powder. In other words, decide what the right answer should be first and then search for ammunition to prove it. You can usually find a way to distinguish cases on the other side; if all else fails, just say they're wrong. By the mid 1960s, when I was studying in the classroom, law schools were just beginning to experiment with practical legal training for credit.[46] I did not avail myself of it. My only real-life preparation for law practice was the summer internship in Phoenix at Brown, Vlassis and Bain, where I learned more than in three years of law school.

At that point, I had not yet faced Mitchell's rants at me for pursuing a non-lawsuit remedy for my client, the Ramah Navajo Chapter, which later catalyzed me to leave DNA and go to work for my former client to help it start its own school. Only after our lawsuit to keep Ramah High School open fizzled did I stumble onto a way to really help them—not with a lawsuit but with self-help. With much outside assistance from private foundations, BIA insiders, politicians and a unanimous, enthusiastic Ramah Navajo community, we managed to storm the political barricades in Washington, D.C., make national news with a grassroots project to fix up the school building and empower our clients to become active participants in their own solution. The result was over 100 Ramah Navajo high schoolers back at home getting a local education in their own community school, which their parents and community controlled.

46. Joy, P. A. The Uneasy History of Experiential Education in U.S. Law Schools, 122 *Dick. L. Rev.* 551 (2018). Available at: https://ideas.dickinsonlaw.psu.edu/dlr/vol122/iss2/4

AN UNEXPECTED GIFT

The New Mexico State Department of Education closed Ramah High School in June 1968, a month before I arrived in Window Rock. Although the judge, a crusty but genuinely sincere and sympathetic man named Frank Zinn, was concerned about the situation, we had framed the case in such a narrow way that he could not find the legal authority to provide the remedy we wanted—an order to keep the school open. So, the school did close, leaving the Navajo children without access to a local public high school.

Young male Mormon missionaries in their late teens and early twenties would be sent to Indian communities in the West to lure families into giving up their young children to be raised in clean, white, Mormon homes, mostly in Utah. Desperately poor Navajo families, often enticed by bags of food, gave up their small toddlers to these young men with the promise that they would be well cared for in Utah. Now deprived of access to the dormitory at Ramah or even a local high school, the Navajos were especially vulnerable to this form of coercion. The dormitory run by the BIA had provided food and warm beds for the kids for many years while keeping them close to home and within the bounds of their Navajo world.

So, this was the situation in the school year of 1968, after Ramah High School closed. One Ramah Navajo parent of a star pupil the year before Ramah High School closed told how his daughter was now in the BIA-funded Albuquerque Indian School. He and his wife had not seen or heard from her since the school year started because they lacked the means to get to Albuquerque and they could not communicate with her because they had no telephone and could not write or read English.

My promotion to lawyer in charge of the lawsuit coincided with its nosedive. I was in charge of a sinking vessel. Vard Johnson had moved to Omaha, and I had just passed the bar. It was up to me to resuscitate the case. But further litigation seemed hopeless.

It was now December 1969. Ted Mitchell had sent me east to interview prospective lawyers at top law schools. I happened to be interviewing at my alma mater, Yale Law School (YLS). I was sitting in a small room furnished with some nice easy chairs, a desk and a phone. Suddenly and unexpectedly, the phone rang. On the other end was a former YLS classmate named Cal Grant, who graduated after me, completing a four-year Bachelor of Laws (LL.B) undergraduate degree and then a law degree (*juris doctor* or JD). He must have tracked me down through Ted Mitchell. He was now a cub lawyer at one of New York's finest Wall Street firms, Cleary Gottlieb Steen & Hamilton, and he told me that his new client, Ann Maytag Shaker, had just founded a nonprofit called the Ann Maytag Foundation whose mission was to assist American Indians. He asked if I would come to his office the next day with a list of possible projects in the $2,000 range, which he would review and pass on to his client to consider. Overnight, I jotted down four or five ideas.

The next morning, I took a bus and subway to Wall Street for our 10 a.m. meeting. One of the ideas I had scribbled down was a donation to the Ramah Navajo Chapter to see if it could start its own school from scratch. Grant was already familiar with the general situation with Ramah's public high school, having been in the DNA library one day the previous summer. I explained that our lawsuit had failed, and the Ramah Navajo kids were now off in federal Indian boarding schools or elsewhere away from home. I told him about my attempt to open a satellite of Rough Rock Demonstration School at Ramah and how I was turned down by Dillon Platero. No Indian community or tribe had started its own school from scratch since the "Five Civilized Tribes" (Cherokee, Choctaw, Chickasaw, Creek and Seminole) after the Indian Removal Act of 1830, when, over the course of two decades, about 60,000 people were forcibly moved to Oklahoma on what became known as the Trail of Tears, classified by scholars as a genocide, since thousands died of disease along the way or shortly after arrival. The Five Tribes had developed an innovative school system of nearly 200 academies featuring texts in their languages, and they had a 90 percent literacy rate. However, between 1830 and 1898, in three separate Acts of Congress, the U.S. government had forcibly shut down their tribally controlled school system.[47]

47. Manuelito, Kathryn. The Role of Education in American Indian Self-Determination: Lessons from the Ramah Navajo Community School. *Anthropology & Education Quarterly* Vol. 36, No. 1, Indigenous Epistemologies and Education: Self-Determination, Anthropology, and Human Rights (Mar 2005), pp. 73-87.

The Ann Maytag Foundation's benefactress chose the Ramah Navajo Chapter for a seed grant of $2,000, provided it incorporated as a non-profit, tax-exempt entity.

I found this letter that I sent to Chavez Coho, announcing the gift and suggesting a meeting.

January 20, 1970

Mr. Chavez Coho
Councilman
Ramah Navajo Chapter
Ramah, New Mexico

Dear Mr. Coho:

A newly organized foundation in New York, the Shaker Foundation, has informed me that it will donate $2,000 to the Ramah Chapter to help provide quality education for Ramah Navajo children. The money will arrive after the Ramah Chapter's school committee incorporates itself in New Mexico as a non-profit corporation.

The money is intended to help Ramah Navajos develop and operate their own school system under their own control. The idea is to develop local schools for all grades run by the school committee (elected by the Chapter) along lines similar to the Rough Rock Demonstration School.

The only condition for use of the money is that the school committee file the necessary incorporation papers. That is an easy process and requires only about $5.00.

Leo Haven and I both think the incorporation idea and the grant of money are very important for Ramah. After trying to win the lawsuit in Gallup, this new approach will allow the Chapter to seek other sources of aid for improving its children's education. Moreover, the new corporation, perhaps to be called the "Ramah Navajo School Board, Inc.," would be able to pursue court action against the state and B.I.A. as well as seek funds for its own school system from private and other governmental sources.

What is so especially heartening about the offer of money from New York is that it means that chances are excellent for even more money once the school committee becomes a corporation. Eventually the idea could lead to a Ramah-Navajo school system including an elementary and high school with dormitories run by the school committee with teachers and programs of the people's own choice. No more would the people have to depend on the local state school boards or the B.I.A. for the assistance and funds so badly needed and wanted by the Chapter.

```
Mr. Chavez Coho
January 20, 1970
Page 2

        It is important for everyone in the Chapter to learn
about the proposed corporation and the donation of money.  If they
approve, papers will have to be signed and further meetings held.
We suggest you call a special chapter meeting as early as possible
(but not for January 30th or 31st) and let us know about it so
we can be there to answer questions.

                        Sincerely,



                        Michael P. Gross
                        Attorney

MPG/vt/1 20 70p

cc: File
    Chrono
     /
```

Letter from Michael Gross to Chavez Coho, 1970

I assisted by drafting "The Ramah Navajo School Board, Inc." and by filing the papers in Santa Fe, since the Navajo Nation had not yet created a corporation code. I brought the necessary incorporation papers to a Chapter meeting on Friday, February 6, 1970. At this historic Chapter meeting, the packed membership (up to then the largest indoor gathering of Ramah Navajos) heard from Dillon Platero and DNA's Deputy Director, Peterson Zah, who later became Navajo Tribal Chairman and then its first President when the Council changed the form of government some years later. After inspiring comments from several of the Chapter members, who spoke in favor of the proposal, they voted unanimously to accept the money.

I was most impressed by a woman named Bertha Lorenzo, who was then close to 60 years old. She spoke first in Navajo and then in English, saying, "It is time we Navajos did something for ourselves." She stunned the whole audience, and her conviction resonated intensely with the crowd. Everyone who spoke after her recommended that her words be heeded. The prepared resolution was quickly adopted unanimously 55-0.

The $2,000 from the Ann Maytag Foundation would fund my first trip to Washington, D.C., along with the new Ramah Navajo School Board, to persuade the BIA to fund the new venture. But first we wanted to pack in more meetings. The Monday following the community meeting, I wrote a letter to Rudi Frank, the program development director at the Office for Economic Opportunity:

February 9, 1970

Mr. Rudi Frank
Program Development
Community Action Programs
Office of Economic Opportunity
1200 Nineteenth Street, N. W.
Washington, D. C.   20506

Dear Mr. Frank:

Last Friday the Ramah Navajo Chapter, a community of 1500 in a remote area of western New Mexico, met to form their own school board. Five members of the Chapter were elected to serve terms on the board ranging from one to five years. The new school board is filing incorporation papers with the State of New Mexico which will grant it non-profit corporate status under the name "The Ramah Navajo School Board, Inc."

I write on the school board's behalf to inquire about OEO funding for a school at Ramah run by the school board and modeled after the Rough Rock Demonstration School. The Ramah people are particularly interested in building a facility to bring home their 70-100 high school aged children presently attending distant Federal boarding schools. If a high school were built, it could complement Rough Rock which presently only handles grades 1 to 8.

At the school board organization meeting last week, the Ramah Chapter heard of the operations of Rough Rock from Cam and Anita Pfeiffer. The reaction was enthusiastic. Several Chapter members spoke, and all were anxious to found a Rough Rock type school under their own control and direction for Ramah. The five persons elected to the new school board are outstanding:

Chavez Coho	–	Navajo Tribal Councilman
Juan Martine	–	Chapter President & new School Board President
Bertha Lorenzo	–	School Board Vice President
Bessie Begay	–	School Board Secretary-Treasurer (pre-school teacher at Ramah).
Sam Martinez	–	(several children on the honor role in local elementary schools).

Mr. Rudi Frank
February 9, 1970
Page 2

They eagerly await news from OEO about the chances for Federal
financing of their school project.

We would be happy to furnish you with any additional
information you might need and look forward to hearing from you
concerning this new venture.

Sincerely,

Michael P. Gross
Counsel for The Ramah Navajo
School Board, Inc.

MPG/vt/2:9:70p

cc: File
Chrono
/

Letter from Michael Gross to Rudi Frank

In March of that year, we received our gift from the Maytag Foundation
with a personal letter from Ms. Maytag Shaker.

THE ANN MAYTAG SHAKER FOUNDATION
SUITE 1000, 52 WALL STREET
NEW YORK, NEW YORK 10005

March 27, 1970

Michael P. Gross, Esq.
Dinebeiina Nahiilna Be Agaditahe
P. O. Box 306
Window Rock, Arizona   86515

Dear Mr. Gross:

I enclose a contribution from The Ann Maytag Shaker Foundation to The Ramah Navajo School Board.

I was very pleased to hear from Carroll Grant of the success you have encountered in obtaining funds for the School.

I am only sorry that prior commitments prevent me from meeting with you next week personally but I look forward to meeting with you in the future. Please keep me advised as to the progress of the School.

Very truly yours,

Ann Maytag Shaker,
President

Letter from Ann Maytag Shaker to Michael Gross

The first grassroots all-Indian school board drew national attention and was mentioned in President Richard M. Nixon's message to Congress on Indian Affairs in July 1970, the statement generally credited with ushering in the Indian self-determination era. While the Ramah Navajo community's leaders were instrumental in securing federal monies to start their own school from scratch, much credit belongs to outsiders. Especially critical was the help they received directly from the White House. While I was still preoccupied by the Ramah Navajo lawsuit against the local public school district, a woman showed up in my office in Window Rock. I had known her slightly at Yale Law School. Her name was Barbara (Bobbie) Greene. She was a third-year law student at my alma mater and had heard about the Ramah Navajo school case. She told me she was writing a paper on Indian education. Would I be willing to sit down and talk with her? I sure was, and good thing I did. Not only did we become lifelong friends, but she played a critical role in the then-evolving Ramah Navajo story and adoption of the whole new policy of Indian self-determination.

After graduating with honors in June 1969, Greene became a White House Fellow and was assigned to Leonard Garment, a White House staffer under John Ehrlichman. She began telling Garment about the tragedy called Indian education. Together they formulated an idea—a new law to give Indian tribes the right to run their own federally-funded Indian programs in place of the bureaucrats of the BIA and IHS.

Nixon was intrigued. His main inspiration was borrowed from the searing report by the Kennedy Sub-Committee on Indian Education, which I had read in draft form that fateful first summer of 1968 in Window Rock. Kennedy lambasted public schools and federal Indian boarding schools whose enrollments were comprised of kidnapped Indian children. Yes, kidnappings. When hungry parents are bribed with food with the promise that their children will also be well fed, I call it "velvet kidnapping." He denounced the whole federal policy of forcing them to become "Anglos," as white people are called in New Mexico. Remarkably, though bitter political foes on opposite sides of most issues in national politics, Robert Kennedy and Richard Nixon saw eye to eye on Indians. One reason for Nixon's affinity may have been that his Whittier College football coach, Wallace "Chief" Newman, a California Native American, was his mentor and idol. Had Kennedy survived, he might have been the Democratic nominee for President in 1968, in which case it is doubtful that President Nixon would have adopted his policy suggestions about reform of Indian education.

My brother sent me this statement from the Richard Nixon Presidential Library and Museum:

The Richard Nixon Presidential Library and Museum includes presentations and resources highlighting President Nixon's pivotal role in advancing Native American self-determination during the 1970s. Notably, the library has partnered with the First Americans Museum to host conferences such as "Tribal Self-Determination Revisited: President Nixon's Lasting Impact on American Indian Life," which explore the transformative policies initiated under his administration.

Key Legislation and Initiatives Supported by President Nixon:

- Indian Self-Determination and Education Assistance Act (1975): This act authorized tribes to contract with the federal government to manage and operate programs serving their communities, thereby promoting greater autonomy.

- Indian Education Act (1972): Aimed at addressing the unique educational needs of Native American students, this legislation provided federal funds to support educational programs and services for Native American communities.

- Return of Blue Lake to the Taos Pueblo (1970): President Nixon signed a bill returning the sacred Blue Lake and surrounding lands to the Taos Pueblo tribe in New Mexico, rectifying a long-standing grievance.

- Alaska Native Claims Settlement Act (1971): This act settled land claims with Alaska Natives, transferring titles to 44 million acres and providing $963 million in compensation, facilitating economic development and self-governance.

These initiatives marked a significant shift from previous federal policies, promoting tribal sovereignty and self-determination. The Nixon Library's exhibits and events continue to shed light on this important aspect of his legacy.

To bring a fuller perspective to the political climate of this time, I must mention that President Nixon was a complicated man. He was highly intelligent and did a lot for the Indian self-determination movement as well as the environmental movement. Yet his foreign policy was a disaster.

Despite campaigning on a platform that opposed the Vietnam War and promising to end the draft, Nixon—advised by Henry Kissinger—was ruthless in his handling of the U.S. involvement in Vietnam. Early in his presidency, he suggested peace talks with Hanoi while secretly authorizing Operation Menu, an expansion of bombing missions over Cambodia and Laos. His plan was leaked to the American press, and this ignited massive anti-war protests at the end of 1969, damaging his attempt to be seen as a peacemaker. The Moratorium Day marches drew millions of Americans into the streets in October and November. The human costs were mounting—by then about 45,000 American troops and nearly a million Vietnamese had been killed.

With Nixon's backing on Indian affairs, however, Bobbie Greene went to work. She and Garment played a large role in drafting Nixon's Special Message on Indian Affairs, July 8, 1970, to Congress. That paper highlighted the new idea of Indian self-determination, making a powerful reference to Woodrow Wilson's League of Nations declaration and mentioning Ramah's soon-to-be-dedicated, new locally controlled high school. He used Ramah as an example to support his radical reexamination of federal Indian policy.

Not long after, I sat in the White House with the five elected members of the Ramah Navajo School Board—Sam Martinez, Chavez Coho, Bertha Lorenzo, Juan Martine and Bessie Begay—talking with staffers about the Ramah Navajo situation and our hopes for a new school. In Washington, we also received advanced help to set up meetings from Don Olson, a Vista volunteer on the Navajo reservation, who spoke Navajo. We also met with Senate staff at one of those meetings, Sam Martinez, a large man who spoke his native Navajo as well as English, Spanish and Zuni well enough to get by, got up in the well of the Senate hearing room and said in halting English to aides, senators and representatives from key offices: "We want to teach our children to speak English and to saddle horse."

The Ramah Navajo School Board: L to R: Sam Martinez, Bertha Lorenzo, Larry Manuelito, Chavez Coho, Juan Martine, Mike Gross
(absent: Bessie Begay), circa 1971-1972

At a meeting in the BIA's main office on a big downtown boulevard,
our team was bunched on one side of the room on a couch and some
office chairs. Bertha Lorenzo, along with two other members, was seated
on the couch closest to the door. We had been negotiating all morning
and were anxious to secure a commitment from them. And then, when
things seemed permanently stalled and everyone was getting tired, Mrs.
Lorenzo, in her finest Navajo garments and a turquoise and silver hairpin
neatly setting her Navajo bun, declared, motioning to the door, "We're
not letting you out this door until you give us the money."

On the instructions of Louis Bruce, the Commissioner of the Bureau
of Indian Affairs, the BIA had prepared a proposed contract for the sum
of $368,068, as detailed in my letter to Cal Grant, who had gotten the ball
rolling just a few months earlier with the initial gift from the Ann Maytag
Shaker Foundation.

April 6, 1970

Mr. Carroll Grant
Cleary, Gottlieb, Steen and Hamilton
52 Wall Street
New York, New York

Dear Cal:

 Its unbelievable. The reality of the letters I carried back on the plane with me containing the BIA's commitment is beyond me. Did we really sit down to talk about possible Navajo projects for the Shaker Foundation only last December?

 Its not only the letter, but the school board itself. Those five people with their determination and guts made it happen. Last Friday they told the BIA they wouldn't leave the building without a commitment. Yesterday they told the BIA they would't leave Washington without a dollar figure on paper.

 We had a small celebration in Washington the evening after Bruce signed the letter with the $368,068 amount. Not much, just the school board, aides of the senators who helped us, B.J. Stiles from the RFK Memorial, Don Olson, and me. We would have liked to have you there.

 But there will be other occasions. The school board sincerely hopes you will come to visit and so do I. Remember, you've got a place to stay. Just let me know when and where you'll arrive.

 I'll confer with you this week about the letters to Mott, Bernard, and Weinstock.

 Meanwhile, my personal thanks for what you've done to help Ramah.

   Yours,

   Michael P. Gross

Letter from Michael Gross to Carroll Grant

April 6, 1970

Mrs. Ann Maytag Shaker
The Ann Maytag Shaker Foundation
Suite 1000
52 Wall Street
New York, New York

Dear Mrs. Shaker:

I wish to extend my personal thanks to you for the assistance
you gave the Ramah Navajo School Board in their effort to create the
first Indian controlled high school in the country.

You have probably already learned of the success of the
school board's trip to the East last week. Not only will the Ramah
Navajo high school be in existence by next September, but its creation
will significantly reform Indian education across the country. For
the first time the Bureau of Indian Affairs, in writing, recognizes
the right of local Indian communities to contract for monies currently
being spent or which otherwise would be spent to educate Indians in
boarding schools. It was the Ramah Navajo School Board's proposal
that resulted in the BIA policy change.

It is my hope that the Ramah project, started not more than
3 months ago because of your interest, will serve as a precedent for
other Indian communities. You may be interested to learn that certain
Alaskan natives have inquired already as to how they can copy Ramah.

Sincerely,

Michael P. Gross
Attorney at Law

MPG/ld

cc: Chrono
     File

Letter from Michael Gross to Ann Maytag Shaker

Nixon had urged Congress to adopt a new policy called the Indian Self-
Determination and Education Assistance Act (PL 93-638). Four years
later, in January of 1975, it was passed by Congress and signed into law
by President Gerald Ford. The nationwide shift in federal Indian policy
ended "Termination," which had abruptly cut off all federal assistance

to Indian tribes deemed "ready to become full Americans." The Indian self-determination policy has dramatically turned Indian policy upside down and led to greater self-governance in native communities throughout the United States. Its principal mechanism for achieving this goal is to transfer control over federal Indian monies to tribes themselves. It remains the core of federal Indian policy.

OUR SECOND TRIP TO WASHINGTON

No one on the original Ramah Navajo School Board was under 50 except Chavez Coho's daughter, Bessie. Walking the halls of Congress was tiring, especially at that age and especially for Bertha Lorenzo, who walked with a limp. After Don Olson left in September, in addition to my lawyering duties, I became the tour guide and organizer of logistics for the school board while in D.C. We still had much business to attend to—other federal agency grants had to be sought, and the country's first Indian-owned radio station had to be funded. Being an outpost and so far away from Window Rock, the Ramah Navajo lacked a means of communicating with the outside world. Washington, D.C., was the center of our universe because that's where the money was. The board and I must have traveled to Washington at least a dozen times in those first years.

Walking around Capitol Hill isn't easy. We would often go from the Senate office buildings to the House office buildings. Even when we took the Capitol subway, this was a long walk. You had to go down to the sub-basement from whichever office you were in last and find your way to the office of the senator or congressman you were seeking and walk down long corridors to get to the office. I was the youngest of our delegation (the term used by Congress members and their staff when constituents visit). Because I was young and vigorous, I would always be in front acting as the scout.

On one trip after a difficult day on the Hill, we eased into taxis and made our way back to our hotel in downtown D.C. on Rhode Island Avenue NW. The hotel was smack in the business district, which featured restaurants, shops and office buildings. We were all exhausted and hungry. Where to eat? Preferably nearby. I vaguely remembered a restaurant right around the corner from the hotel. So after a short rest, we agreed to meet in the lobby and walk around the corner to this place I knew. Sure enough, the restaurant was there just where I had remembered. It had a large picture window in front covered with a thick red velvet curtain. The doorway was around the corner from the window. To get in, you had to enter a small passageway perpendicular to the sidewalk. The glass door was also covered in a full-length red curtain.

I stood in front as usual, waiting for the rest of us to catch up. I vaguely remember some loud honkytonk music issuing from within but paid no attention to it. Nor could I see through the front entrance. I began ushering our delegation through the door as the music got louder. I began to hear tittering from members of my group already inside. When everyone was in, I followed and confronted the following: The staid and proper school board members were lined up in single file next to the front door, the men holding their cowboy hats in their hands. All were staring at the center of the room where a large lazy Susan rotated slowly with a nearly naked lady gyrating in the center. The ordinary restaurant I had remembered was now a strip club! I later joked that instead of immediately turning around, our little delegation lingered a few minutes and enjoyed the show.

TŁ'OHCHINÍ
(LITTLE ONION GRASS)

Now tasked with starting a brand new, Indian-controlled high school from scratch, there was much ground to cover. Major repairs of the old Ramah school structure, especially the roof, had to be made in time for the start of the school year, just a few short months away. The local Navajo War-on-Poverty office donated an additional $60,000 for its renovation. But work on other fronts was needed as well: hiring teachers and other staff; bringing Ramah Navajo high schoolers back from boarding schools and making them aware that they were going to have their own school; buying books and other materials; securing a fleet of minivans for transporting the kids from their scattered, isolated hogans to Ramah; developing—with a great deal of Ramah Navajo input—the curriculum for the new school; buying insurance; organizing and arranging logistics for food preparation; and renovating and converting the dilapidated, abandoned stone building next to the high school into a cafeteria.

During one week in July 1970, the absurdities, culture clashes and ominous forewarnings presented by our summer program for Navajo high schoolers coalesced, as they returned from boarding schools in Albuquerque, Utah, California and elsewhere, or in some cases from home, having dropped out after their local high school was shut down in 1968. In my view, the students' participation in creating their own school would help them become owners of their own future. The plan was to give the kids a typical, American-style summer camp experience—academics for a while, sports, boating on the Ramah Lake, excursions to national parks and monuments, and at least token participation in renovating their own school building. The 120 or so kids living in our surplus army tents were supervised by hippie, college-age counselors from around the country.

As "Temporary Coordinator," a title I chose to indicate that I wasn't going to be around long, my role was to oversee the logistics of the summer program—hiring teachers, renovating facilities and dealing with the State Department of Education, which had created a calamity for the Ramah Navajos by ordering the closing of the high school in June 1968.

Reality set in quickly. First, there was a drought that summer and the lake was a mud bath. No swimming. Next, safety concerns nixed the idea of having the kids work on renovating their own school. Third, we were oblivious to the culture clashes that might follow from placing a horde of Navajo teenagers in the middle of a sedate but remote Mormon village 45 minutes from the nearest law enforcement—bad enough in itself, but made even more acute by being supervised by long-haired, Anglo college hippies from the coasts, all living on top of each other in twenty surplus army tents. What could possibly go wrong?

The kids arrived in June and were immediately dispatched to the tents. The counselors had arrived in various ways—some in their own cars, most by train or bus to Albuquerque or Gallup. Several were in law or graduate school; the rest were undergraduates.

Teachers had begun to arrive and were assigned to faculty housing built 30 years earlier by the BIA. They were largely isolated from the kids, busy huddling with each other and members of the Ramah Navajo Chapter designing the curriculum, ordering books, figuring out schedules for classes—in short, designing a whole new school in a few weeks. Two counselors were grandsons of deceased Supreme Court justices. One teacher, a Harvard-trained anthropologist named Tom Cummings, had been on digs around New Mexico, spoke Japanese from his service time in Japan as well as Chinese from his time teaching in Taiwan at the Taipei American School, and had lived on the Navajo Reservation. A kind soul, he lived near the school, next to the ball field that accommodated tents for the kids. He had a wicked sense of humor, spoke in Boston-accented English and was a soft touch. He'd lend you his last dollar or give you a meal anytime you needed it. His refrigerator was always stocked with treats (and, yes, some booze, which he monitored loosely). Given his intense hospitality and friendliness, his house quickly became a locus for socializing.

Several romances blossomed, including one between my brother Tom, who was in charge of the summer program, and Maria, a girl from Connecticut, which led to a marriage that is still going strong. He was paid separately out of a small grant from the Association on American Indian Affairs. His credentials included degrees from Princeton and the Yale School of Management, and that summer he was enrolled in

Harvard's School of Education, where he was working on another master's degree.

The makeshift main kitchen, along with the dining room for kids, staff and counselors, was housed inside a long-abandoned WPA building, a still-handsome massive stone edifice next to the recently abandoned high school. Local Navajos, supervised by an Anglo builder from Ramah village, jury-rigged the old structure into a workable kitchen and cafeteria. Don Olson, our Kennedy Memorial Foundation fellow, was our quartermaster. No one knew how he had secured surplus army tents or kitchen equipment from an old federal installation. Logistics were a never-ending problem. Excursions to Albuquerque and elsewhere for supplies made up somewhat for the absence of the lake for swimming. A local Mormon opened a trailer park on the western side of the village on NM 53. Some faculty housing was available for rent from El Morro National Monument, eleven miles south on the same highway. Books began to arrive. My wife Andi and my law school housemate Bob Kellogg's wife Jane became the fledgling library's unpaid librarians. (Once school started, Bob became the math teacher for all grades.) Congeries of teachers were planning the curriculum after polling the Navajo parents, community leaders and school board members. Orders had been placed for supplies of all kinds, from blankets to bathroom supplies, delivery to take place in two months. Don Olson also managed to get some used vehicles and myriad other necessities.

The central focus was on renovating the school itself. Fortunately, the structure was not located within any incorporated municipality. If it had been, building codes and safety requirements would likely have delayed the project. Our deadline for completion of the renovation and opening the school was the first part of September. Luckily, the electricity in the building and gym remained functional all summer, as the gym was a major recreational destination for counselors and campers alike. Meanwhile, Ramah Navajo men worked feverishly to refurbish the structure's roof and make other necessary repairs to the 1950s hand-built and designed edifice. By the end of June, real progress had been made on all fronts, although much remained to be done. So far, things had gone relatively smoothly. Then came the week in which the precariousness of the enterprise made itself felt in spades.

The euphoria began to dissipate in early July. That's when our melting pot began to scald. Set in an unincorporated, isolated village of

300 Mormons far from any population center, surrounded by a Navajo community of some 1500 souls living over an immense territory of some 230 square miles, our enterprise faced inherent risks, dangers, challenges and pitfalls. In July, in ways that were sometimes funny, sometimes poignant, sometimes frightening, the main crosscurrents began to be revealed.

Before going into detail, let me first break story-telling rules by dispelling at least some possible outcomes that could have flowed from that sociological mix but did not. No one got seriously hurt and no one went to jail. Instead of total mayhem, the summer was peaceful and fruitful and led to life lessons of great value for nearly everyone participating. Nevertheless, living through it presented some scary moments.

One Sunday, the day was off to a pleasant start. We staff members had a cookout at a remote cabin on the Zuni River. Along with the camp counselors and other staff, who included the first teachers, both Navajo and Anglo, we had guests who had somehow appeared in various ways, including a couple named Ron and Donna who had been teaching at a public school in Zuni but who had been turned down by the new Ramah Navajo School Board for jobs as art instructors because they were hippie flower people, too hippieish for the staid Navajo Board. Ron's long hair was knotted in a bun and his chin was covered by a scraggly, brown beard; Donna wore long, colorful, flowing skirts. Both wore sandals everywhere. Although some of the summer counselors were similarly dressed and groomed, they were only around for the summer. The teachers, however, would be permanent and would have long-term influence over the Navajo community's children.

Someone had brought venison steaks, lots of beer and a nice dessert. It was a pleasant, joyous, optimistic party. The rest of the week… well, you be the judge.

We knew the work week to follow would be frenzied. The federal Office of Economic Opportunity (OEO) was sending a staffer to review its $25,000 grant for the fledgling, untested Ramah Navajo School Board to see how it was working out. This whole project was an experiment—the first time an Indian tribe or community on a reservation had started its own school from scratch in modern times.

Representatives from the newly formed Edward Elliott Foundation had funded a similar amount for books. Its founder John Elliott, along with sole staffer John Williams, came to Ramah for the same reason the OEO sent its rep—to see how this self-help Indian project was getting along. Earlier, in March, at the tail end of the Ramah Navajo School Board's historic last trip to Washington, D.C., to secure federal monies, the board members and I had traveled to New York to meet those foundation folks and to be put in touch with other sources of funding as well. So the board members and the Edward Elliott Foundation principals already knew each other.

Money for the renovation had come from the Office of Navajo Economic Opportunity (ONEO), which had received a sum from the Office of Economic Opportunity in Washington to undertake War-on-Poverty projects and programs around the country. ONEO was headed by Peter MacDonald, a WWII vet and member of the famous Navajo Code Talkers Marines, who had been recruited too late in the war to serve on the battlefield.

Back in the summer of 1970, partially because of the national media attention we had attracted, the Ramah Navajo persuaded MacDonald to support their school board's school renovation project. As I recall it, ONEO contributed $60,000 to hire Navajos to work on the repairs and reconstruction of the facility during the summer. It was partly this work that the OEO inspector was to review.

The two Johns from the Edward Elliot Foundation came to the cookout that Sunday at Zuni and were expected to stay the full week. The school board was considering applicants for its key position, executive director. And policy decisions of other kinds had to be made. I was planning to go to Gallup to buy a new van for the Ramah Navajo School Board. All the while, counselors were expected to keep our kids occupied, safe, fed and active in ways that would foster their "ownership" of the new school.

One constant feature of the week as it was throughout the summer was noise. As Navajo workmen were banging away at the old school structure, kids got into fights. Weekends produced a steady stream of runaways, mostly to Gallup or Grants, but occasionally to Albuquerque. Our counselors would go look for them and usually found our kids and brought them home.

Fortunately, Andi and I had lodging in the dilapidated, barely functioning wreck of the Merrill house (now renovated and commemorated with a historic plaque with the names of all its prior occupants except the two of us), about four blocks away from the new school site. We were thus shielded from much of the bedlam and noise. People would just show up to see what was going on, including distant relatives, old college friends, acquaintances of acquaintances, candidates for jobs, etc. Several stayed in our "loft."

One in particular, whom I shall call Nancy, was an artist and a good friend of a former high school friend of mine. She would leave an indelible mark—an emblem of the craziness of the whole operation, the era in which it was happening and the ongoing culture wars of the time. Our adventures with her began bright and early Monday morning.

We were expecting a visit from the OEO inspector, and I was pretty antsy. We only had his name—a long African or Muslim name, lost in the mists of time. His was to be the first of several inspections by our funding sources. Meanwhile, Nancy had parked herself in our run-down abode in the "guest room" up the broken staircase. She was smart, had a biting sense of humor and an assertive personality. A non-stop talker with an opinion on everything, Nancy was unafraid to insert herself into any conversation within earshot. As with most of our guests that summer, she had invited herself. All the while she was with us, she kept talking about her ongoing therapy and how she had been advised "to let it all hang out." And boy did she. Although I don't remember Nancy being at the elk steak cookout, she must have come that Sunday because the first memorable incident involving her occurred bright and early the next morning, the day our funders were expected to visit.

My office—and our command center—was in an old surplus World War II-era aluminum Airstream trailer that Olson had commandeered from somewhere unknown. The trailer was parked directly on the ballfield east of the old Ramah High School facility with one side close to the school building and the other side with a view toward the ballfield.

Soon after I arrived at my desk, at about 8 a.m., I happened to notice out the south window a man walking briskly towards the trailer, obviously the OEO inspector. I had not met him before, but his appearance quickly gave him away. He was a tall African American man dressed in a brightly colored dashiki, sporting the largest Afro I had ever seen, reaching nine inches in all directions. Turning around and looking through my north-facing window, I saw Nancy, striding boldly towards the trailer from the opposite direction. Then, she too, saw Mr. OEO. Instead of continuing towards the door, she abruptly turned south towards him. Now, Nancy was fairly imposing herself, with her flowing hippie skirt and her own long hair and various necklaces. She too, constituted a snapshot of the times. Besides that, she had a booming voice, which she was about to employ. At that point, I lost sight of them both but could still listen. And what I heard has remained solidly seared into my memory as one of the most excruciating utterances I have ever heard. A few seconds after they both disappeared from view, Nancy literally screamed at the top of her lungs in the most amazing tone of triumph and exaltation and inappropriateness I ever heard: "OH! I HAVEN'T SEEN ONE OF *YOU* SINCE I LEFT NEW YORK!"

It was ghastly. I instinctively shrunk into my chair but there was no place to hide. I was so embarrassed that I can't remember Mr. OEO's response—I was too ashamed. Nancy went off somewhere else, maybe sensing that the trailer could not accommodate Mr. OEO, herself, my staff person and me.

Moments later, Mr. OEO knocked politely on the trailer door. I answered and began mumbling some kind of apology for her, although my mind had gone numb. The subsequent interview was pleasant. I must have explained what we were doing and taken him around the campus. All that I remember is that he was very diplomatic and wound up giving our program high marks. But that incident was only the first involving Nancy. More adventures were to come.

A day or so later, Nancy decided to accept Tom Cummings' invitation to go on an excursion to the Hopi villages. "Tell me, Mr. Cummings, is there a Mrs. Cummings?" she asked. That afternoon, Nancy managed to get into an argument with a Hopi woman selling pottery outside of her home, over the price of one of her pots. The woman had told Nancy that the pot she was interested in cost $50, but Nancy proceeded to insist she had said $15, not $50. The argument caused Tom to cringe with embarrassment, as he recounted it to us later.

Back to the day of the inspection, after the Nancy encounter with Mr. OEO, I collected myself and showed John Williams and John Elliott around our campus—the library-in-progress, the main school building under construction and the makeshift dining room/kitchen—and introduced them to the school board. As disorganized and rambling as the project may have seemed to those of us in the middle of it, the two Johns were as nice as could be and praised what they saw. They talked with folks on their own after touring the school.

On Tuesday evening we had a meeting with the Navajo school board in one of the classrooms. Don Olson was present as was my brother Tom. We reported on the OEO inspection and brought the Elliott Foundation people by to say hello. After that, however, an event happened that brought home to me more graphically and personally than I ever experienced before the nature and psychology of discrimination in this country. My brother had encouraged a friend of his from graduate school to apply to be the executive director for the school board. The man had excellent credentials and would have been an ideal person for the job in my opinion. However, he was African American, and that nixed it for the board. They blatantly indicated they would not hire an African American.

Never before had I experienced cross-minority bigotry, and it simply floored me. The thought that the oppressed minority we outsiders were trying to help could themselves be prejudiced along the same fault lines displayed by the rest of American society shocked me. Having participated in the Meredith March Against Fear in 1966 as a Brown University tutor at Tougaloo College, the episode was acutely painful to me personally. Hearing people who themselves had suffered so badly from white supremacy and ingrained racism speak about another minority in the same racist manner literally made me feel nauseous. In that moment I determined that I would quit if they decided to reject this candidate before he was at least interviewed. I don't remember what I said, but I did express my feelings of outrage to the board, somehow in a manner which did not totally blow up my relationship with them. Nevertheless, I was truly disgusted.

Later, I talked about my feelings with my brother, who was equally emotionally affected. We agreed we would tell the candidate what had happened and that we would back him if he came for an interview anyway. The candidate, however, withdrew his application. To this day I think that was the worst moment of my career in Indian affairs. Both my brother and I contemplated resigning. Don Olson spoke with us and helped put things in perspective, saying that resigning would not solve anything, and that cross-minority prejudice is common and must be understood as part of the reality that stems from human nature. In later years, the Ramah Navajo School Board did hire other minority people, including Blacks. A Black person, in fact, later became principal adviser and consultant to the school board. I attribute the board's bias in 1970 to the fact that they had picked up the white European prejudice against Blacks while segregated in the army during WWII.

My brother and I still brood about that event. Cross-minority prejudices affect many. I have relatives in Israel, cousins once removed. Their mother was my mother's first cousin and has since died. When I visited Israel in 2000, she voiced outrageous views about Palestinians and Arabs generally. How could Jews—perhaps the most despised minority in world history—harbor such views against fellow humans? The mysteries of human psychology remain.

Student in front of tent, Ramah, NM, summer 1970.
Photo by Michael Gross

Two students on tractor at camp, Ramah, NM, summer 1970.
Photo by Michael Gross

GO-GETTERS: CONVERSATIONS WITH BESSIE RANDOLPH AND BEVERLY COHO

On January 30th and February 26, 2024, my daughter Ashley and I interviewed Bessie Randolph (formerly Begay) and her sister Beverly Coho, daughters of Chavez Coho. Chavez and Bessie served on the original Ramah Navajo School Board (RNSB). Beverly served 22 consecutive years (2001-2023) on the RNSB and the Board of Trustees.

These interviews were combined and edited for brevity and clarity.

Ashley: Could both of you talk about the history of the Ramah Navajo? Have they always been separate from the big Navajo Nation?

Beverly: Yes. Prior to being sent to Fort Sumner, Ramah Navajos were already living in the Ramah Navajo area. Some were not gathered up [at the time of the Long Walk]. They stayed behind and they did not go to Fort Sumner.

Ashley: Did any of your ancestors have to go to Fort Sumner?

Beverly: Our ancestors did, not our parents but their grandparents. So, my great, great grandparents went to Fort Sumner.

Ashley: Did anyone pass down stories to you about it?

Beverly: I think I met my maternal grandfather, but he was such a blur in my mind. I was just a little baby, so I really never heard Fort Sumner stories directly from my grandparents. It was slow, hand-me-down information through the lineage and of course, when we got to school, there were some books on it, but we don't know whether we should believe those books or not.

Ashley: When the Ramah Navajo came back from Fort Sumner, were they able to go back to their traditional land?

Beverly: I guess they came back from the east, naturally. They saw Mount Taylor as the major landmark, and from there, they veered towards the left from Grants and arrived back in Ramah. They tell us that Ramah had seven original Navajo families right after the return from Fort Sumner. From there they regenerated at a prolific rate, and the population bloomed, and here we are. By now, there may be 3,000 to 4,000 of us. I must add that the returnees discovered that white settlers had taken over some of the customary land used, so the Navajos were moved to the south of Ramah.

Ashley: And what did the families do to get by?

Beverly: We were very strong. Around the 1960s, 70s, a little bit into the 80s, our parents were running the show. They had quite a bit of sheep, goats, cattle, horses, pigs and chickens. They were running little ranches, and they had farms where they grew their own crops like corn and various types of vegetables and some fruits. Their homes were self-sustaining. There was not any convenience store around the block, no Wal-Mart that we could run to. We had meat, eggs, bacon, goat milk, vegetables of all sorts and the three sisters—corn, beans and squash. We also had potatoes. We had chokecherries and wild berries from the mountains. Then we had Navajo tea. We had yucca for our shampoo. You could live out there without ever going to the store.

Ashley: How many kids were there in your family?

Beverly: There were four siblings, three girls and one boy. Right after World War II, the baby boom began. There were families with more than four. Many of them had five to 15 children. Sam Martinez had 15 children. So that's why we had a lot of students to go to school, but no school.

You know, not everybody was born in the hospitals. There was a mortality rate of infants that we don't know about. What we heard parents say is that you had another brother, and then this happened. Or another sister, and this happened.

Bessie: Beverly was the first one in our family that was born in the hospital. The rest of us were born at home. I heard that my parents lost a child before my oldest sister. At some time, there might have been another one who was stillborn.

Beverly: I'm sure other families suffered more losses. Now, the number of children is limited to two or three.

Bessie: And birth control was also reinforced in recent years. The government just said the word, and the doctors introduced different kinds of birth control, whether or not the mother accepted it.

Ashley: Can you tell me about your father? You talked about him going to boarding school, I think, in Crownpoint and Fort Wingate.

Bessie: Yes, according to what he told me, he first went to Fort Wingate boarding school.

Beverly: I saw his record when I went to school in Fort Wingate. He went from beginner up to third grade, and his report card was right there in the old file. So that's probably when he essentially stopped school.

Ashley: Do you think he chose to stop, because it was a hard experience?

Beverly: According to the information I have, he got sick. Either some boys fought him and beat him up or he was trying to play a little football there, and a whole bunch of boys pounced on him, some big guys, and he was just a little guy. But he got seriously hurt.

Bessie: Yes, he had some broken bones, broken ribs and plentiful serious injuries. And he had to be taken home and was given medication at home. When he got well, the family moved out to Cerro Alto, and nobody could find the family to bring him back to school because his parents said that he didn't need to be back in school because of the serious injuries. He continued to help the family with the livestock and dry farming. And of course, he exercised.

He told me about running very early in the morning. He increased his running distance. Cerro Alto is a large mountain where the family lived. He started out from the east, and would run about a quarter of the way around the mountain, and would come back home. It probably took months and months until he could run around the whole mountain. That was one of the disciplines that he did on his own, for his own health. He used to tell us, "Go run, go run! It will help you be healthy and that way you will get rid of a lot of bad things."

Those are some of the experiences he had and the strong thinking he had about how to succeed, how to improve the ranch, how to help the family at home. He used to carry large logs over his shoulder back to the house; many of those heavy jobs he did. Those were some of the stories that I heard as I was growing up. He was always working, taking care of home and livestock.

I know he was involved with the community—he was a judge when he was only 20 and also, for 32 consecutive years he was the council delegate from our area to the tribe's bigger council/government. He increased his knowledge and had a better understanding of English and speaking ability when I was growing up. He educated himself.

Beverly: I noticed you had a question earlier about our mother. She did not go to school in the Western contemporary way. But she was more schooled Navajo tradition-wise. She was able to weave, make moccasins, silversmith, take care of the sheep, take care of the household, be a farmer and rancher when our father was away in Window Rock. Her name was Nellie H. Coho. Her sister, our aunt Alice Henio, helped her.

Bessie: She did a lot of sewing and weaving. She planted all kinds of food and had a lot of know-how and taught a lot of community members how to do things for yourself.

Beverly: She was an herbalist, a Navajo traditional medicine woman. People who were ailing would come to see her. She would go up into the mountains with her prayers, and bring the right herbs down and show people how to mix and consume them, and get well.

She used to show her artistic craft at the Wheelwright Museum in Santa Fe. They asked her to bring her weaving loom. We would go with her to translate for her.

Ashley: You mentioned that your father would talk about the treaty of 1868 and the promise to Navajos to get an education.

Beverly: After the forced trip to Fort Sumner and probably four years there, there was a time for Navajos to come back. We Navajos had to promise to lay down our guns and not be furious and warlike anymore. If we behaved and submitted ourselves to being reservation-type residents, we were either promised or offered some things in return. And one of them reportedly was education, where for every 30 Indian children there would be a teacher, and there would be a building in which these children could go to school and learn Western contemporary education. This is in Article 6 of the Navajo Treaty of 1868.

Next, there's a dispute on this one: some say that there were promises for healthcare in perpetuity. But others say no, there weren't really any promises made. But to this day, we hold the federal government responsible for paying the costs of education, and for paying the cost of our healthcare. And somewhere along the line, there came provisions for other types of care like public safety, which is law enforcement, and social services including aid to families with dependent children and who have no income. If people needed counseling and a way out of our supposedly wayward ways, we should have counseling provided to us, or if our children were acting out and not progressing in school. And then there were also funds for higher education. All these came later, and to this day, we have contracts with the federal government for each of these services, even for housing. But the federal government would not build us a complete house. It was mainly for repairs on a limited basis, like for a roof, maybe for a window or door or floor—nothing extravagant, just a small room to live in. We call them "matchbox houses."

These were some of the things that evolved later, but the main provisions were for education and healthcare. From the beginning, they were put into the Treaty of 1868 between the federal government and the Navajo leaders at Fort Sumner at the time, like Chief Manuelito, Chief Ganado Mucho, Chief Barboncito and others. Then, when the Navajos were released, instead of getting a nice ride back, they all had to walk 300, 400, 500 miles back to where we assumed our original place of living was.

When attorney Michael P. Gross and his school board colleagues went to Washington to speak to officials about the Treaty of 1868, be it congressional leaders or federal programs staff, they told them, "You haven't fulfilled your promise that you made in 1868, over 100 years ago now, 102 to be exact. Where is our teacher? Where is our school building?" So that was used as an effective leverage in gaining commitment from those they spoke to in Washington, D.C.

Ashley: That's a really important point. So, there was a one-room schoolhouse built in the 1950s near the Chapter House? Or was it built in the 1940s?

Beverly: The very early beginning was in the late 1800s. There was a one-room schoolhouse in the actual Ramah Mormon town. I'm sure that wasn't for us Navajos, probably just for the white people that came from the state of Utah.

For us Navajos, a one-room schoolhouse was built for various grade levels in about 1943, in Mountain View, which is eight miles north of Pine

Hill and 12 miles south of Ramah Town, there in the original Ramah Navajo center. The third graders sat on one corner, second graders in another, first graders, another. Beginners didn't even speak English at that point. I didn't go there but my two sisters and brother did.

There were no buses. Somebody bought a pickup truck, like an old army truck or something, with no seat belts and no seats in the back. All the kids stood in the back while riding to school with their hair blowing in the wind.

Bessie: We were picked up Monday morning and brought to the school. At the beginning, we mostly played there with toys, mud, water, drawing, most of those things at the beginner level. We ran around outside and played on the swings and whatnot. We would go to the dining hall.

In later years, there was a small building designed with some beds, double beds. We had one person there to take care of the girls. For the boys, they had a hogan, which was used as a dormitory. There was no running water. Electricity, I believe, was from a generator.

There was one teacher for beginners through third graders. She was busy with all four groups. In first grade, we learned numbers and counting. We started on the ABCs, and then we learned about different kinds of arts. In second grade, we learned about math and did some reading. We did some crafts there. We would go on to learn about nouns and pronouns and all that in the third grade and probably adding, subtracting and multiplication.

Every morning, we would say the pledge of allegiance, and we did some singing. We learned together, but we could go home on the weekends in the army truck and come back on Monday.

Ashley: You were really young when you began to stay in a dormitory, right? I mean, how did that feel for you when you were just 6 or 7 years old?

Bessie: Yes, we had to stay there, and it was cold with no heat or running water. We learned what was good for us from playing outside in the dirt and doing what we could, I guess. But, when we went to fourth grade, we were sent out to other states for boarding school, in New Mexico Fort Wingate (near Gallup) or to Albuquerque or Santa Fe. We would join bigger groups of students at the boarding school. There would be first through 12th grade. In addition to Navajos, we would meet students from a lot of different tribes like Apache or from different pueblos.

I don't know about how other students did in California and Nevada or Utah or Oklahoma. In Albuquerque, I repeatedly struggled to finish school. It took me about ten years to get a diploma. But I felt that if I had gone to school at home and been taught by my parents, I would have been taught more, because in Indian school, it was more like military school. You had to go by the hours and always in a group. We were disciplined in a lot of ways and were punished for little things. We stayed in a fenced area. When I finished 12th grade, I felt like I had only learned up to the level of an eighth grade education, whereas if I had gone to public school or stayed at home, I would have been wiser and had more knowledge and more understanding of what was going on in the community, as well as in the world. I think I missed out on a lot by attending an Indian school.

Ashley: It sounds almost like prison.

Bessie: I don't know much about the military, but I think that's what they go through—boot camp. It was very strict, even at Ramah dormitory where I went.

Beverly: In the early years at Mountain View, it was a school but not really a school, meaning that the curriculum standards weren't really there. It was just gathering a bunch of Navajos who only spoke Navajo and no English, and getting them acquainted. Most families taught their babies up to three or four years old, but we hope parents teach their children a lot more now. But back in Mountain View in the 1940s, these children were getting their introduction to the practices of the dominant society.

But then the federal government got bolder. In the 1950s, they opened up the Ramah dorm right on the edge of the old Ramah High School. It might have been in its first or second year when I got to school, the 1957-58 school year. It was run military-style. We marched around quite a bit all over campus, even to go eat. We stood in line by height, boy-girl, boy-girl. And if any of us were out of line, we immediately had to do some strenuous exercise right then and there, like do a duck walk on the side-walk back and forth, or kneel on the court in the corner of a room, or take ten laps around the tennis court, or something to that effect. And at no time were we supposed to utter any Navajo words, whatsoever. If we were caught, immediately we went to the soap room, where there was a big old bar of soap, maybe about three inches in height, three inches in width, five inches long. They would chop a block off of that and stick it in our mouth, and we would have to stand there, simply for speaking Navajo.

We were supposed to say, because we couldn't write, "I will not speak Navajo anymore." We would say that 100 times in the presence of a matron. The majority of these matrons were non-Indians, but there were some Indians beginning to be hired.

For the boys, if they did something bad, there was a hill right behind Ramah dormitory, and then there was an arroyo on the other side of the perimeter there, and the boys would roll big blocks of sandstone from the hill all the way across campus and into the arroyo. That was the punishment they received.

So, that's the kind of school we went to. We rarely got our jackets washed for us. Our sleeves were sometimes very hard with snot.

One day, somebody's parents saw that. They had a big old meeting down at the Ramah dorm in the recreation hall. None of the children were allowed in there. Only my brother Bennie Cohoe was allowed to go in because he was the student body president. These parents had had it with the Ramah dormitory staff. "How come our children were disciplined so harshly, and how come they are neglected? How come they are not properly cared for?" So, they hashed this out, and we saw some slight improvement from that point on.

But still, it was no sin for a full-grown adult, a matron, to put on boxing gloves and to box a student. That was another form of punishment. I can now see in my mind who was rolling down the rocks, who was being punched out by a boxing glove, who was taking their ten laps, who had soap in their mouth. Traumatic!

Ashley: Did you get boxed?

Beverly: No one boxed me. No one put any soap in my mouth. I was very tame. I didn't goof off. But that all goes back to the discipline that our parents gave us at home. No one got out of line at home. We each had to do our chores, and we were able to perform well at home, and with me it carried on at the boarding school. I didn't want to get punished.

Ashley: How old were you, Beverly, when you went to stay in the dorm?

Beverly: In 1957, I had turned six years old.

Ashley: And how long would you be at the dorm? How often would you go home?

Beverly: In early September we would check in and stay there until we went home for Christmas, and then be back in the dorm in January. We stayed there until the beginning of summer vacation, which was late May or early June. And this went on for 12 years until I graduated.

The whole purpose of this assimilation was that somehow somebody wished our skin would turn white, and that our ways would turn away from our Navajo. So, the more we were kept away from our parents, our grandparents and our comfortable surroundings of Navajos, the better. I think that was the mentality at that time. It was pretty harsh, and this is no lie. And all the while, we were going next door, just about half a mile away, to the Ramah Elementary School.

When I got to school at six years old, I didn't know one word of English. I understand that my father used to have a dictionary under his bed, and that he would try to read it. A couple of days before I left for the dormitory, he tried to help me. He let me know what my name was in English: Beverly, and furthermore, to how spell that: B-E-V-E-R-L-Y. You know, it was kind of long. Who gave me the name? Maybe it was really popular then. Like my sister said, I was the only one born at the hospital.

So, I got to school and my long hair was cut off into what we called a 'German helmet.' They cut our hair right by our ears, all the way around to the other ear. It was chopped off and our bangs were cut straight across. We wore denim coveralls. All of us had to dress the same, and we wore a white t-shirt underneath. The boys had their hair cut off too, with only an inch sticking out from the middle of the top part of the forehead. So, we all looked the same, wearing denim coveralls.

We would stand in line. Somebody would walk by and say, "I want all of you standing there to call out your name when I point to you." And some of the kids didn't say anything, they just stood still. So, they went down the line, and then it was my turn to really shout it out.

I said, "L Y!" That was the only thing I remembered that my father was trying to teach me: I didn't remember the B e v e r. The kids looked at me. (Laughter.) So much for the impression I was trying to make.

Mike: What's your Navajo name?

Beverly: Something about our Navajo name, it's known only to us as individuals. We use it only for ceremonial purposes. Our Navajo name is how the holy people know us. We identify ourselves with that to the holy people. But that day, it was 'L Y.'

Ashley: You said there was a baby boom and there were too many coming to the dorm.

Beverly: In 1965, there were about 200 children in the dorm. They actually called it a hall, because there were no rooms; it was just a long hall with bunkbeds. The little girls stayed in one, the little boys in one, older boys had their own wing, the older girls had their own wing. They were able to roll in more bunkbeds than what the fire department probably allowed, in order to accommodate more kids. Little boxes were bought for them to store things like underclothes and other hygiene items. There were no lockers. We got as crowded as we could get before somebody ordered that we couldn't have that many students in there.

So, they shut down the dorms for us older kids, meaning ninth grade on up. That was in about 1965, when I had to transfer over to Fort Wingate boarding school, even though I had already gone to Ramah High for one week. Many of us my age and older got sent off, so the attendance at the public school fell even more, and pretty soon somebody ordered that school to be closed. I guess it wasn't worth the trouble for the maintenance costs on the school building.

Ashley: Where were the local Mormon kids going?

Beverly: Well, they tried to continue going to the old high school, but once it shut down they were bussed over to Zuni in McKinley County. Most of the Mormon kids lived in McKinley County, so there was no issue about boundary lines. About 97 percent of Ramah Navajo kids lived in Cibola County. There were a few around the Ramah town in McKinley County.

Ashley: And the school in Fort Wingate was a BIA school, or was it Catholic?

Beverly: It was a federal BIA boarding school, a huge school, 9th through 12th grade. There were over a thousand students. In my graduating class in 1969 there were 161 students, whereas my graduating class in Ramah might have been 15 students. I don't know who chose for me to go to Fort Wingate. Others went to Albuquerque; Riverside, California; Oklahoma; Chemawa in Salem, Oregon; Stewart in Reno, Nevada; Intermountain in Brigham City, Utah. We were all scattered.

We thought it was bad not seeing our parents when we were at Ramah dorm, but it was much worse when we went to the boarding schools, because we couldn't come home. But my dad always made a point of driving to see us. He was a councilman at Window Rock, so he would stay in Gallup and drive back and forth to his daily council meetings. Fort

Wingate was just 12 miles east of Gallup. Every now and then he would swing by and pay a visit or watch a basketball game with me.

Ashley: Was it as military-like there as Bessie described?

Beverly: At Fort Wingate it wasn't really military-like. By the late 1960s it had simmered down. At Ramah our uniform—a white t-shirt with overalls with suspenders—had a buttoned L-shape on the butt to open and shut. Some of those boys were awful when we were in line for lunch, boy-girl, boy-girl, they would try to get at your button without you noticing. Then they would call out, 'hey!' And everybody would run over there. Naughty!

Ashley: Kind of a design flaw. So, when your dad and other leaders like Juan Martine wanted to re-open your own school at Ramah, why did they want this kind of school when it had been so bad?

Beverly: They wanted a school, period. For that reason, they visited several sources, like the Cibola School District, the Navajo Nation, other branches of the State of New Mexico, even the federal government office in Albuquerque. There was no help from those sources. They just wanted a school, they weren't thinking much about what type of school.

Ramah Navajo Community was so under-developed—except for the little gravel road that went through town, nothing else was improved. We knew that there had to be a boarding house of some sort with a school alongside it so children could stay there. But we thought that hopefully this time, it would not have a military flavor to it, but have empathetic people who would work as matrons or instructional aides. It would be our own people who would be motherly toward our own students.

Ashley: Did they envision also a school where Navajo language and Navajo history would be taught?

Beverly: Definitely. The founding philosophy was that the school would be taught in such a way that Navajo culture would be enhanced, not just reading and writing or speaking. At the same time, Western contemporary lessons would be learned, and students would be capable of using both English and Navajo so that they would be bilingual and could function 'in all worlds,' which is what they said. For us Navajos the founding thought was along those lines because our elders knew that we could do well and live well on whichever side we chose.

Remember I said there were a bunch of sheep, goats, cattle, horses? Drought set in, the land base was becoming smaller, and there was encroachment from non-Indians who moved nearby. In their spoken teachings our parents told us, "You can no longer just try to function at home. You need to go get an education, which we didn't have." That would be one of the reasons why education was important to them, because they didn't have it. They saw how society was changing. People were functioning more and more in different ways than in the Navajo way, so we had to learn their ways, and learn how to make a living over there too. So if we were fortunate to live in both realms, we could function even better. That was the hope.

Then in 1968, two years after the school was closed, the Ramah Band filed two lawsuits unsuccessfully to keep the school open and to have transportation to public school in Gallup or even to Zuni. They made an unsuccessful appeal to the Navajo Nation for support. And then they decided that if it's to be, it's up to us, which is tied to the core of Navajo culture.

T'aa whi aji t'ee go. If it's to be, it's up to me. That's what it means. It's a prelude, I guess, to self-determination that's instilled in Navajo minds. Our parents would say, "Get out there, assert yourself. Do something for yourself. If something's going to be for you, it's up to you." It was ingrained in the previous generation before us very well, so that it was like a fertile land on which Mr. Gross arrived. And that's why their minds just gelled so well. You know, the Ramah Navajos there, these founding leaders that you keep mentioning, they were go-getters. Mike was also a go-getter, and they just meshed together, started making plans, and that's how it got started and finished in beauty!

The school board was incorporated on February 10th, 1970. February 6th was the day of the chapter meeting held in the Ramah Navajo Chapter House. Our father went to visit each hogan to say that we would have an important meeting. "Put your sheep in the corral. Don't graze them. Keep them in there and come out to the chapter meeting. If you need transportation, I'll be driving by at such and such a time." He would pack them up in his truck. At that time, there were no double cabs. There was a single cab, but he would put them in the back of the pickup truck and haul them in. Juan Martine and Sam Martinez hauled in others in their pickup trucks, and some others who wanted to help did the same, Lee Pino, Curley Biggs, Bertha Lorenzo....

There was a large audience in Chapter House. And then there was food: frybread, mutton stew and coffee that the ladies were making outside. They asked, 'What should we do? The government promised us education 100 years ago. We don't have anything here for our children. Our children aren't learning anything. We went everywhere. Nobody wants to help us. They don't think that Ramah Navajos should learn Western contemporary education.'

So they had that meeting, and they discussed it, and Mike was present. A Navajo girl was a translator. They took an hour and a half to explain what others said. But they sat there hours on end because it was important.

At one point, Rose Henio, a community lady, an elderly Navajo who was not educated, made a motion from the floor. She said, "I make a motion that the Ramah Navajos start our own school, based on the fact that we've exhausted all our possible sources going here and there, and nobody wants to help. We even went to Rough Rock, they're not willing to break off a piece of what they're doing and give us a part of it, so let's do this. We are resilient people. We have bright ideas. We can do something with our hands, yes, but beyond that, we can do something with our minds. Here's the man who is going to help us," she said, pointing to Mike.

So, that was the motion. Leo Narcisso Martine seconded the motion. The vote was overwhelming. Everybody got up, and that's what happened at the Chapter House with no opposition.

Four days later, Mike went to Santa Fe to get the Ramah Navajo School Board incorporated as a private, not-for-profit organization by the State of New Mexico, to provide charitable, benevolent, social and educational services, as needed by the Ramah Navajo community. That was the Chapter resolution that was passed as well.

The first year, people from the East came. We got the foundation monies, and kids were enrolled, and they had tents, and they started off with summer school and whatnot. The building was rebuilt by the Ramah Navajo railroad workers who would go to different states and work on the railroad to make money to make a living for their families. All those men came back, and they were the ones that were up on the roof pounding nails. They were Navajo.

There were no sanitation or health workers among us. We built an open fire outside, and these Navajo ladies made fry bread and stew. That was what the students ate. We began to get a few teachers.

From 1970 to 1975, the Ramah Navajo School Board, Inc., operated Ramah Navajo High School in the village of Ramah by leasing that former public high school that was renovated by our own people. Every Ramah Navajo student returned to attend the new school.

Our women folks were not educated but they were good drivers and became the bus drivers. They hauled in the students. But then Mike worked out something. Remember, McKinley County prohibited buses from crossing the county lines. With his magic, we were able to run the buses into the community in Cibola County, to bring those kids into McKinley County daily to go to school.

Some of us had been at the dormitory in earlier years. I don't remember what the capacity there was. I think at one point, we had 200 students, boys and girls. My brother Bennie Cohoe was student council president both at the dormitory and at Ramah High School. We were taking over and outdoing the white kids at basketball and academically. We were outshining each one of them and getting the hang of English.

Then in 1975, the school board continued to work with the federal government to build a new school altogether. They kept going to Washington, D.C. They didn't have travel per diem money. The school board leaders and Mike stayed at Mike's relatives' homes. Five board members and some staff went. They would rent three motel rooms, maybe four or five to a room, and they had brown-bag sandwiches from his relatives.

They visited the Shaker Foundation, the Kennedy Foundation. There were about four or five different sources of funding to help raise money. I think they got about $368,000 dollars from Washington, D.C., to start the school. They got $68,000 from ONEO. That was figured out by Mike and Don Olson together with Chavez Coho and Peter McDonald.

Mike: A fortune in those years.

Beverly: They started constructing new school buildings for the elementary grades up to high school at Pine Hill with the appropriation from Congress. The appropriation didn't go through right away due to bureaucracy. The new school was opened in 1976, including a kindergarten and health clinic. The Ramah Navajos were the first Indian tribe to operate their own health clinic; the Ramah Navajos were the first Indian tribe to build their own school from scratch.

They were the first Indian tribe in the lower 48 states to enhance their communication by getting a radio station, KTDB, a year after KYUK-AM in Bethel, Alaska. We didn't have telephones. All the roads in the community were dirt roads. There was no electricity or gas line. It was just out in the boonies, where the windmill was, and we were climbing around in the mud up there in the winter and in the dirt in the summer.

Local community people gave up their land use right there and said, 'Here, we'll make room. We'll move the sheep a little bit.' A man named Billy Coho was asked, and he obliged to do that. So, they made room right there where the school now is at Pine Hill, so that all the development could take place. And of course, there were dedications all along. There was a school opening dedication at the old Ramah High School in September 1971. I think there were about 12 seniors that graduated that spring. We had visitors from all over, and there were always familiar people on stage like Bessie, Mike, and the rest of the school board members. I just sat in the audience. I was in college then, so it was important that I fly back home to observe.

Ashley: Bessie, why did you want to be on the school board?

Bessie: I had been working with the Peace Corps starting in about 1966. I worked several years as a teacher's aide, and I was able to become a teacher for about 20 four- and five-year-olds. When there was a chapter meeting, I would go to the Chapter House and listen in to see what they were talking about. I experienced the feelings and emotions of the community. I went to several meetings and just listened. I actually didn't feel like I wanted to be on the school board. But when they talked about the school board election, the community decided they needed to elect members. People in the audience were nominated, including me, and they voted, and that's how I got in.

Beverly: In those days there was only the one preschool that was started in 1964 in Mountain View so that preschool children wouldn't go into culture shock when they got to school. Bessie was the only teacher there. She was the only high school graduate and later got a bachelor's degree in elementary education at UNM, all through the pushing of our parents. Maybe Mr. Gross suggested that they needed someone who had experience in education.

Ashley: Bessie, were you part of the original group that went to Washington, D.C., to talk with members of Congress?

Bessie: I lost track of how many trips we went on. The community expected us to do what we had to in order to get the school. One day we were writing a proposal. I was the secretary for the group, and it was my duty to write it out on a yellow legal pad. We described the location of Ramah, the problem and ourselves. We talked about our needs, and why the parents in the meetings were in tears—why it was so important to have their children at home and to have a school nearby.

Then we went and told the people in Washington about the promise the government had made a hundred years earlier. We told them we needed their help to get a school going in the community. We didn't type it. We just took that notebook and made copies. Other than my father, none of us had ever been in an airplane before. We took the papers to Washington, D.C., and had a lot of help along the way. One was Michael Gross, and the other was Don Olson, who spoke some Navajo. They knew where to go.

One time we didn't have Mike or Don with us, and we introduced ourselves. It was up to us. We brought our papers and proposals, and we went to the House of Representatives, the Senate, the BIA, the Department of Education, and many other offices that worked on education. I remember Greene Kilberg at the White House.

At the BIA office, we talked about the 1868 promise the government had made to provide one teacher for every 30 students, and the agreement made at Fort Sumner, when the government released us Navajos back to our own reservation. Four years were spent there with a lot of suffering and losses of our people, but we were able to come back. Our ancestors were released to our Four Mountains, which is what we call the Navajo reservation. We told them that the promise was about a hundred years old, and we hadn't seen a school for our children in Ramah, NM. We went to look for the name Ramah on a map, and it wasn't written anywhere. What we did was to put Ramah on the map.

Ashley: Can you describe the day the new Ramah school re-opened?

Bessie: We worked day and night, and we were always on the go. Ninety-five percent of us Navajos had no education. We were worried about our children's future. We got a little money here, a little there. A lot of people from the community helped to build the new school and register the students. We hustled to get the old school renovated and open by the end of the summer. It was very exciting. Everybody in the community was involved. We had bus drivers, cooks. What we really needed at that time was dormitory space. We had space for the elementary students. Some of the parents brought in the students, others came on the bus, sometimes in bad weather. Even in the mud and through hardship, students came.

Beverly: Because I was in college that fall, I didn't witness the opening of the brand new school. However, I flew back in September to witness the ceremony to dedicate the opening of the Ramah Navajo High School. There were elder folks down to newest generation and everyone in between. They stepped out in their finest regalia with all the bling. This was a very special day, the most optimistic day of the year. It marked a new start, a new chapter, a chance to engage with students, colleagues. In Navajo we say, "the dawn of a new day, a new year." When speakers went to the podium to make their remarks, they expressed a great deal of hope. Whatever had happened in the past, it happened. Let's seize the opportunity. Certainly, there was excitement as well as anxiety. It was a new experience, wondering if it would succeed. There was room for all those stomach-churning feelings.

At the same time, it was a beacon of hope, not just limited to the Ramah Navajos. We were mingling with white people from all over, other people from Big Navajo, and representatives from other tribes. People wanted to meet with our leaders to one day replicate the model in their communities. Others wanting to do that was a mark of Ramah's success. The speakers included the student body president and other children. We did it good old Navajo-style, with an open pit fire and grilled mutton, along with mutton stew with fry bread. Journalists came out in numbers and stories were written up. On other days, people from other nationalities came, like from China.

Ashley: Thank you for describing it in such a beautiful, clear way. We're truly grateful for you.

Beverly: The real person who was there was my sister, Bessie, along with her father Chavez.

THE DEDICATION OF THE NEW RAMAH NAVAJO HIGH SCHOOL

On September 12, 1970, the newly refurbished Ramah Navajo High School was dedicated "under new management" at a colorful ceremony in the front parking lot. A stage had been built with chairs arranged in a semicircle for the school board and me as toastmaster. Andi and I were dressed in our best version of Navajo finery—she in a gathered, flowing skirt and Navajo jewelry; and I in my cowboy boots, a button-down shirt with a Navajo bolo tie, and a leather vest. Numerous dignitaries were present. Ed Foreman, the rightwing Congressman representing a swath of western New Mexico including Ramah, sat in the front row with his big American flag pin prominently displayed on his lapel. Representing President Nixon, who sent a congratulatory telegram to the dedication, and sitting next to her friend Bobbie Greene (later Bobbie Greene Kilberg) was LaDonna Harris, former wife of Oklahoma Congressman Fred Harris and founder and president of Americans for Indian Opportunity. Together with Ramah Navajo members, BIA officials and a smattering of Ramah Mormons, the crowd sat on folding chairs in the warm New Mexico sun. The vibes were good, everyone was jolly, refreshments were served, and all the folks mingled pleasantly.

The following Monday, the *Gallup Independent* splashed the dedication across its front page. Alongside was a photo of a BIA helicopter, which had crash-landed nearby after taking off from a grass field next to the parking lot. No one was hurt, but the paper gave it equal billing on the front page with the dedication.

Later that week, all hell broke loose. The local papers claimed that the staff of the new school were anti-war hippies who didn't stand to salute to the flag. We then collected signed statements from each of our staff swearing they had not shown any disrespect for the flag, nor had I witnessed any from my perch on the dais. Many did have long hair and beards with peace symbols on their lapels; the women wore flowing dresses and flowers in their hair. No one mentioned Vietnam. But the article's tone left no doubt that the local papers believed the new school was part of the hippie wave taking over the country, marked by their breakaway style of dress and hair and known for their pot-smoking and anti-war sentiments.

Amazingly, many Mormon youth enrolled in the reopened Ramah Navajo High School despite the fact it was now under Navajo control. The new Indian-run school was near their homes and saved them a half-hour bus ride each way to Zuni High School. They too, had been beleaguered by the closing of the high school in the summer of 1968 and welcomed the newly reopened and refurbished edifice despite the fact that it had come under Navajo control. Of course, the buses did not venture out on the Ramah Navajo Reservation to pick up Navajo kids to take them to Zuni, which would have taken twice as long each way.

From the unexpected gift of $2,000 to the Ramah Navajo from the Ann Maytag Foundation in February 1970, it had taken only eight months to obtain over $370,000 in operating monies for the first Indian school started from scratch under Indian control in modern time. During that frantic summer, it was of course impossible to complete all of the necessary tasks to open the school while at the same time managing and providing activities for upwards of 50 Navajo teenagers living in make-shift tents on the ball field. But somehow it all got done. One special problem, however, was bureaucratic jealousy.

New Mexico State Education officials, who had unthinkingly and mechanically warned the Gallup-McKinley County School District (GMCSD) year after year that their small high school would be shut down if enrollment was not increased, started poking their noses under the new Ramah Navajo tent. Somehow the officious ex-Marine who headed the state Department of Education, Leonard DeLayo, still believed he had jurisdiction over the now Navajo-run school. He was not at the dedication, but reportedly had been intensely upset about the negative news stories about the closing of the Ramah public high school and the inadequate plans for ensuring the Ramah Navajos a high school education. The week after the dedication, DeLayo insisted on inspecting the school, even though he had no legal authority over it. I accompanied him. While roaming the hallways looking at the gym, examining the desks and chairs, looking for dirty windows, he stopped at a water fountain. He took out a tape measure and measured its height from the floor. He then announced that the drinking fountains were not regulation height above the floor, making harrumphing noises as if the building were about to collapse because the fountains were three inches too tall. His tone suggested he would have to order shutting down the school, which of course he had no power to do. It was ironic that during the years the building had been a public high school, no one complained about the height of the drinking fountains. As karma would have it, I heard that DeLayo's car suffered a flat tire on the way back to Santa Fe.

But somehow—despite the hippie staff, living in tents, Navajo kids running off to Albuquerque on weekends, the near tragedy of the jeep that turned over with kids jumping off it, and dealing with meddlesome state officials—it all came together. It was now time for the dedication to take place.

Mike at podium at dedication of the Ramah Navajo's first
self-determination school, Ramah, NM, 1970. Photo by Andrea Gross

Mike and Andi at dedication in front of buses, Ramah, NM, 1970

SPEAKING FROM EXPERIENCE: AN INTERVIEW WITH MARY COHOE

After addressing the high school graduates at Ramah Navajo High School in May 2021, Mary Cohoe sat down with my daughter Ashley and me to discuss her family history and how she came to work for the Ramah Navajo School Board and Pine Hill Schools, shortly after the founding of the new high school in the fall of 1970. This interview has been edited for brevity and clarity.

Mike: Please say your name and tell us where you were born.

Mary: I'm Mary Tsinnajinnie Cohoe. I was born in Ganado, Arizona, when my mom was working at a school nearby in Klagetoh.

I'll start off with talking about my mom a little bit. Actually, I credit my maternal grandfather, *Shichaii*, for his commitment to valuing education. He must have been a young boy when he heard about the Long Walk of the Navajo People and the long walk of people going back to their homelands. But remember that in the Treaty of 1868 there's a phrase—not a full paragraph or a full sentence, but there's a part of a sentence that says that for every 30 Navajo children, there will be a teacher. And then it goes on to say that the teacher will be provided a house, so I figured my grandfather must have known about that. He made sure that one of his children went to school, and that was my mom. My grandfather lived after the Long Walk people went back to their lives and went to a different place to live, and so my grandfather lived in the Torreon area, about 25 miles west of Cuba, New Mexico.

He made sure he selected my mother to go to school because the government had demanded that Navajo children go to school. Her first school was the boarding school in Crownpoint. She has her own stories about being picked up from my grandfather's place and taken to Crownpoint, where she got her hair cut, and her English name. Later she went on to

Fort Wingate, and then ended up at Albuquerque Indian School. My mom graduated from high school in 1933.

My grandfather valued education, so he made sure he provided the transportation. There were no accommodations such as buses or cars on the reservation at that time, so my grandfather took my mom to school at the beginning of school every year on horseback from Torreon to Albuquerque. Sometimes they would have to spend the night along the way, and he kept the fires going so they could get to Albuquerque afterwards. Leaving my mom at Albuquerque Indian School, my grandfather took the two horses to Bernalillo to catch a freight train. The railroad people allowed him to put his two horses on the freight train that used to go into the Cuba mountains close to home. The train would stop, and he would take his horses home. So that's how my mom went to school. He was going to make sure that the Treaty of 1868 was fulfilled by having one of his children go to school, so there would not be another Long Walk.

Ashley: Did he see it as the key to exerting Navajo rights once his daughter was educated in American schools?

Mary: No such thing. He was just trying to satisfy the U.S. Government.

Ashley: When she started elementary school, was it a BIA school in Crownpoint?

Mary: It was the government school, administered by the BIA, or maybe it was the Department of War at the time. She went to Crownpoint, Fort Wingate, then Albuquerque Indian School. At the end of her junior year, during the summertime, my mom went to work as a maid over at Chaco Canyon, before it became a national monument. She worked there for the summer, and she met a very good childhood friend there. They reunited 40 years ago at Chaco Canyon.

After high school, in 1944, my mom was given a job in Klagetoh, Arizona. Around that time, at the end of World War II, the government needed teachers, and she was selected since she had a high school education. Later, she became a teacher and principal at the Torreon Day School, the one that's there now, west of Cuba, New Mexico.

I was born, but my mother had a job to do, so I was given to my aunt and uncle, my dad's brother, Uncle John Tsinajinnie. I was raised by them in Klagetoh until I was eight years old. I went to school in Klagetoh. My first language, of course, was Navajo.

Before first grade, I got very sick. I think I spent close to a year at the hospital in Ganado Sage Memorial Hospital, and that's where I started hearing English, probably from the nurses there, and so I knew English and Navajo. When I was discharged from the hospital I must have been maybe four or five years old, and I don't remember much of my days at that time. All I know is that I was very young, and I was able to go to school in Klagetoh.

Then, when I was seven and eight years old, I went to Crownpoint Boarding School. It was just terrible. I'm so glad that that particular boarding school is leveled now.

Ashley: What was so bad about it?

Mary: Well, we couldn't go home. The distance between Torreon and Crownpoint at that time was more than 70 miles each way, all dirt roads, so my sisters and I couldn't go home on weekends like other students were able to do. And the caretakers were just mean. You could not speak one single word in Navajo, or you were physically punished, and I mean physically punished and other stuff.

Ashley: So, like spanked?

Mary: I don't remember being spanked, but I remember being hit. We had to sit up against the wall in a row. And if we moved, we got punished.

Ashley: Mary, did you wonder why you were there at school?

Mary: No, I never questioned it because I had to go to school and be in third and fourth grade. Then, lo and behold, there was a public school in Cuba, New Mexico. The Torreon trading post owners had kids too, so we were the first ones. There were three kids from the store owner, and I think three of us from my mom's family. We started going to school at Cuba Elementary. We started out in the cattle truck—that was our bus. Then later on, we were able to sit in the back of my dad's pickup truck because it had a cover. And then later, because there were only dirt roads and sometimes they were muddy or snow-packed, the store owners got us a four-wheel-drive jeep, and we were packed in there like sardines. We were so proud of that little jeep. We asked the owners of the store to paint it yellow like the school buses at Cuba Elementary School. We were the only ones in a red jeep, so since that was our bus, we had our jeep painted yellow.

Ashley: Who were the others? White kids? Or were there are a lot of Navajo kids?

Mary: No, mostly Hispanic and just a few of us Navajo students. Now, I think the percentage is like 65 percent Navajo going to Cuba schools. By that time, I was in the fifth grade, and I wanted to do a lot. It never registered that I was a Navajo person or that I was a different person.

One day, there was an announcement at Cuba Elementary that we were going to have a band. And by noontime, everybody got in line if we wanted to join the band. I did not know what "band" meant, but I wanted to join something. I heard people in front of me say, 'I want to play this instrument, I want to play that instrument.' I thought, what in the world are they talking about? And then I remembered one of the comic books, I think it was *The Three Little Pigs*. One of the little pigs used to play flute, going through the woods. So, when it was time for me to say which instrument I wanted to play, I said flute. It was accepted. Oh, my gosh, I said the right thing! I said a flute.

After school I went home, by this time on buses, and I told my parents, I'm in band and I'm going to play the flute. And my mom and dad said, "No, you're not." They got out the Montgomery Ward catalog to the musical instrument section and they said, "You're going to play the clarinet." I said, "Okay." So, they bought me a clarinet in Albuquerque. So, that's how I started my music career, with what started out as a comic book flute. I went on to middle school and graduated from Cuba High School.

By this time, my mom was the principal at Torreon Day School, and she made sure that we did not talk about getting a job. We did not talk about having a boyfriend. She demanded that we talk about having a college degree—not just going to college, but having a college degree. Then we would be on our own. So, through high school I only did band. I didn't do sports. One of the band teachers was a graduate of Highlands University, so I said, I'm going to Highlands University to major in music, and that's where I went. I majored in music for three years and changed majors in my fourth year.

Ashley: Was clarinet still your main instrument?

Mary: By that time, I just loved it—the college band, the marching band, the orchestra, the musicals—everything musical at Highlands University. And I learned how to play all the clarinets. At the time, I was the only one allowed to play this mysterious instrument that came to Highlands University. Everyone was so excited. It was unveiled that the new instrument for college was called the contrabass clarinet. Guess who was asked to play it. I loved that instrument, so I was able to play the contrabass clarinet for Highlands University. Yay! I mean, it was heavy. But one time I took it back to my college room, and I was hugging it. Now, I have no idea how to finger a clarinet, though those were my musical days. I played in the marching band and the pep band, the concert band, the musicals, the pit orchestra, and on and on. It was required for everybody to have physical education (PE), and I discovered I could run. So, I changed my major and planned to become a physical education teacher.

I taught at public school for a couple of years, and then the Vietnam War came about, and I discovered that I was eligible to apply for this program. Did you see the interview?

Ashley: The one on New Mexico PBS, about the Vietnam War?

Mary: Yes, New Mexico PBS. My brother and I were very close, and he was drafted by then. But instead, he and his cousins and other friends decided to join the Marines as a group, so they went to the Marines. And there were other family members who served. I had an uncle who was killed in action in World War II.

I thought back on it. I didn't know too much about the Code Talkers at the time. But still, I qualified to be in this program to go to Vietnam. I was single, had a college degree, was healthy, and wanted to do something different. So, I went to interview after interview. My first interview was with the American Red Cross in Denver, and they paid all my expenses to get to the interview. Even though there were protests against the Vietnam War, I went to training in Washington, D.C., where a huge protest march was expected. I don't know if it was with Martin Luther King or a Vietnam protest march. For safety reasons, my particular training class was held in Virginia at one of the universities, and then from there, we went all the way across the country to the Bay Area, San Francisco, and we waited there for about four days. Our orders had us leaving from Travis Air Force Base, going to Honolulu, then on to Manila, and from there to Saigon. I spent a tour there in Vietnam, and then I came back.

When I came back in the summer of 1969, I was accepted to join a group of Native Americans going to universities. One group went to Boulder, Colorado, the other one to UCLA. So, I went to UCLA as a graduate student then. The rest of the students were all undergraduates, and I think the studies were maybe called Indian Studies, I don't remember, but it was sort of like social studies. I was able to get some credit hours there—it was not my intention, but it was something to do. It was drilled into our mentality that we could not have any non-Indian friends. My closest friend at the time was my undergraduate roommate from Michigan. To this day, she's still my best friend. I thought, what am I going to do? She is my friend. So that was that.

Then I was recruited by Highlands University to enter a master's program in Guidance and Counseling in Education. I was offered a fellowship because they were looking for an American Indian. There were only ten slots and I was the tenth one.

I traveled to Window Rock, Arizona, for a meeting with the group that ran the Department of Education for Navajo Nation. There were three people, two men and a lady. At that time, everyone was Navajo. They needed teachers there, again all Navajo, no non-Indians were allowed to work with Navajo education. That was the mentality again, that only Navajo people should be teaching Navajo people. No white people.

All of a sudden, here comes an attorney who had just come back from Washington, D.C., with Navajo people, and they were going to start a school. This attorney was not Navajo, but he was introduced as an attorney, and his name was Michael *Gross*. You got that, Mike?

Mike: How do you spell it? [laughter] What do you remember about that day?

Mary: The meeting was in Window Rock, with Dillon Platero, Sam Billison and Catherine, the only one who's still around. It was in the summer. You took their first five school board members, and you went to Washington, D.C., to meet with the commissioner. When you came back, you went to this brief meeting where no white person was supposed to attend. You were allowed to say something, and it sounded strange—that these Navajo people were going to start a school.

So that was how I heard about the Ramah Navajo school, I think it was the spring of 1970. My colleague and I went to Window Rock because we were doing a research paper about Navajo education. We thought, what is this about, starting a school for Navajos? We didn't talk to you, Mike, but you were there. That was the first time I had ever heard about the Ramah Navajo. I didn't know there were Navajo people at a place called Ramah.

Ashley: So, did that conversation make you want to come and join the school?

Mary: It was a different idea at the time. My colleague and I went back to finish our paper, and I got my master's degree. Then I went home and sat around for almost a month—I didn't want to do anything. And then my mom says, you need to go get a job. So, I started applying here and there. And I got offers from different schools. By that time, I was asking myself whether I wanted to work with Navajo students or Native American students, because of what was drilled into me at UCLA, as well as that strange attorney saying that they were going to start a Navajo school.

I was offered positions to be a guidance counselor at about three or four different schools in the Southwest. My mom had retired from the big school by that time and was a Head Start teacher after her retirement. She knew about this place called Ramah Navajo Chapter. She loaned me her car and money for gas and a motel, and she said, 'Go to Ramah.' Somebody else also told me about the Ramah Navajos. I looked at a map thinking, where is this place? I found the school, still down in the village of Ramah, and I had an appointment for an interview. My interview lasted about three hours because I did not speak Navajo at the time, even though I could understand it. I had to have a translator, and that was the late Abe Plummer. I was drilled by those founding board members, especially Mr. Chavez Coho. He drilled and drilled me. Why did I want to work with the Ramah Navajo? I had all my credentials. I had teaching experience. I had my master's degree and was ready to go to work the next day, and on and on. And still that was not enough credibility.

Finally, I said, "I am one hundred percent committed to doing this." And I was finally accepted to work for the Ramah Navajo School Board at the Ramah Navajo High School.

Ashley: With the different places you had applied to, why did you decide this was where you wanted to commit?

Mary: Because it was not only different, but it was the beginning of something that was different from other schools across the nation. My first job was to be the PE teacher, along with being a Navajo language teacher. That didn't really add up to anything, so I started running the front office, doing filing, which is not my forte. I did the filing and answered the phone just to stay busy. And I would hear Abe Plummer. He was yelling on the phone. I don't know whose staff he was yelling at, maybe the late Senator Joseph Montoya's staff. The main office was in the hogan. When

Abe Plummer was talking to the congressional staff, that whole hogan was vibrating. That was the old Ramah Navajo High School.

Then I heard about how divided the village was. We had students from the village of Ramah for about a month. Then one day, no one showed up. Only maybe two girls came back to school. I think the non-Navajo students went on to Zuni or Gallup, I don't know where they went. They might have gone to boarding school.

Ashley: Do you remember why?

Mary: In the village of Ramah, they said that this school was ridiculous. I'd say the Mormons, I guess about 95% of them, were totally against Navajos having that school, and they did everything they could to get it closed down by the Albuquerque Area BIA Office and the Department of Education in Santa Fe. Do you remember that, Michael?

Mike: I don't know about that, not that it's not true. But what I remember is that there were a couple of Mormon teachers like Joe Weight, and there may have been one or two others who taught from the Mormon community. They were very supportive. By and large, from my observation, the town was fairly welcoming.

In the previous summer there were counselors from various colleges who signed up to be counselors during the summer. Were you there for any of that?

Mary: I came in the fall.

Mike: There were a couple of Mormon teachers at the Ramah Navajo School that year and later on too, for that matter, so the town wasn't entirely against it at all.

Mary: I would say about 90 percent. Only two students from Ramah Village graduated from the Ramah Navajo High School when the school was still in Ramah.

Mike: In fact, they were upset about having to send their kids to Zuni, being bused by the Gallup-McKinley School Board. The Navajo kids, since they lived in Valencia County, were outside the school district and could not take that bus, which was one of the major problems for the Navajo kids. They weren't going to be able to get to a public school anymore. That was one of the big selling points in Washington, D.C., about funding the school through the BIA. So, you weren't in on that. But that's the reason that the old high school in Ramah became the first location for the school.

We got the Ramah Navajo community to form its own school board, and we got big money for the actual costs of educating the kids through hiring teachers and all that for the school year. That's how that school got saved, to help the Mormon kids, too. They went there, too.

Mary: Most of them left, except for two girls.

Ashley: Do you think it was racism?

Mary: Yes, yes.

Mike: Well, wait a minute. The Zuni School was all-Indian as well.

Mary: Well, they were probably at public school, or they were already in session, but there was like a thick line, a thick block between the Ramah Navajo and the Mormon village of Ramah.

Mike: As I understood it, at the beginning of the first school year, half the Mormon kids went to the new Ramah Navajo High School, and after two weeks, most of them disenrolled and went to Zuni with the Gallup-McKinley school bus.

Mary: One morning, Mike, the Mormon students from the village of Ramah did not arrive. Only two of them came back. I don't know where the others went.

Ashley: Could you describe the five original board members a little bit? Bertha Lorenzo, Sam Martinez, Chavez Coho, Bessie Begay, Juan Martine. Can you tell me about their backgrounds and what they were like as people?

Mary: Chavez Coho was at one time the Chapter president. And then he took over being a council delegate for a cousin of his, and so Chavez Coho was a councilman through the terms of Tribal Chairman Sam Akia, Raymond Nakai, Paul Jones and Peter MacDonald. Chavez Coho was a rancher. He had cattle and sheep over on the edge of the reservation, southeast of Pine Hill, on the highest dead volcano, Cerro Alto. That's where he owned a ranch.

Bertha Lorenzo had a family as well, and she was called a community leader or some sort of a community liaison; she was like a social worker, doing what social workers do—helping out families and communicating for them.

Juan Martine was referred to as a Christian and had a church, I think, for a while.

And Sam Martinez was a traditional person. He knew the cultural songs and cultural ways of doing things the Navajo way. He was not a medicine man but a cultural specialist, a traditionalist. Sam Martinez was the youngest.

Bessie Begay had a high school education, so she was the secretary. She was able to speak English and able to write. She was the only one with a high school education.

Mike: Mary, I want to ask you a question, but please feel free not to answer it if it is somehow disturbing. Chavez Coho hardly ever spoke English. I knew he could understand a lot of English, but as far as I can remember, he hardly ever spoke in English. Bertha was the main spokesperson for the board when we went to Washington, D.C. Does that dovetail with your understanding?

Mary: Yes, because I think he only went up to the third grade at Fort Wingate School. He was not literate or a fluent speaker in English, but he knew the Navajo ways. But Chavez Coho was the leader of the entire community.

Mike: How informed do you think Chavez was about what was going on, where the money was coming from, and why we went to Washington, D.C.? Did he understand all that?

Mary: 200 percent.

Mike: That's a very important insight. I never asked that question before. It was hard for me to tell, because he didn't like to speak English. But I knew that he could understand a lot of English and would speak if he wanted to speak.

Ashley: So, if Bessie was the only one with a high school education, why was it so important to them to start this school?

Mary: According to what's written—Michael knows more about this part when McKinley County School District closed down Ramah High School as a public school—the Ramah Navajo children then had to go off the reservation to go to school: places like Riverside, Oklahoma, Albuquerque Indian School, maybe Fort Wingate. They had to go away from home to go to a school.

So, the time came when the community selected these board members to try to reopen Ramah school as a public school. But they lost. Instead, Gallup-McKinley School Board said, we'll run buses up to the county line. That didn't work either. Because like your dad said, the Ramah Navajo

Reservation was at the time in Valencia County, now Cibola County. Something had to be done for education. When people write their dissertation or research papers, that's what usually comes up: families wanted their children going to school back home.

Ashley: Sending them to school and having an education was very important to them, even if they didn't have that much education themselves.

Mary: Yes, that's correct.

Ashley: I was wondering about the curriculum. When you first started, were teachers teaching Navajo language and history?

Mary: The curriculum always included Navajo from day one. And the curriculum was just really basic, the four core areas: English, math, science, social studies, and Navajo, probably following the Department of Education out of Santa Fe as a guideline. At the time, I don't think the school board as the board of trustees for school curriculum said "We'll follow the school guidelines." That didn't come until in the early 2000s. What they followed was what the BIA required at the time, out of the Albuquerque area office.

Ashley: I know you haven't worked at the school your whole career, but you worked there, then you left, and then you came back. What are you most proud of when you think about working at Pine Hill School in the broader landscape of American Indian education?

Mary: Probably about fulfilling my commitment to education. I'm thinking of my mom's education, my grandfather's expectation, raising my children here, and just keeping the school moving on to the next step.

I told you about how the village of Mormons tried to close down the school. In fact, there was one bus driver who was not Navajo. She even wrote to the president of the United States to say that the Ramah schools should be closed. There were even a couple of Navajo ladies who said the same thing. Why? I don't know. So, just like me wanting to play the flute in the band way back when, I just thought something has to keep moving.

Mike: What did they say was wrong with it?

Mary: They never said. Can you imagine? That's a good question.

Mike: There were a couple of Mormon teachers at the school.

Ashley: It's interesting that it seems the school faced more opposition than you realized, Dad.

Mary: It seemed like there was only one family that always supported the school, and that was Kurt Clauson's sons. They ran Cowboy Stopover.

Mike: The Clausons were friendly. Stuart Clauson lived on the road to Zuni.

Mary: Even Stuart got harassed by the people who opposed the school. But he still went on, and he helped smooth out the grounds at the old high school. He built the trailer park because we started out with our housing units in mobile homes. It was good business for him, but he still was supportive.

I didn't know at the time that the school board was asking for permanent buildings out at Pine Hill. A survey went around the community as well as neighboring communities. What kind of a school should be built for Ramah Navajo students? I remember that question in a survey. Supposedly the results said, we want a permanent school building that does not look like a government building or a BIA building. We want something that looks permanent, and to make sure that there's a hogan shape, and an area somewhere to have a fireplace in each building. So that's how it started. Those fireplaces are not standard anymore. They're all closed now, but each building had included one. The clinic had a fireplace, the kindergarten had a fireplace. The elementary school, the high school, those four buildings had fireplaces, but not anymore. So, that kept me going, besides my children's father being from here.

And then, of course, I talked about the State Department of Education as well as the BIA—we had to keep up ADA, Average Daily Attendance. When the monsoons came and the roads were impassable, with my Vietnam experience I said, "There's a way to bring the kids in and they can stay at the dorm." The dormitory was still under the BIA at the time.

I estimated how much it would cost to rent helicopters, and Tom Cummings helped me by going to certain foundations back east, and we rented the helicopters. And by this time, it must have been the spring of 1972, because the KTDB radio station had just started. It was Abe Plummer who went to the radio station and announced that a helicopter would be landing close by to their homes, and that the kids would be picked up and be taken back to Ramah dormitory. So, with that we were able to fulfill our obligation for the Average Daily Attendance so we could stay open.

Mike: So, you had a helicopter?

Mary: Yes, and that was never told, never written, never publicized. But we did it. Those helicopters were not what I had in mind, but it still worked. The helicopters that I had gotten used to were called 'Hueys.' They're no longer part of the military, but that's what we rode in every day in Vietnam. Instead, they brought out a two-seater besides the pilot, and somehow, we transported enough kids to be able to keep our attendance up.

Another part that I enjoyed after coming over here to Pine Hill was just keeping track of the congressional appropriations in the last phase of the construction here. All the buildings were built in phases, and I was responsible for the last phase, which was an addition to the gym. I coordinated all that and I enjoyed communicating with congressional offices. That was my job for a while. I wasn't paid for it, I just volunteered. My other position was as division director for many different departments. I enjoyed that and just kept things moving, which is very different from how it is today.

Ashley: Did your kids graduate from Pine Hill School?

Mary: No, they didn't. It got to be political around here, so I put them in private schools. One graduated from Rehoboth. My second daughter graduated from St Catherine's Indian School in Santa Fe, and then St Catherine's closed, so my youngest daughter transferred to Santa Fe Indian School. In order for my youngest daughter to attend Santa Fe Indian School, I had to get an okay from the Navajo Division of Education Committee. I followed that committee around to wherever they were having meetings to get their okay so my daughter could go to Santa Fe Indian School. But then Bennie and I said, just forget it. They required an agency superintendent's approval, and by that time, Ramah Navajo had its own BIA agency, so we had a superintendent for a Ramah Navajo agency. We got his signature, his approval, and my youngest daughter graduated from Santa Fe Indian School.

Mike: How much did the community understand in the beginning about how the school was organized and where the money was coming from to open the school?

Mary: I'm just guessing that they knew it came from Washington, D.C. At that time, maybe across the nation, BIA was not very popular, so when you and the school board started working with Congress in Washington, D.C., the thinking was that the money came from Washington, D.C. It did not come from Navajo or the local BIA office in Albuquerque.

Mike: Did they understand that we went to Washington, D.C., to get the money from Congress?

Mary: Yes, though I understand that whenever the school board traveled anywhere, mostly to Washington, D.C., they had prayer groups during the travel time to make sure that they were successful in whatever they went to Washington for, and in this case it was for education. That's so unheard of these days, right?

Ashley: They don't do those prayer groups anymore?

Mary: No. They're so political with each other.

Mike: Let me ask one last question, Mary. Had anybody, including you, ever heard of the Ann Maytag Shaker Foundation?

Mary: I don't think so.

Mike: They were the small start-up foundation that I coincidentally got in touch with through a classmate from law school. But they gave the first $2,000 that funded the school board's trip to Washington, D.C. That's how the whole thing got started. That was how the Ramah Navajo School Board got founded.

Mary: I don't think the current board knows that part.

Mary Cohoe, Mike and Roger Martinez (former RNSB member)
at 2022 Pine Hill graduation ceremony

FOUNDING THE COALITION
OF INDIAN-CONTROLLED
SCHOOL BOARDS

After the dedication of the new Ramah High School, the time had come for me to move on. I had been in contact with the Native American Rights Fund (NARF), which expressed interest in retaining me part-time as its Indian education expert. I was to be paid a half-time salary and all expenses. John Echohawk (Pawnee), from a renowned Indian law and social justice family, served as NARF's first and longtime executive director. He co-founded the organization in 1970 with funding provided by the Ford Foundation and California Indian Legal Services. In 1971, NARF moved their office to Boulder, Colorado, where they still operate more than fifty years later.

During the latter part of 1970, after I had made the connection with NARF, John spent a few days at Ramah with me. This visit took place in mid-December just as a record-breaking cold wave swept into northern New Mexico and Arizona. At Ramah, temperatures dropped to minus fifty degrees for a solid week. It was eerie. There was not a breath of wind the whole time. John, my wife and I had to sleep on the living room floor under blankets and as close to the fireplace as we could get. The heating system in this jury-rigged home, built in the 1930s, had broken down because the propane on which we depended for heat had gelatinized and wouldn't flow through the pipes.

My pickup of course would not start, and we were running low on supplies. So, one morning, desperate for mobility, I decided to do something totally in keeping with my reputed—but about to be deflated—intelligence level. I built a small fire under the engine. I let it burn for a while. I had a water can near me just in case. So far, I was pleased that the truck had not blown up. A few minutes later I tried to start the truck. Nothing happened. I tried again. Same result. I was smart enough not to build a bigger fire and so gave up my desperate efforts at mobility. Luckily, we survived both the cold wave and my stupidity.

Later, after the cold wave started to fade, we had a visit from Edgar Cahn, a noted scholar and author of a book on Indians[48], civil rights and poverty law. He was interested in seeing what was going on in this remote part of western New Mexico. He and his wife, Jean Camper Cahn, had powerhouse names in the rising field of poverty law. I picked him up at the Gallup airport and drove him to Ramah. He stayed on our living room floor as well. I never heard from him again.

I was now off on a new career path, aiming to help other Indian communities and tribes replicate Ramah. Other Indian tribes and communities were beginning to hear about Ramah and wanted to do the same thing. I was receiving requests, directly or through NARF, from tribes and ad hoc parent groups around much of the country.

After resigning from my work with the RNSB in the fall of 1970, Andi and I took a road trip in our new Ford F-100 pickup to Montana to visit Jim Goetz, a friend from law school. It will be recalled that Goetz had arranged the blind date for me with Andrea Hughes, whom I married in June 1969. We stayed at Jim's cabin in the mountains outside Bozeman for a few days. While there, I had told him about the Ramah school and my new part-time job with NARF.

Goetz was teaching history at MSU while waiting to get admitted to the Montana Bar. He immediately made news in Montana when, after flunking the state bar exam, he sued the Montana State Bar Association on grounds that as a holder of a law degree from a non-Montana law school he was required to take the Montana bar exam, while those who had graduated from the state's only law school at Montana State University were exempt from taking the exam. He won his case, opened his practice in Bozeman, and became one of Montana's most highly regarded lawyers.[49]

My engagement with NARF did not require me to move to Boulder. Indeed, my first engagement after Ramah came directly from a

---

48. Cahn, E. *Our Brother's Keeper: Indians in White America,* (Plume, 1975).

49. After opening his practice in Bozeman, Goetz became one of the best known and successful lawyers in the State of Montana, having represented Charles Kuralt's estate litigation among other significant matters, especially in land and water law.

reservation in Wyoming. I was still negotiating my new arrangement with NARF when I got a phone call from Dennis SunRhodes, an architecture student at Montana State University at Bozeman, who had been talking to Jim Goetz. He explained that he was a member of the Northern Arapaho Tribe located on the Wind River Indian Reservation in Wyoming.

SunRhodes told me a complicated story about his home community and their desire to form a reservation school district to bring a high school closer to home and under Indian control. The two public school districts in Riverton and Lander had been enrolling Wind River Indians in their respective high schools off-reservation. Complicating the situation was the fact that the Northern Arapahos shared the same reservation with the Eastern Shoshones, though historically they were blood enemies. When the Northern Arapahos suffered defeat by the U.S. Army in the Plains Indian wars, they "temporarily" had been removed to the reservation already established for the peaceful Eastern Shoshones, which has now resulted in a permanent reservation for both tribes.

Wind River is immense and beautiful, bounded by the Wind River Mountains to the west. The Indian kids from both tribes went to elementary schools on the reservation but, because there were no high schools on the reservation, the kids were being bussed to high schools in Lander and Riverton, at least a half- to a three-quarter-hour bus ride each way for most students. Dennis told me how badly they were treated at these off-reservation schools. Not only were they ridiculed and treated with contempt because of their long hair and unusual names, but they were denied the chance to participate fully in afterschool activities, especially sports. The buses to and from the reservation ran on a restricted schedule each way, stranding them at school if they wanted to join a team because there was no late bus home. Nor could Indian parents exercise any control over their children's education, being heavily outnumbered in school elections. These were some of the conditions the Kennedy Subcommittee on Indian Education had talked about in its thorough and frightening report on Indian education, which I read that first summer in 1968.

Dennis explained that the Northern Arapahos, with some support from the Shoshones, had mounted an effort to redraw high school district lines using a state initiative to reorganize all of Wyoming school districts. The idea was to create a Wind River Reservation high school district. They had backing for their redistricting project from the progressive Episcopal missionary Father Duncombe, the same good soul I mentioned in a previous chapter who was tragically killed by a youth at Ethete, the principal community on the Wind River Reservation.

In 1971, NARF sent me to Pine Ridge, South Dakota. Pine Ridge is part of the Great Plains, largely barren except for wild grasses and rolling hills. By contrast, and coveted by the Sioux as their ancestral homeland, the Black Hills, about 90 miles to the northwest of the Pine Ridge Reservation, are covered in forests, and with low mountains and wild game. The Pine Ridge Reservation has precious little of those. All the lands set aside for the Sioux tribes contrast sharply with the Black Hills. Their reservations look barren. Though previously guaranteed by a now-abandoned treaty that reserved them for the Sioux, white trappers and homesteaders were allowed to settle in the Black Hills. In the early 1980s, the Great Sioux Nation including Pine Ridge won, or more accurately their attorney won, a $100-plus million-settlement to compensate them for the lost lands.[50] The funds still sit in a U.S. government account earning interest, now worth more than a billion dollars; the Sioux nations steadfastly demand return of the precious Black Hills instead.[51]

This story recalls what happened to the Ramah Navajos. White Mormon settlers from Utah armed with land patents from Santa Fe kicked out the Navajos from the best-watered land and forced them into more barren land to the south and west. The U.S. military sat idly by. The Sioux tribes still covet the Black Hills as a spiritual place—theirs by treaty.

We were sitting in a small conference room at Loneman Day School on the Pine Ridge Reservation. Birgil Kills Straight and Gerald Clifford had heard about NARF's new ability to provide legal assistance on Indian school matters. They asked for assistance, and I had been dispatched to answer their request. I first got there in late 1971. Pine Ridge is home to the Oglala Lakota Tribe, perhaps the best known of the several Sioux Nations. Crazy Horse was an Oglala. Gerald One Feather, then a council delegate and later tribal president, was present, along with a couple of others. Under discussion was Loneman, a day school run by the BIA about 20 miles north of Pine Ridge, the administrative headquarters of the tribe. It was in a dire state of disrepair. The five Oglala and I were discussing Ramah and how it got its own school. They wanted to do

---

50. *U.S. v. Sioux Nation of Indians*, 448 U.S. 371 (1980)

51. Why Are the Black Hills Sacred to the Lakota Sioux?
https://www.thecollector.com/black-hills-sacred-to-lakota-sioux/

something similar: convert Loneman Day School to local Indian control along with several other Pine Ridge community schools, such as Kyle. These schools and others around the reservation were suffering from neglect, low morale and consequently poor education. I told them about Ramah: how its kids had lost access to any local public school and were forced into federal boarding schools or Mormon Placement foster homes in Utah, and how after a lawsuit to keep their only public high school open failed, they had used self-help based on a $2,000 gift from a small foundation to launch their pioneering, self-determination project to start their own school from scratch.

I also mentioned that there were several other Indian communities that had heard about Ramah and wanted to follow in its footsteps. Suddenly I had an idea: "Why don't all these fledgling school boards or informal committees like yours form a coalition of grassroots Indian organizations?" I suggested there would be strength in numbers. By joining the new coalition, a powerful megaphone would be created shouting out the fundamental problem in Indian education, a lack of community or parental involvement, and its solution through local control. The organization would help each member get its own school by bringing greater attention to each one's situation.

I recounted how Ramah got started and how it had attracted Richard Nixon's interest. I told them about Wind River and its long effort to create a reservation-based, Indian-controlled public high school on the Wind River Reservation. I told them about a group at Northern Cheyenne and the Crow Agency in next-door Montana, where local leaders were gathering to adopt the Ramah model. I told them about the Menomonie in Wisconsin and the Meskwaki at Tama, Iowa, where parent groups had formed to create Ramah-type schools. "You all could form a coalition for Indian education reform," I went on. "The guiding principle would be tribes helping other tribes get their own locally controlled schools, the way Ramah and Rough Rock have done."

The response in the room was electric. We agreed that the working principle would be that all members would join in helping the member community furthest along in its organizational, logistical and political planning, and then once it succeeded, move on to the next in line.

The group jumped at the idea and agreed to form what soon became the Coalition of Indian-Controlled School Boards (CICSB). I suggested that from my own involvement through NARF, it seemed to me that the group on the Wind River Reservation in Wyoming was the furthest along. It had already organized and was engaging in a state process to create its own public school district coterminous with the boundaries of the Wind River reservation. But no one knew how long that would take.

So it was that in that modest room at Loneman Day School, our small group enthusiastically agreed to form the Coalition. Returning to Santa Fe, I drafted and filed articles of incorporation for nonprofit status using NARF's address in Boulder, Colorado. Prospective coalition members joined us for a joyous signing party in Boulder shortly thereafter, where we also planned a trip to Washington, D.C. With monies from the American Association on Indian Affairs and one or two other small foundations, we made plans to reassemble in D.C. to assist Wind River. In a flash, we were off to the capital to implement the working principle of the Coalition.

On a bright day in October 1973, we assembled in Washington, D.C. That trip was interesting for several reasons. For one thing, it had bipartisan support. President Nixon favored Indian self-determination and educational reform. So did Senator Ted Kennedy, who had assumed command of the Special Senate Subcommittee on Indian Education in the wake of his brother's death. But for me it was of great significance too. For one thing, I roomed with Birgil Kills Straight in a flop house hotel a few blocks from the White House called The Presidential (now defunct). Birgil snored but not just snored; he bellowed his sounds. I am sure it kept even the President in the White House awake. I wound up making a makeshift bed in the closet, but I couldn't sleep there either. Birgil was unfazed. He slept well.

It was a volatile time. The Vietnam War was still raging. On the Indian front, Dennis Banks, a firebrand Indian activist, had lit up Washington, D.C., after spending time with other militants on Alcatraz Island demanding its return to Native Americans. Our group managed to get meetings with Senators and Congressmen from Indian country, high-level BIA and Interior Department officials, plus, thanks to Bobbie Greene Kilberg, a full-page spread by Bill Greider in the Sunday edition of the *Washington Post*'s weekly magazine. It contained almost all the salient points concerning Indian education, the CICSB's struggle to reform Indian education at Wind River, and the formation of the CICSB.

Our meetings and the Greider article worked. By midweek we had a commitment from the BIA to give the Wind River Indian Education

Association $50,000 to open an alternative private school using an empty building in the Episcopal Mission's complex on the reservation at Ethete.

The very next day, we got a phone call advising us that we would have a meeting with the Commissioner of Indian Affairs' top deputy that week. We did, and the outcome was as gratifying as Ramah's had been two years earlier. And so, the Coalition's first foray into the national governmental arena concluded successfully.

On my family front, within three years of adapting to my new home in Santa Fe, Andi and I had two daughters: Ashley in 1971 and Lisa in 1974. In August 1974, my mother died at age 57 from complications of cancer. Her condition was undoubtedly caused by a heavy smoking habit. At the time, I had taken a break from legal practice and was teaching at a new law school in New Hampshire, affiliated with Franklin Pierce College. My father tried to carry on his business, then located in Englewood, New Jersey, while caring for my sister Nicky, who by then was 11 years old. Meanwhile, I longed to return to Santa Fe. Although I enjoyed teaching, I had maintained contact with my Native American clients.

Anxious to return to New Mexico, I persuaded the law school to allow me to go back and run a Franklin Pierce externship program for students while teaching courses in Indian law and related subjects part-time. Most of the students made good use of their time in Santa Fe, learning about significant differences in our society. One of them has become a leading, nationally known advocate to abolish the death penalty.

In the spring of 1977, my father sold our family house in Bergenfield and moved to Santa Fe. Parenting Nicky fell to my brother Tom, who remained in the East while my father became an integral part of my growing family.

In New Mexico, my father's true personality, previously hidden, burbled to life. He joined the local temple and was immediately elected president of the B'nai B'rith men's club. He had never been in charge of such an association or club before. From the introvert I had known all my life, he transformed himself into a funny public speaker with an ebullient style. He lived over our back fence in a rented stand-alone guest house on the eastside of Santa Fe. He found a job as a tailor for a local haberdashery; the owners' family still remembers him fondly. He became friends with our Congressman Bill Richardson, whom I had assisted with a legal problem during his first victorious campaign for Congress. Richardson always called my father Charlie, which made my father proud. He prized the form letters Bill's campaign team sent out every time he ran for office. He actually thought they were written and signed by Bill to him alone. When I told Richardson that story, he laughed and laughed.

One night a week my father played chess at a local club. One of his favorite opponents was a local state appeals court judge named Lew Sutin, himself a local character. My father and Sutin also had chess games under the back portal at our house. These were happy times for my father. My wife and I had a rental property on the other side of Santa Fe that had been a headache to rent, so we sold it to a widow who had been in my father's bridge circle back east. She eventually married my father and the two of them lived there until my father died of a heart attack in November 1996. Though his last years were painful, his time in Santa Fe was among the happiest of his adult life.

My sister Nicky and her husband Danny raised their two daughters in Nyack, New York. Various cousins live in California, New Jersey and Massachusetts. All seem to have prospered. I thought everyone in America should, could, and with hard work would eventually prosper as civil rights were extended to all in the 1960s. I was badly mistaken.

A FRONT RUNNER IN INDIAN-LED EDUCATION: AN INTERVIEW WITH BETTY GRESS

I met Betty Fredricks Gress in 1972, when she worked for the Coalition of Indian-Controlled School Boards (CICSB). In 1978, Betty Gress went on to establish an Indian health clinic in Denver, which is named in her honor—The Betty Gress Clinic. In November 2022, my daughter Ashley and I sat down with Betty to learn more about her personal history and the purpose and accomplishments of the CICSB. This interview has been edited for brevity and clarity.

Mike: The Coalition of Indian-Controlled School Boards (CICSB) is the story of Indian education reform in this country. Essentially, I'd like you to tell us who you are, where you come from, what your tribal affiliation is, and where you're living now. The central topic is your involvement with the Indian education reform effort that essentially started, in my view, under the Richard Nixon presidency.

Betty: Before we get into the interview, I would like to preface with an important Indian Education Act that was very beneficial to putting the CICSB on the frontrunner map of making reforms for Indian education. PL 92-318 had just been passed in 1972 by Congress, and funds had been appropriated. However, Congress then impounded the funds! Therefore, the first order of business for CICSB was to file a lawsuit to get the impounded funds released.

Abe Plummer from Ramah, a CICSB member, had engaged Mike to file the lawsuit to release the impounded funds, which didn't take long, and the CICSB had a lot of work to do to meet the requirements of the Act. This Act was perfect in getting the CICSB off and running.

The Indian Education Act had three major parts:
• Part A stipulated funds for the public schools that Indian students were attending.
• Part B was very helpful to CICSB as it provided start-up funds for Indian-controlled schools and funds for organizations to apply for, to work with these schools. CICSB was successful in obtaining the funds from Part B to hire more staff to help get schools more established.
• Part C of the Act was beneficial for adult education programs.

The CICSB was so thankful for this law because it met the needs of Indian-controlled education reform.

Ashley: Where were you born, and where did you grow up?

Betty: I am Betty Fredericks Gress. My maiden name is Fredericks, and I grew up on the Fort Berthold Indian Reservation of North Dakota. I'm a member of the Mandan, Hidatsa and Arikara Nation. I used to live on my family's ranch in the bottomlands near the Little Missouri River in North Dakota until the Garrison Dam came and flooded the bottomlands out. Then, we had to move to the uplands of Twin Buttes, North Dakota.

I was the youngest of nine children. We had what we called a "school camp" to attend because the bus didn't come down to the Little Missouri in the breaks of North Dakota. We all caught the bus and went to a BIA school about ten miles away in Elbowoods, North Dakota. Because of the span of 17 years between the oldest and youngest children in my family, it just worked that when one was graduating, another would be starting school. My brother Tom teased me, "You're not going to be able to go to school next year because nobody is graduating." I was devastated even though I was only five years old. I wanted to go to school because I didn't have anybody at home to play with. My dad said he didn't want me to go to school until I was six years old, but after he left for St. Paul, Minnesota, to ship the cattle that fall, I begged my mom, and she took me to Elbowoods. They accepted me into the first grade. When my dad got back, he didn't have the heart to make me stop going to school. So, I went to the BIA school in first through third grade in Elbowoods.

When Elbowoods was flooded out, they moved us over to the public school system, in a little town about 16 miles from our Twin Buttes home, which was called Halliday Public Schools. I was in fourth grade, and I remember how embarrassing it was because we had not advanced to appropriate, grade-level tasks in the BIA school. My teacher would give us homework and say, read the chapter and do the questions at the end. It was something we'd never done, and so it was kind of a hard thing, but thank goodness I had a mother who read a lot, and she was very proactive in education. She wanted us all to do the best we could.

Out of nine children, eight of us got a college degree, which was pretty amazing. Even Kenny, my brother who went into the service, worked in Washington, D.C., and then he went to school in Maryland and got his master's later in life. My sister Buddine was a cowgirl and two of my brothers, Buzz and Pete, were cowboys. They rode broncs and steer-wrestled, and she was a barrel racer. All three attended New Mexico State University on rodeo scholarships to study and participate on the rodeo team.

Ashley: Would you also talk about your parents? Did they go to school as well?

Betty: Yes. My dad went to a BIA boarding school called Pierre Indian Learning Center, and he would run away from there, so my grandma and grandpa decided he didn't need to go back. I think he just went up to the eighth grade. My mom went to Pipestone, Minnesota, also a boarding school, until she graduated from the eighth grade. Then she went to Flandreau Indian School for high school.

They got married—I think when she was 20 or 21—and they started ranching down in the beautiful, rich bottomland. My dad, with some help, built our frame house. We didn't have electricity because it was too far from utility hook-ups. But everything was available there. You don't think about those things until you don't have them anymore. For example, we had strawberries and asparagus that were wild. We had plentiful amounts of June berries that we kids loved. Our mother canned 80 quarts one summer, and she put in big gardens. The soil was so fertile that she could plant anything, and it would grow—like musk melons and watermelons, which were hard to grow up above. We raised pork, beef and chickens. The only thing we had to buy were staples like flour, sugar and salt, and she grew the rest. She made wild plum and chokecherry jellies and jams, syrup and plum butter. But when we moved up above, most of that was gone.

Ashley: You had to move up because of flooding?

Betty: Yes, the Garrison Dam came through. The Army Corps of Engineers was in charge. It's a pretty sad story because they were going to put the dam near Williston, North Dakota, but the townspeople didn't want it there. And, of course, eminent domain could impact townspeople too—but the government could take our lands without our approval. We bought and leased land up above in order to keep our livestock functioning. I remember when our chairman went to Washington, D.C., to sign off on the dam. His name was George Gillette. He was crying because he knew he was signing off a lot of our lands to the Garrison Dam. It was a big change for our family because we had to move away from the bottomlands, an ideal area in which to grow up and continue our ranching livelihood. I was probably about nine years old when we moved to the uplands.

Ashley: So, school overall was a good experience for you, but it was challenging when you went to the public school, right?

Betty: When I went to the public school, I felt like I was dumb. We didn't know about reading chapters. We were still coloring in third grade when we should have been doing much more. I had lots of friends, but it was a bad experience with respect to the fact that I felt very behind in school. It was just one year that I went to Halliday. When we got to Twin Buttes, another BIA school, there weren't a lot of students there. A lot of students from the community went away to the boarding schools, so there were maybe four people in fifth grade, six in seventh grade. We had few teachers—the principal of the school was teaching sixth, seventh and eighth grades, and the school only went to eighth grade. Sometimes he would leave and go to Newtown, which became the headquarters for the tribe. The principal's main concern was to get out of Twin Buttes and into a bigger area to be a principal or a superintendent.

I think we got cheated on our education at Twin Buttes, but because our mother read to us and had us do our homework, this was a tremendous help. My dad also valued education.

On the reservation, they separated us into what they called segments: we were the southern segment, and there was the northeast segment, the northern segment, and so forth. They named them, like White Shield, Parshall, and our area was Twin Buttes, where most of the Mandan lived. And then Newtown was the new Elbowoods, where the BIA administrative staff worked. The BIA had a lot more say at that time. We didn't have sovereignty, which came later.

When I got to sixth grade, the principal would head off to Newtown and put students in charge. My dad was the chairman of the Parent-Teacher Association. The principal always put me and my friend Gertrude in charge. We'd ask him, what should we have the kids do? And he'd always answer, any two pages out of the math book. And that's the kind of education we got. I didn't learn until I got to college that you should have lesson plans. Gertrude and I thought we were real cool because we were in charge of the kids.

When Elbowoods closed its doors, my brother Pete was an excellent member of the basketball, football and track teams. Frankie Fiegel, who was the barber in town, was friends with my dad. My dad was very friendly with all the townspeople. Frankie told him, "John, they're talking about the kids from Elbowoods coming to Halliday. They said, we're not going to let those Indians come in here and take over our basketball organization."

And Dad said, "Well, Frankie, they're not going to have my son in their school."

My sister Duveen had just graduated from the University of North Dakota in home economics, and she got a job teaching in Watford City. They had a high school there, so my brother Pete enrolled in Watford City. He was a sophomore in high school at the time, so he didn't go to Halliday.

When I went to high school, I went to Killdeer, which was the next town over from Halliday. My sister Juanita and brother Tom also went to Killdeer. But we had to pay for boarding to attend. We would stay there for five days, and our parents would come and get us on the weekends to go home. But we did that because of the prejudice that was in Halliday.

I went to school in Killdeer for two years. I was kind of sickly when I was younger. I got sick and was in the hospital for a full semester. Then I transferred to Halliday in the spring. I went there for a year and a half, and I graduated from there. I got along just fine. I was a cheerleader, and I worked for the superintendent's office, doing office management. It was actually a course, and they were very selective as to who they allowed to enroll. It was enjoyable. I didn't feel discriminated against myself, except that I noticed some off-color things. Some of the students were ignorant, you know.

Ashley: Where did you study?

Betty: I studied at various places. I started at Minot State in North Dakota, and I wanted to be a counselor. I wanted to get my degree in psychology and education but couldn't study psychology at Minot. My sister Juanita and brother Tom both graduated when I was a sophomore. My junior year, I transferred to the University of North Dakota. It was built on such a tremendous Greek system, and I had already gotten into a sorority at Minot, which was national. It was kind of a bad experience there. It was all flatlands up there and just different and really cold. I wanted to go to a warmer place.

After that junior year, I went to work in the southern part of the state where it was warmer and decided not to go back to the university. My oldest brother Ken took care of us after my dad passed away when I was a senior in high school. He worked for the BIA, so he knew the education director in the area office, Peter Schmidt. He had him find me a place to work, and I ended up at Cheyenne River Boarding School as a counselor. I was there for two years and was planning to go back to school.

Webster Two Hawk was working in Rosebud, and he came to Eagle Butte and enticed me to go to Rosebud to be the adult education coordinator, so I did that for a year. When I was there, the tribal chairman, Cato Valandra, called me into his office, and I thought, what in the world did I do? It just so happened that Rosebud tribal members were chosen to be in the movie, "A Man Called Horse," and they chose Rosebud children to be in the movie. He called me in to see if I would go along and be a tutor/teacher for the kids so that they could keep up with their education while they were filming on site in Durango, Mexico. Richard Harris was the main actor.

I did that, but when I was there, I just didn't like the food and hardly ate anything, just getting along on bread. They would serve you a nice-looking steak, but I think they just butchered and served it right away. It tasted horrible, and I was used to good beef because I grew up on a ranch. I just quit eating everything. Anyway, I got sick. I got peritonitis. It was an evil sickness, and I nearly died from it.

My sister Buddine was teaching school in California.. She flew down to Mexico to be with me when they put me into surgery. I stayed at her house that semester, and she adopted a little boy. I just took care of her son and got ready to go to school for the fall semester. I got into Northern Arizona University in Flagstaff, Arizona, so that's where I got my degree in psychology and education.

Mike: I would like you tell us about your role with the Coalition of Indian-Controlled School Boards.

Betty: Yes, in 1970, I went to the graduate teacher corps program in Billings, Montana, and that's where I met my husband, and we got married. Then I went to work for Phoenix Indian School, so I had some experience in the boarding schools.

By June of 1972, my husband was not happy there because it was too hot. He worked outside as a journeyman lineman. So, we headed north and stopped in Boulder to visit my brother Tom who had just graduated from law school there. He said, why don't you just leave your furniture here? He was working for NARF (Native American Rights Fund) as an intern, so he knew that the Coalition had been established, and he told me they were looking to hire staff. So, I called Birgil Kills Straight, who was the chairperson. I went down and gave him my resume.

I had planned to have the summer off. My husband was going to his friend's place in Red Lodge, Montana, to go on a pack trip, and I was going up to my home in North Dakota to be with my mom and later, visit my sister who was a teacher in Cheyenne, Wyoming. But the Coalition wanted people in there right away because the Indian Education Act (P.L. 92-318) had just passed.

They called me, and asked, "Could you come to work tomorrow?"

I said, "Well, I think I need at least a week to get organized a little bit." Within a week, in early July, I went to work for the Coalition.

Ashley: And what was your job, Betty?

Betty: I was hired as an education specialist. The funds got released in August of that year, and by September we had to meet strict deadlines to submit proposals to the administrators of P.L. 92-318, the Office of Education in Washington, D.C. I had to put a workshop together quickly and call the people who were in charge of the organizations setting up Indian-controlled schools. There were about ten members eligible to apply for Part B funding to get their schools started. I found people who were good proposal writers. We had about four or five consultants come in. Our first grant was $250,000, which was the start of the Coalition. We made it on the map right away because of Mike.

Mike: You were essential, in my opinion, to the formation of the Coalition of Indian-Controlled School Boards.

Betty: In 1970 and 1971, Mike, you were working on getting it off the ground, setting up the 501(C)3. The Office of Native American Programs funds were approved in 1972. When Congress impounded the funds, getting them released was a big deal.

Gerald sent me to Washington. I had to land on my feet for everything, because he used me for a lot of different tasks. The Indian Education Act required hiring a deputy director within the Office of Education. They hired Dr. William Demmert, and he didn't have any staff, so Gerald asked me to work for Dr. Demmert, who was a very pleasant person to work for. I stayed for two weeks until he could hire an assistant.

Mike: What did you find interesting about the Coalition? **Betty:** The Indian control. When I had been in the graduate teacher corps program, I was stationed at Busby, Montana. There was a physical fence around the school and the community lived on the other side of the fence. There was no interaction between the school and the parents. The kids came over to their dormitories and went to school. But the parents only came and picked up their students on the weekend. I'm not even sure if they came for teacher conferences. I don't recall meeting with any of the parents when I worked there. And I knew, because my parents had been very involved in our education, that having the parents involved was crucial to the success of the educational process.

They told me that they wanted us to train the school boards so that there could be Indians on the school boards and to find the teachers to be in the classroom, and hopefully they could be Native American. That sounded wonderful to me, so different from my experience of education, which was not something you'd want to have.

Ashley: Was Busby School started by the tribe?

Betty: No. It was a BIA school, but they were interested in starting an Indian-controlled school on the Northern Cheyenne reservation. The two people involved there were Ted Rising Sun and Sylvester Knows His Gun.

Their dream was to have their own Indian-controlled school. And as it turned out, Busby did, maybe three years later. Sylvester lived in Lame Deer, Montana, and Ted lived in Busby, Montana. They were friends and they were part of this movement.

Ashley: So, you had worked in Busby, and you saw the disconnect between the parents and the school administration. And also, problems in the classrooms.

Betty: Yes. For example, they needed a home economics teacher, and so they found one. But her husband also needed employment. Even though his background was as a shop teacher, he was given the job of teaching the fifth grade. He had a big ruler that he would slam on the desk to tell the students to be quiet. He was supposed be my mentor and he had me making the lesson plans. I had to just figure everything out on my own. At the end of the semester, I withdrew. I didn't think I needed to be there doing his job. I was not happy there. My experience with the BIA schools was a bad experience.

Ashley: Did the Coalition help start the Indian-controlled school there at Busby?

Betty: Yes, there was Busby, Wind River, then Menominee, and Loneman Day School at Pine Ridge, South Dakota.

Mike: In my memory, the Indian school reform movement had already begun without a name, so to speak. There were various places like Wind River, and the Menominee and so forth, who had wanted to be in control of their own schools when they heard about the Ramah School.

Ashley: How did the Coalition help with starting these schools?

Betty: We went and worked with the school boards to provide school board training. Then we also helped them to testify when they had various hearings on Capitol Hill about Indian self-determination, which catalyzed Indian control of schools. Our director, Gerald, met with several of the Indian-controlled schools and went to Washington, D.C., to testify on various issues with regard to Indian control. I know Mike was very involved in the testimony. The first big thing CICSB did was get those funds released, and that put us on the map. And we also were respected by all the Indian organizations and tribes right off the bat. So, the Coalition made a name for itself, and we were able to get those impounded funds released.

Mike: In the decade of its existence, the Coalition gave birth to a wealth of Indian-controlled schools, which the majority of Indian kids attend today unless they reside too far from one and attend public schools.

Betty: Yes, we had about ten members to start, and when the Coalition ended, we had about 100 members.

When I was the acting director at one time, Maurice John, who was from the Seneca Nation in New York, was our board chair. We were invited to testify on the Vocational Education Act[52] (Smith-Hughes Act of 1917). There was one percent set aside for Indian instruction, and in order to get that approved, we had to testify. Mike, you came and helped me get it written.

The Coalition was in business for ten years, and then what we called "Reaganomics" killed it, because when President Reagan came into office, the federal funds dried up. The unfortunate thing is that we lost funding for teacher training too. We worked with the colleges like Minot State and some other colleges. We would have instructors come out on the reservation and offer courses. Students who worked as classroom teachers' aides could take those courses and the schools would pay for that. Previously, most teachers and teachers' aides were non-Native. We had teacher-training programs that would focus on getting the aides to graduate from college and become teachers, and we had a high success rate. We got funding from the BIA and from Part B of the Indian Education Act, so we had two funding sources. We also went to New York and met with the foundations and were able to obtain funds from them.

The Indian Education Act is still in existence today. All those acts we were involved in are still going on today.

Mike: I want to understand the death of the Coalition of Indian-Controlled School Boards.

It may have been engineered somehow in Washington, D.C., but I don't know.

Betty: We lost our teacher training funding through the BIA. The only funds we had then were from the Indian Education Act, and that wasn't a whole lot.

So, basically, the Coalition did a lot of work and got a lot of Indian-controlled schools. Through our efforts, we got the P.L. 92-318, the P.L. 93-638, and the Vocational Education Act approved. I think the Coalition did a lot for Indian education. The coalition lasted ten years. When I thought it was getting bad, I called you.

Mike: You and I tried as best we could to try to rescue it, but there was no way to do it. The coalition effectively ended in 1981.

Betty: But the Coalition accomplished many things before it ended.

---

52. Brittanica. https://www.britannica.com/topic/
Vocational-Education-Act-United-States-1963

Ashley: Could you tell us about the story of Hannahville, Michigan?

Betty: That was a really interesting story. Hannahville Organization called us up; that was Gloria McCullough and her brother-in-law Jake McCullough, who was their chairperson. They were Native people who had lost their language and pretty much lost their tribe, and they were trying to get it back.

They had a relationship with a person from Canada who was familiar with their language and their traditions, trying to bring back their culture. They called us wanting to establish an Indian-controlled school because the Native kids went to a school with a lot of Scandinavian students, and didn't get along well. Once the Native kids made it to high school, they would drop out of school, so few of their kids managed to graduate.

We met with the head of the public school. The administration was all for helping the Native American students, so Bill Roberts and I wrote to the administrator of the Johnson-O'Malley Act at the time. We proposed educating not only Native students but teaching the non-native students about the culture and Native Americans in general. And it got funded and was approved.

We brought the Ramah model, and Mike, you were involved in this. We testified at the Michigan State Department to get start-up funds for Hannahville. A couple of the school board members from the Ramah Navajo School Board were there and testified too. It was a pretty decent amount, $90,000. That wouldn't be much today, but it was enough for them to get going and try to locate additional money and get approved for a contract school.

I thought it was very admirable for the state education department to make those funds available to a tribe in Michigan. They said that if the state wasn't doing its job in educating the kids, then the money should be available to the tribes to get their own schools. They were very supportive. That was amazing.

Ashley: Do you have an idea whether that school is still going?

Betty: I don't, but I know Hannahville still exists. They get housing as a recognized tribe. I worked for HUD, the Department of Housing and Urban Development, at the end of my career. The tribe is still going, so I would think that the school might still be going.

Sometimes it was scary starting Indian-controlled schools, like the one in Hammon, Oklahoma. There were vigilantes, and we had to have our meetings in people's homes because we were scared to be out in public. The non-native community was trying everything they could to keep an Indian-controlled school from happening. And our clients told us that when we weren't there, when they were trying to meet and organize, that they had some vigilantes up on the roofs. That was a scary thing.

Mike: What kind of feelings do you have looking back on your work with the Coalition?

Betty: I think we made a lot of progress. I have good feelings about what we did and probably the best thing is that the laws that we supported still exist today as part of the Indian Education Act and bolster the ISDA (Indian Self-Determination Act). We have more Indian-controlled schools, and we have more Indian teachers in the classrooms. We have more trained natives on the school boards who hire their teachers and have a big say in the educational path for their students, which was non-existent before the Coalition got started.

I don't regret being a part of it. I just feel very happy about what has taken place. After my experience of feeling hampered at Busby, I realized that the dedication that parents invest in their children's education is what is essential for their success. The Coalition was an important part of a movement that helped that happen.

Mike: Thank you, Betty. Thank you.

THE OMAHA, BLACKBIRD BEND AND REUBEN SNAKE'S CROSSING-THE-DELAWARE TALE

W hile working part-time with the Native American Rights Fund (NARF), I was introduced to other issues facing Indian country, besides education.

The Omaha Tribe of Nebraska borders the often unpredictable flow of the Missouri River. So does the Omaha Tribe's neighbor to its north, the Winnebago Tribe, and of course the States of Nebraska and Iowa themselves. All three share the river's notorious shiftiness as their common eastern (or in Iowa's case, its western) border. Every few years, the Missouri River gains or loses territory on one side of the river or the other. These changes are subject to the whims of nature—sometimes here, sometimes there, at times adding land and other times subtracting it from the opposite sides of the river. Some changes in river flow are minuscule, other times more dramatic. Those close to the river are accustomed to these changes. Usually, the shifts—big or small—affect only river navigation. Those who use the river for commerce know how to navigate these changes without creating legal problems, but interesting dynamics sometimes develop, as was the case with our client, the Omaha Tribe.

C. Bryant Rogers had just joined our legal crew. I recruited him for his exceptional knowledge of Indian law and hard-driving work ethic. I first met him in 1976 when he flew with me to South Dakota after Bobo Dean of the Hobbs, Straus, Dean & Walker law firm in Washington, D.C., had phoned me and asked me to fill in for him at a self-determination negotiation for the Oglala Sioux Tribe at Pine Ridge, which he could not attend. That negotiation led to the first-ever P.L. 93-638 contract for operation of a local BIA day school. Dean told me the firm would send a law clerk, Bryant Rogers, to the negotiation. He had not yet been admitted to practice law. A few years later, after graduating from law school, he migrated to Indian country in New Mexico, and began work for Zuni Legal Aid on the Pueblo of Zuni, Ramah's next-door neighbor. At my invitation, Bryant later joined our firm in Santa Fe. Our relationship evolved to the point where he played a prominent role in the rest of my legal career and became one of my partners. He went on to become one of the leading legal experts on Indian self-determination and continues, after my retirement, to confer with me on past events and legal theories in connection with this book project.

Bryant had first-rate credentials: a Harvard Law degree and an unbeatable background in Indian law. Hailing from Mississippi, Bryant impressed me in all respects with his intelligence, background in poverty law and his interest (and already considerable experience) in Indian affairs. While still in law school, in his third and final year, he wrote a chapter on Indian law for Harvard Professor Laurence Tribe's brilliant tome entitled *American Constitutional Law*.[53] He was enrolled in Professor Tribe's constitutional law course and suggested to Tribe that his treatise should include a chapter on Indian law. Prof. Tribe agreed to include an Indian law chapter in the treatise. Later, the law review students doing research for that part of the treatise had repeatedly approached Bryant for help on that. Bryant was behind in completing his third year paper and had missed most of his commercial transactions classes due to work on that paper and volunteer work at the Boston Indian Center. He proposed that he draft that section of the treatise after final exams and that that Indian law chapter of the treatise be accepted as his third-year paper. Professor Tribe agreed to this, and Bryant completed the chapter, which was duly inserted in Professor Tribe's treatise with suitable reference to Bryant's contribution. He still managed to graduate with his class.

Bringing Bryant into the Omaha Tribe's situation, I told him about the moderately sized accretion of the Missouri River that had exacerbated a major legal problem for the Omaha Tribe. They owned a large tract of several hundred acres on the Iowa side of the river, on a swath known as Blackbird Bend. That land was protected reservation land of the tribe then occupied by a non-Indian tenant, Harold Swanson, per a BIA approved lease, but Swanson was in breach of that lease for non-payment

53. Tribe, L. *American Constitutional Law, 3d* (University Treatise Series) 3rd Edition. (Foundation Press, 2000)

of rent. They requested my legal help to deal with that ongoing trespass on the land he had leased—a large parcel of land that was flat, fertile and bounteous, producing annual crops of various grains. This was a part of the Tribe's 1854 reservation land that had ended up on the Iowa side of the Missouri River after an avulsive shift[54] of the path of that River.[55] When they called me to do something about Swanson, they said he hadn't paid rent for a number of years. The prior tribal councils and local Bureau of Indian Affairs had, after many delays, finally cancelled Swanson's lease based on his breach of various lease terms, but that cancellation was subject to further appeals. They now wanted help from our firm to disabuse Swanson of the belief that he could continue using this land without paying the required rents, to evict him and to collect past rents to address those issues. We sued Swanson and obtained a temporary restraining order preventing Swanson from disposing of the crops grown on the leased lands. We also brought two actions in federal district court against Swanson, seeking an accounting and the immediate removal of Swanson from the leased lands and against the government and certain government officials for breach of fiduciary duty in failing to take appropriate action against Swanson. *Omaha Tribe of Nebraska v. Swanson*, 736 F.2d 1218, at p. 1220.

Swanson's lease provided that his rent was based on the amount of proceeds he earned from his crops.

After flying from Albuquerque to Sioux City, Iowa, the nearest interstate airport to the Omaha Reservation, we rented a car and drove the 100 or so miles south to the tribe's headquarters near the Missouri River. It was autumn in the upper Midwest, a beautiful time of year. The cornfields

---

54. Usually only gradual shifts in a water course called *accretions* affect legal boundaries. But accretions on the Missouri River are rare. The living river has an unruly habit of shifting course abruptly and relatively frequently. Basic water law holds that sudden shifts in a stream flow are called avulsions and that avulsive changes in a river's course do not alter property lines. Only rarely do these raise serious legal issues, but on occasion, they do. Such was the case now for the Omaha Tribe.

55. *Omaha Tribe of Nebraska v. Swanson*, 736 F.2d 1218 (1984); *Omaha Indian Tribe v. Wilson*, 614 F.2d 1153 (8th Cir.). cert. denied, 449 U.S. 825, 101 S.Ct. 87, 66 L.Ed.2d 28 (1980); *Wilson v. Omaha Indian Tribe*, 442 U.S. 653, 99 S.Ct. 2529, 61 L.Ed.2d 153 (1979); United States v. Wilson, 433 F.Supp.67 (N.D.Iowa 1977).

along the river were heavy with grain. The weather was sunny, and the Missouri flowed ferociously beside us. Dorothy could have appeared flying through the fine Midwestern air holding her basket, it was so idyllic a day. This was Currier and Ives country, scenes from the pastoral America now fast vanishing. If it hadn't been for the many social problems of still-struggling Indian tribes in that part of the United States, the picture would have been perfect. When we arrived at the Omaha Tribal Council Chamber near the river, we were greeted warmly by their members. They were all men dressed in everyday garb, no jackets or ties. We, however, looked like big-city legal honchos, decked out in suits and ties, and carrying briefcases.

By the time the new Omaha Tribal Council sought our help in getting its land back, Swanson had been making noises about owning the land outright, which of course was nonsense and infuriated the new Council. None of Omaha's neighbors were affected by Swanson's defaults—neither the Winnebago Tribe nor the State of Nebraska had suffered any financial losses because of the avulsion. They had no land in Iowa. But the avulsions did call attention to the Omaha Tribe's problem with Swanson. Fortunately, before our travels to meet with the Omaha members, we had boned up on the law of rivers, floods and errant tenants. The legal problem was straightforward, and had already been resolved in the Tribe's favor in prior litigation affirming that none of the avulsive shifts in the river's route had altered the reservation status of the Blackbird bend land which was a part of the land confirmed to the Tribe as reservation land in 1854. The avulsions did not relieve Swanson in any way of his legal obligation to pay rent. For one thing, the bulk of the land he farmed was not part of the current avulsion. Nor did his argument that somehow the land now belonged to him under the prescriptive easement doctrine save him.

On the plane from Albuquerque to the airport at Sioux City, Iowa, and then in the car on the way to the U.S. District Court in Iowa, Bryant and I again went over our plan for the hearing on our pending motion for a preliminary injunction to bar Swanson from harvesting and removing crops still in the fields. We believed that the federal Iowa Northern District Court (located in Sioux City, Iowa)—the state in which reservation land at Blackbird Bend was located—had jurisdiction over our lawsuit, instead of the U.S. District Court in Nebraska, where the bulk of the Tribe's reservation lands were located, but no party had been able to convince the court of that. From the start of our trip, Bryant fretted about what he considered to be a vital fact that we would have to prove if the case went to court: how do we prove the U.S. District Court of Iowa had jurisdiction over this suit? Establishing that jurisdiction involved convincing the Court of several facts and circumstances, including that Iowa was located east of Nebraska.

Finally, shortly before our one and only in-person hearing in court on the case to obtain the preliminary injunction hearing against Swanson, we came up with a strategy. Why not just ask the judge to take judicial notice of the fact that Iowa lies east of Nebraska and the other factors required to establish the Iowa federal court's jurisdiction? We did, and he did.

Based on that ruling and our other claims against Swanson, a full settlement on the Tribe's claims against him was reached.

> The primary provisions of the settlement were Swanson's recognition of the tribe's right immediately to possess the land. Swanson's abandonment of his administrative appeal, and Swanson's agreement to transfer crops and money to the tribe in satisfaction of accrued rents. *Omaha Tribe of Nebraska v. Swanson*, 736 F.2d 1218, at p. 1222.

The problem we faced was that the Omaha Tribe had not complained about unpaid rent for several years. The doctrines of waiver or estoppel or even the normal state statute of limitations respecting such claims might have applied here. That might have protected Swanson if enough time had passed, usually several years before the land automatically changes ownership.

If all else had failed, the United States Interior Department might have been liable to the tribe for its derelict failure to monitor the situation in disregard of its trust duties to do so. Until the Omaha Tribe, through our firm, filed suit against Swanson, the BIA had scarcely shown a smidgeon of interest in the problem.

Then came damages. Our calculations were, of course, estimates. The unpaid rent alone plus the lost use of the land by the Omaha Tribe brought the theoretical damages for trespass to an enormous sum. However, our claim for damages was itself hampered at least psychologically by the length of time the tribe had allowed Swanson to occupy the land without demand for his past due rent.

Several factors contributed to our assessment of what we should demand in a trial should the case not be resolved before then. We conferred with our clients, and although Bryant and I thought we had a good chance of recovering damages for lost rent, the tribe was more interested in regaining possession as quickly as possible. We managed to accomplish that mission—negotiating the settlement which involved immediate recovery of the land for the Tribe without having to submit to the Court's deciding the case. That settlement also transferred "certain stored crops and $70,000 to the Tribe in satisfaction of earlier accrued rents"[56] recognized as part of the Omaha Reservation at least since the ruling in *Wilson v. Omaha Indian Tribe,* 442 U.S. 653 (1979).[57] The case served as an educational exercise not only for the Omaha but also for us as legal counsel.

We then aided the tribe in a novel way, as we had for others, helping Indian tribes make money through casinos. I felt a little queasy doing that, but Bryant convinced me that so long as the activity was legal and did not injure anyone, we should not judge the propriety of an activity sanctioned by the tribal government. Once it recovered the land, the tribe created one of the first Indian casinos on it, a profitable enterprise on Blackbird Bend. This success helped persuade Congress to legalize gaming on Indian reservations around the country.

Unforeseen events sometimes occur in rural areas. As professionals, for example, Bryant and I always showed up in formal clothes wearing jackets and ties. Unexpected occurrences, however, can spoil this professional veneer. For example, remote Indian clients often lack restaurants near their headquarters. More significantly, the Omaha and Winnebago Reservations are among those lacking eating establishments where formal business attire is appropriate. The nearest eatery to the tribal offices was a small, one-room luncheonette lacking even tables to sit at. Bryant and I joined a few tribal leaders at this eating spot, which featured sandwiches and shakes. I ordered a malted milkshake. It was thick and would not pour. In frustration and without forethought, I lifted up my soda fountain-style paper cup, and, in front of my clients and Bryant, spilled the milkshake all over my suit and tie. The owner felt badly about that and

---

56. *Omaha Tribe of Nebraska v. Swanson,* 736 F.2d 1218, 1220 (8th Cir. 1984).

57. Imperfect Victory: The Legal Struggle for Blackbird Bend, 1966-1995 Mark R. Scherer https://core.ac.uk/download/pdf/61078387.pdf

refilled my shake. And then I did it again! So much for maintaining the dignity of our profession; so much for big city lawyers coming to work for Indians in the hinterland.[58]

After that episode, perhaps trying to make me feel better, Reuben Snake Jr., Tribal Leader of the Winnebago Tribe, told us another story about his tribe. The Winnebago were also interested in the frequently changing course of the Missouri River, and cooperate with the Omaha on river issues. Reuben was a gregarious man who had been a priest for the Native American Church, also known as the peyote religion. On this one occasion Reuben—he liked being called by his first name—had organized a demonstration to bring attention to the Omaha problem and some of his Tribe's own river issues. Five or six towering, stocky tribal leaders—all dressed in elaborate feathered 'war bonnets,' beaded vests and jewelry—were going to row across the Missouri with local TV cameras rolling. Plains Indians are generally big people—much taller than the Southwestern tribal members I had known, and as is often the case, the older one gets the more weight one gains. To support their neighbors' efforts at recovering their land in Iowa, the Winnebago members, dressed in their finest regalia waving in the breeze, wanted to demonstrate in favor of the Omaha's claims to the land across the Missouri, as they pushed off in their Washington-Crossing-the-Delaware boat.

Headdresses fluttering and oars paddling in unison, they advanced about ten feet into the Missouri when the boat began to slowly sink! Not containing his laughter very well, Reuben went on to describe what followed. Quickly the extravagant scene dissolved into a mass of soggy humanity. At first they struggled to stay afloat and then gave up, somehow managing to disembark from their mighty, now half-submerged rowboat. Standing in knee-deep water, sopping and bedraggled, they waded ashore in the muck and mud with cameras still rolling. Reuben Snake enjoyed this description very much, his formidable belly shaking throughout. And so did we.

---

58. The author wishes to record that he has never since spilled a milkshake or malt on himself.

THE MOST ISOLATED CHAPTER: AN INTERVIEW WITH JOHN LOEHR

My daughter Lisa and I conducted the following interview in October 2022 with my late friend and former Alamo Navajo School superintendent John Loehr. Loehr helped the Alamo Navajo Chapter to establish their own Indian-Controlled School. Also present were his wife Meg and my wife Andi. Alamo Navajo Chapter is located two hours southwest of Albuquerque and 220 miles southeast of Window Rock, Arizona. This interview has been edited for brevity and clarity.

Lisa: How did you get started with the Alamo School?

John Loehr: I was in graduate school and working for the University of New Mexico on a federal grant program, and I had just been assigned to teach education courses on several pueblos and Indian reservations. I taught courses on various reservation sites, and Alamo was one of them. I had just been admitted to the doctoral program at UNM, and I was the bottom kid on the totem pole. When it came to going to Alamo, there were no volunteers. It was considered tough duty and not very interesting. But I thought it'd be interesting. I knew a little bit about the nearby town of Magdalena and its mining history, so I accepted the assignment.

I was the only member of the seven or eight people in our graduate school group who did go to Alamo. I was teaching a couple of classes down there in 1977. I had 15 or 16 students.

There was no telephone, no paved road, lots of dust, no sewer system, no community water system. There was virtually nothing going on down there. Education was provided by the Bureau of Indian Affairs in Magdalena, which was about a 30-mile drive on a bad road. You couldn't get there in bad weather. It sits at almost 7,000 feet. The wind blows constantly, and it gets very hot there in the summer. There were an enormous number of health problems, as well as logistical and organizational problems on the reservation and little capacity to compensate for this.

I was asked by one member of my class, a fellow by the name of Jackson Pino, who was an excellent silversmith, if I would meet with the Alamo Navajo Chapter and talk to them about the purpose of this University New Mexico program and tell them how to start their own school. I met with them, and they listened and asked questions. The chairman of the school board asked me to help them get started. I told them that, yes, there had already been one of those schools created in New Mexico, the Ramah Navajo School, an effort headed by Michael Gross. I said I didn't know him, but maybe I could call him and ask about grant money so we could start writing proposals.

The levels of education and numeracy on the reservation were pretty nearly zero. There had only been one college graduate in the history of Alamo. She was a teacher's aide at the Bureau of Indian Affairs school in Magdalena. When I got back to Albuquerque, I picked up the phone book and tried to call Michael Gross.

When I reached him, I told him who I was and that the Alamo Navajo had some interest in starting their own school. He said, "I don't know anything about the Alamo Navajo Reservation." And I said, "It's 40 miles west of Socorro, up on the high plateau and is quite a primitive place." We agreed to meet and we began making a plan to help Alamo, the first step being to find some money to support a planning effort.

Mike: When did you get your pilot's license?

John: I got my full pilot's license in 1974.

Mike: And I took your lead and wanted to copy you.

John: I had already learned to fly in Alaska in 1962. So, getting a pilot's license was a very easy thing for me. I soloed after 1.3 hours, and I took the exam early. I bought an airplane immediately because there were tremendous tax advantages to ownership. It looked as if I was going to be spending more time down at Alamo, and the drive could be brutal and time-consuming.

John Amarant [from Mike's Santa Fe law group] was not admitted to the bar at that point, but he was doing organizational consulting work with Native Americans. He was an energetic guy and understood how to write proposals. I met him and we quickly became friends, and are to this day.

Mike and John were very gung-ho. We wanted to raise a little money so that we could sustain the administrative work and try to get some proposals going under PL 638 to start a contract school at Alamo.

Lisa: Can you just explain what PL 638 is?

John: That's the federal law that gives Indians the right—based on their original treaties—to operate their own institutions, programs and organizations. It came about during the Nixon administration. And at the time, it was not really understood to be the boon for Indian independence that it subsequently came to be. It was a bone of contention for everybody in the Bureau of Indian Affairs because they correctly saw it as an opportunity for Native Americans to put most of them out of work.

Mike: That's right.

John: And we worked very hard to put them out of work. We wanted to shut down their school dormitory in Magdalena. It was not a good school system. It had terrible test scores. The dormitories were no fun. They employed a lot of people in the community, which caused some rancor and upset towards us. But our local enemy was really the Bureau of Indian Affairs who wanted to keep Alamo kids in the Magdalena School District.

Lisa: So that was the Indian Self-Determination Act, right?

John: Yes, Self-Determination. Alamo was a different kind of reservation, and there's a lot of interesting local history that's been recorded by some legitimate historians. During the great Navajo roundup conducted by Kit Carson and others, a number of the Navajos from the main reservation fled to Alamo. That area was actually part of the Mescalero Apache hunting grounds and a settlement area. The Apaches welcomed them, and they settled there and intermarried with the Apaches. They ended up speaking a Navajo dialect that was very much infused with Apache. The most common surname on the reservation in Alamo to this day is Apache. And the second most common surname on the reservation is Apachito (little Apache).

Lisa: So, it's its own little world.

John: Yeah, it's isolated and not contiguous with the larger Navajo reservation. There are people on the main Navajo reservation who've never been to Alamo. Now, of course, they are a chapter, and they're part of the Navajo tribe, so Alamo council members travel to Window Rock frequently.

Alamo folks liked to ride with me in my airplane to Window Rock because the drive was long and miserable. Alamo was an idiosyncratic Indian group, and it had none of the advantages politically, economically or administratively of the big Navajo reservation. It was truly a backward place.

Mike: Well, Ramah and Alamo were similar.

John: Yes, they were. I think Ramah probably had more enlightened leadership, at least in the beginning. One of my old classmates from Highlands University, Mary Cohoe—Mary Tsinajinnie, before she was married to one of the Cohos—was a close friend of mine in undergraduate school. She was a very elegant, hard-working, straight-A student.

Lisa: How many lived in Alamo?

John: The Alamo Reservation population was somewhere around 2,000 when I was there.

Lisa: And was Ramah the next closest reservation?

John: No, Cañoncito was, in terms of straight-line mileage. Cañoncito was the closest reservation, north of I-40, west of Albuquerque.

Andi: The Diné name for Cañoncito is To'hajiilee.

Mike: To the east of Mt. Taylor.

John: There was not much interaction between Ramah and Alamo, but I'm not quite sure why.

Lisa: What was your background before you ended up at Alamo?

John: I had a bachelor's degree in sociology from Highlands University, and after I graduated, because of a high score on the civil service exam, I became a child welfare worker headquartered in Las Vegas, New Mexico, with offices in Mora and some other places. My principal duties were adoption and school truancy investigations, and I spent a great deal of time on child abuse investigations in San Miguel, Mora, Harding and Union Counties. That was the great majority of my time—driving out there and making investigations on semi-anonymous reports of child abuse. I did that for a year, and then I finished my probationary period and did not get hired full-time because I was not a political friend of the director of the welfare department, Leo Murphy, an influential Democrat.

I was hired by the West Las Vegas Schools, and I wrote their proposals for the Head Start program and their Neighborhood Youth Corps. I became the assistant superintendent to Ray Leger, and I was a friend of Tiny Martinez's. I worked there for a year and a half directing the Neighborhood Youth Corp and then was hired by the Westinghouse Research Group in Albuquerque.

Mike: What date was that?

John: That would have been late 1965. I was hired by Westinghouse, and that was a transformative experience for me—smart people, a corporation that had endless amounts of money to spend. They were very generous in terms of their salaries and everything else, and I traveled a lot. I learned the consulting game working for Westinghouse. I was there for three and a half years, and then I left to join a start-up effort in California that failed ultimately because of the 1973 business recession, when the investors' money was turned off. I came back to New Mexico in 1974, and that's when I started the graduate program at the University of New Mexico. I bought a little house in Old Town.

I was absolutely bored to tears with the UNM classes. I was depressed by the inadequacy of the intellectual repertoires of both my fellow students and the faculty.

Mike: You were not impressed?

John: No. So, when the Alamo Chapter asked if I would become their founding Superintendent of Education, I said, "Sure." I thought it would be an exciting thing to do. I knew it was a different kind of job and was going to take somebody who understood some things about how the consulting game worked, how funding worked, and how political and government organizations behaved.

I also knew the elements of a good education system. I had learned this because the Westinghouse Behavioral Research Labs in Albuquerque were producing enormous amounts of training and education programs for all kinds of purposes. For example, when I was working for Westinghouse I went to Sharon, Pennsylvania, and supervised the development of a program for the welders who did the seams on the rods for nuclear reactors. They had a high failure rate, meaning one percent. And we were required to come up with a training program that reduced that by 90%. So, one in a thousand instead of one in a hundred failures. I learned a lot about education technology, computer-assisted instruction and basic skill development, all of which were valuable when I went to the reservation.

Lisa: So, what were the first steps with Alamo?

John: The first step with Alamo, everybody agreed, was to get some money to sustain the creative effort. The First National Bank in Albuquerque, which was owned by the Maloofs at that time, had a fellow working there by the name of Bill Shifani. He was from one of the old Italian families that had immigrated from Italy, like the Domenicis, to work in the mines at Raton, and then they ended up down in Albuquerque. Pete Domenici was a lawyer, Shifani was a financial guy. I can't remember who wrote the request to the bank, it might have been me or it might have been Mike. But it was a simple, one-page letter asking for $10,000 to sustain an effort to develop a contract school under the PL 638 Indian Self-Determination Act on the reservation. Their board met, and they gave us $10,000.

I did my research on PL 638 and the Indian Treaty. I can still quote sections from the treaty between the U.S. government and the Navajo Tribe.

Lisa: Do you know when that treaty was written?

John: 1868. It was ten years before the transcontinental railroad came to New Mexico. One of the interesting terms in the treaty was a requirement for the federal government to provide education for the Native Americans, and it even specified the student-teacher ratio: There shall be one teacher for every 30 students, and there shall be a classroom. There shall be books. They didn't say anything about lunch or toilets or that kind of thing, but that was implied as a right by the courts.

Lisa: And you knew about this?

John: I actually went to the library at the University of New Mexico and looked up the treaty cases. It's straightforward, and of course the business about overhead expenses and getting the school building and all of that, that's part of having a school. You can't have a school without a building. And while the treaty didn't say, we'll give you a building, they did say, we'll provide a classroom. And that provision to provide a classroom became the basis of all that construction in Ramah and at Alamo. Ten million dollars for Alamo.

Lisa: So, it says, this is what the U.S. government is going to provide.

John: Yeah. If you stop shooting at us, we're going to give you this. All right. Go to your reservation and be quiet.

My interest in becoming the founding education superintendent at Alamo was enhanced by the fact that Don Kelly, the education department chairman at the University of New Mexico, had called me in and told me that he thought that my graduate career there was at an end. I had just had a public confrontation with one of the great untouchables of the education faculty who thought he understood something about how students learn to read. At Westinghouse, I had studied the most recent research on the difference between phonics, non-phonics, etc., and the new theories were completely at odds with the training of elementary school teachers at UNM.

At a large gathering of academics, I had challenged a "guru," Dr. Miles Zintz, stating that all the legitimate research said that his theory was wrong and that this was not the way to teach people how to read. I said, "We're going to end up in New Mexico with another five or six decades of New Mexico kids whose reading scores are an embarrassment to everybody, and it will be a tragedy for the students."

Kelly called me in the next day and said, "I guess you know you're finished here."

I said, "I thought that might be the case."

He said, "I'm going to give you your salary for the next six months, but you need to go someplace else if you want to continue your graduate school education."

But by that time, the Alamo Navajo School Board had already said, "Come down here and help us on this." And the funds had arrived from the bank, so I agreed.

There I was—the university didn't want me anymore, but Alamo Navajo School Board did—and I thought, go where you're wanted, and that's what I did. In the meantime, I bought myself an airplane because I knew I was going to be going down there a lot, and I didn't like the drive. I did like the tax advantages to ownership that Reagan had fostered.

I had driven to Alamo one day in my Volkswagen van, and I saw the Socorro County road grader working alongside a long, straight stretch of the of the dirt road, not too far from the Chapter House. I stopped and said to him, "I'd like to have a little airstrip built here."

He said, "I don't know anything about how to do that."

I said, "I can put some small piles of rock out to show you. I need a straight and level area, about 2,500 feet long and 50 feet wide, because I'm going to be flying some airplanes in here."

He answered, "Oh, that's not my job, I'm just a road grader here."

I said, "I'll tell you what I'm going to do. Do you like Coors beer?"

"Absolutely," he said.

I asked, "Do you drink whiskey?"

"Yeah, I drink Heaven Hill," he said.

I said, "I'll tell you what, I'm going to give you two cases of Coors and a bottle of Heaven Hill if you take that road grader right now and follow my directions. You level and grade it smooth from one end to the other in the areas between my piles of rocks."

It took him about an hour. The next time I saw him, I had the two cases of Coors and the bottle of Heaven Hill, and I paid him off. That was how the airstrip at Alamo was constructed. It made an enormous difference in terms of access—bringing people there, taking people from there to Gallup so they could go fight with the BIA, picking up Mike in Santa Fe, and things like that. It was a north-south strip and could be tricky when the west winds blew, but it worked for skilled pilots.

I had a very enthusiastic group of students down there. They worked hard, they read their assignments and they were part of our informal team. They were constantly asking me questions about what they could do to help. They understood the politics of the reservation much better than I did, and they were a major influence on their relatives and parents and friends who were members of the Alamo Navajo Chapter Council. They were enormously helpful in the beginning. It set a good tone for things and raised energy levels in the community.

Rosie Pino, Jackson's cousin, said to me once: "I went in there and I told those people they damned well better listen if they want a school here."

I said, "Well, thanks, Rosie. What did they say?"

"They threw me out of the meeting," Rosie said.

"Why?" I asked.

"Because I'm a woman!" she said.

I remember she took me over to Raymond Apachito's trading post. We enrolled Raymond Apachito that day in the class, and he became an enormous positive influencer down there on the Navajo reservation and a very close friend of mine.

Lisa: So, you didn't feel like people were suspicious of you?

John: I never thought for a minute that people were suspicious of me, though surely there must have been some. There were ultimately the normal kinds of jealousies and antagonisms that you would expect in any major start-up with a promise of gainful employment in a small community. And ultimately, when the school board decided not to renew my contract, I think it was because of my unwillingness to give bonuses to one of the relatives of a school board member, who was employed at the school. I had gone through my first contract, and my second contract was expected, and that's the one I didn't get. I got a modestly generous departure payment.

Lisa: So, you didn't sense a distrust of whites?

John: I'm sure there was some of that. I never experienced any of that personally. When I was in high school, my dad represented the [chairman of the] Navajo Tribe, Raymond Nakai, and I spent a lot of time out on the reservation with my dad, sitting in his car, waiting to go to meetings and walking around chapter houses. I'd also served as a trucker's helper delivering water to reservation residents one summer.

Mike: What was your father's name?

John: John Loehr. We lived on a ranch between New Mexico and Colorado, and part of our western border was the Ute reservation. So, there were always Native Americans around. I went to Farmington High School. The student body president was a Navajo by the name of Raymond Tso, a wonderful guy. He went on to medical school and went out to the reservation in his forties. But I never experienced any jealousy or animosity. When things got a little nasty because of the fierce opposition of the BIA trying to curtail our influence and stop us from expanding the school, there was an incident when someone shot some holes in the tail of the airplane, but I wasn't in it, so it didn't really make much of a difference. I thought it might be a BIA employee or a disgruntled reservation resident.

Mike: Did the plane still fly?

John: Oh, yeah, it sure did. Nothing critical was damaged.

At one point, when the BIA was trying very hard to make sure that we didn't steal their dormitory students—we had most of them, certainly, the younger grades—somebody went out and ran a grader diagonally across the airstrip and put up a barbed wire fence to cut it in half. But that came down very quickly.

I think there were some jealousies there because we had the jobs, and they were close to home. We were a source of money and local prestige.

We were a source of people getting a pickup truck that they could take home and drive or a nice lunch if they worked at the school. The school was the major industry on the reservation. There wasn't anything else. There was nothing. I mean, if they didn't drive to Magdalena to work for the BIA, they just sat around and earned nothing. The Alamo Navajo School *was* the industry. We had the buildings, we had the staff, we had the payroll, the library, the cafeteria. We had everything. And, at least for the first few years, we had most of the students.

Lisa: So, you got things rolling, you got money for the school, and you got it established.

John: Yes, we did do that. I met with Bill Shifani at First National Bank. I opened my account there personally and had a long relationship with that bank. They were very good to us. And of course, then we had to start thinking about relationships with [U.S. Senator] Domenici and with the BIA, education boss Larry Holman, and a whole bunch of senior bureaucrats, most of whom were bound and determined to make sure that we failed. But they had to follow the regulations, and they were supposed to follow the intent and the spirit of the legislation. They had to make their opposition more clandestine. They would make us wait for two hours on a bench in the BIA building in Gallup. We would have a 10 o'clock appointment, and noon came and went, and we still hadn't met with them. But they had to meet with us. So, at 1:30 in the afternoon, when they had finished their lunch and had their desk all tidied up, we met with them. That was the way it was during the period of my superintendency at Alamo.

Lisa: Because you were taking money away?

John: Yes. They correctly concluded that we were taking jobs; we were taking "their" money. We were upsetting their security and their status quo. We were successfully competing for the students because the money goes where the students go, and we had an enormous initial enrollment at the Alamo Navajo School. The enrollment at the school my last year there was the highest enrollment ever. We were like used car salesmen. We were out there pushing like mad to get kids enrolled in the school, at every opportunity.

Lisa: So, the school before this, where was it located?

John: Magdalena. It was a BIA dormitory next to the Magdalena public school.

Meg: They lived in the dormitory?

John: Yeah, almost all of them. There were some who didn't if their parents worked and lived in Magdalena, but there wasn't that much work for Alamo Navajos in the town. They were always the last hired and the first fired.

Mike: That's exactly what Ramah had. Ramah had a public school in the town of Ramah, which was Mormon dominated, not incorporated. And the Ramah Navajos sent their kids to that school. I was called in because the public school was shut down. This is background that eventually brought in Alamo and many other schools in other places and helped to get the Indian Self-Determination Act passed. The word spread that Ramah got their own Navajo-led school. I didn't know anything about the Alamo at that point.

John: I had also done some part-time summer work with a good friend of mine, Skipper McGee of the Mormon trading post family, and another named Foutz from another famous Mormon trading post family from Farmington. We would go out with water trucks and help them unload water. So, I'd been around the reservation as a teen laborer.

The Navajo reservation was scenic but a very primitive place in those days. The roads were horrible. The Navajos themselves had just started to own pickup trucks in the middle of 1950s. That had an enormous effect on the Navajo population because it made off-reservation shopping possible. They could go to Farmington. And it took that town about 20 years to figure out that they were a gold mine. Farmington mistreated them for a very long time, but not anymore. Now they are happy to see Navajos walking through the grocery store doors. Now, they all have new pickup trucks, they've got mobility. The roads have improved; it's a different world now.

But Alamo was the last part of the Navajo reservation to access this "progress." When I arrived, there were no telephones, no water supply, no sewers, no paved roads. I took the first dentist to the Alamo Reservation in my airplane. There had never been a dentist out there. I actually took three of them from the University of New Mexico, and they spent three days in their first week doing dental exams on the kindergarten and first-grade kids. And they were appalled. They'd never seen as many serious cavities as they saw out there. They just didn't think it was possible for there to be that many. And then there was a two-year project to repair those teeth and get those kids to stop eating candy from the trading post as their main meal of the day.

I remember that one of the dentists had an air sickness problem. He was in my airplane a lot, and we used a lot of little bags to keep him going. I had to help him out of the airplane once after a rough flight. But the airplane was a big help for getting that work done. It saved us many hours and gave us flexibility. We could do things like fly to Gallup and wait for three hours and have a meeting, and I could get home that night instead of having to go up one day, wait or work all day, and go home the next day. It accelerated our whole process, having the airplane available.

Lisa: So, once the school was up and running…

John: Well, it took a while to get it up and running. The first campus was a temporary campus with leased metal buildings, some of which we ended up buying. Others were returned to the manufacturer. This was the temporary housing that public schools sometimes use. And, of course, we had all kinds of problems with water, sewer, heat, flooding, mud, leaks and other infrastructure issues. There were some very long days—and nights.

For example, the day before the first day of class, there was no drinking water available in any of the classrooms. I drove back to Albuquerque at night, and very early the next morning I bought 23 five-gallon jugs of water, put them all in my Volkswagen van and drove like crazy down to the reservation. I distributed a five-gallon jug of water and some paper cups to each classroom, so that we would be allowed to open the school. We knew there would be a health inspector to stop us on our opening day if we had no drinking water in the classroom.

Mike: Did you have bathrooms?

John: We had a series of portable outhouses.

Lisa: Was there actually sabotage? Did they do something to the plumbing or anything?

John: They didn't overtly sabotage, but they took actions that were clearly designed to stop us from operating our program. We didn't have any buses, for example. They didn't want to give us any buses, and although they had been told by the Washington, D.C., BIA that they had to turn over their fleet of school buses to us, they wouldn't do it.

Lisa: Oh, yeah. This story. Could we hear it?

John: Well, we needed the buses. Our enrollment was far beyond early predictions, and the BIA didn't need all of their buses, and we knew that. I think at that time, our total fleet consisted of two pickup trucks, and we knew that these people were so poor, and their vehicles were in such horrible shape, that they couldn't safely transport their kids five miles to school. So, Abe Plummer and I went to see the superintendent of the BIA dormitories in Magdalena, and I was pretty abrupt with him, telling him we needed the buses we were legally entitled to and we needed them immediately.

I said, "We need those school buses that are parked out there in your yard."

He said, "Well, I'm not going to give them to you."

And I said, "Well, your bosses have told us that you have to give them to us and that you know that. You're breaking the law by not turning them over to us."

He had a small tray on his desk with a bunch of keys in it. I could read what bus numbers these keys went to because I could see them right outside the window in the lot. He argued with us that he was not going to give us the buses, and that meant that we weren't going to have a school day. That was going to be a real problem for us in terms of attendance requirements and everything else. I looked at Plummer and he looked at me. I reached across the desk and grabbed the keys.

He said, "Put those back!"

"No, these are the keys to the buses," I said.

"Yeah, but you can't have them," he said.

"We're going to get in that bus right now and take it out of there," I told him.

And that's what we did. He was screaming at us as we walked down the hall, and Abe said, "Keep walking, keep walking, you go through the door, and I'm going to stop him."

I got in the bus, started it up and drove away. (I did not have the correct license for this!) About a half an hour later, Plummer showed up in our pickup truck and just couldn't stop himself from laughing. I asked what had happened after I drove off.

He said, "Well, he called the state police, and they came. And I told the state police no, that *he* was the thief, *he's* the one who didn't have the right to the bus. We were the ones who had the legal right to the bus. The superintendent wanted the police car to chase you out to Alamo and arrest you. I said the cop wouldn't do it."

And he wouldn't. We had a copy of a letter from Washington telling the superintendent to give us the buses. Plummer showed it to the cop. He backed off because Plummer convinced the guy that the BIA were the bus thieves. We were the ones who were entitled to the bus, not the BIA.

Lisa: And you picked up all the kids?

John: I didn't pick up any kids. I drove right to the school and turned the bus over to our school bus driver, who had the right license and left immediately to pick up the kids.

Mike: Abe Plummer had worked at Ramah.

John: I think you recommended Plummer because we felt it was necessary to have a knowledgeable Navajo at Alamo who was familiar with contract schools. And I had known Plummer before. I think I met him when I was at undergraduate school, but it was a brief encounter. I knew his brother, Marshall Plummer. Marshall was quite an extraordinary guy—a big, tall, handsome, smart fella. I think he may have introduced me to Abe. They were an impressive and well-known Navajo family.

Abe Plummer was easy to work with. I got along with him and gave him all the space he needed; he gave me all the space I needed. He never once interfered in any way with the education program at Alamo. He had a far wider view, and he was essentially a major protector of the effort down there because, you know, he was a native Navajo, and he kept the evil forces pretty much at bay. So, I didn't have to worry about that.

Lisa: What was his exact title?

John: I think he was Executive Director, and I was Superintendent of Education.

Lisa: And before he got involved at Alamo what was he doing?

John: I think he was working at Ramah. He knew the federal regulations and he certainly understood the legislation. He knew the BIA inside and out because his brother Marshall worked for them. Marshall was a fast-rising manager in the BIA at that time, as I remember.

I was very much at the center of all activity because almost everybody needed a ride in the airplane. My lifetime of flying when I gave it up was 4,320 hours, which is seven times as much as the average private pilot flies in a lifetime. I owned three airplanes in my 35 years of flying, and about 1,500 hours was for the Alamo work.

Lisa: So, you had a few challenges in the beginning of setting up Alamo. You couldn't get the buses; you didn't have water.

John: Well, the bus situation was a funny kind of challenge, but the really interesting thing was trying to get the community organized around the objectives and purpose of the school. There was always a competition between what's going to be best for the kids and, can I have a job? I was always adamant, even obsessive and aggressive, about insisting on the objectives of the school. I had written out the school objectives in two sentences, 36 words long: "Our objective is to ensure that every Alamo Navajo student is literate and numerate. We want them to be independent learners, and we want them to be able to handle any intellectual challenge in their lives." That was basically it.

So, we wanted to bring them the advantages and conveniences of modern life—a toilet that flushed, a telephone that rang, a house that didn't flood out immediately after a rainstorm. And we wanted the kids to have their teeth in good shape. But the major purpose of the education program there was literacy and numeracy. If I didn't say that 85 times a day, every day I was there, it was because I was falling asleep.

Most of the people in Alamo accepted that and seemed to agree that this would be good for their kids. Later on, as the school expanded, and other influences came in, there were issues raised about: "You're not doing enough to protect our culture."

My retort to that was always: "I think the best way to protect your culture is to have literate and numerate kids—people who can read and add up a two-digit column." That usually stopped that argument.

Lisa: There was no Navajo tradition?

John: Alamo had a very weak Navajo tradition, compared to what there was on the main Navajo, because they had been taken in by the Mescalero Apache, and their language had been altered by intermarriage, and they were isolated from the big reservation as much as if they were in Dallas, because there was a hell of a drive to get to the big Navajo, and you couldn't make that drive much of the year. The shortest distance was north, right up to I-25 and then left and over to Window Rock. Or you could go down through El Morro, through Ramah and on up. But that was a long trip, and if the weather was bad, as it often was in the winter, there wasn't much of a payoff for those people going to Big Navajo. The tribal councilmen from Alamo were the ones who ended up in Window

Rock and Gallup. But they always had to go back home.

Lisa: Did you have a high school at Alamo school?

John: We started with a kindergarten program through sixth grade. We added the junior high and high school program. And that was the real threat to the BIA. Then we created a preschool program. We even had adult education. I think the highest enrollment at Alamo was in my third year there. We had something like 720 students altogether. So, of roughly 2,000 people, we had one out of every three in our school. Non-literate, non-numerate parents were coming in at night to take night classes. Our library had almost all its books checked out by Alamo parents.

We brought in mostly outside teachers because there was no pool of teachers on the reservation, although we were trying to produce this. We did this successfully. We hired a librarian from Oklahoma, who was a friend of Quanah Parker's great-granddaughter, who we also hired at Alamo. She worked hard and was a good teacher.

Mike: Say who Quanah Parker was.

John: The famous Comanche chief, one of the more successful, who dealt constructively with the Anglos, well enough to get rich.

This librarian was focused and articulate and came with good recommendations. She came to me quite upset one day and said, "We've got to stop this."

I said, "What is it that we have to stop today?"

"They're not bringing the books back," she said.

"Who's not bringing what books back?" I asked.

"They come into the library, and they check these books out, and they never bring them back," she said. "I know where they are. They're sitting on their kitchen table at home and in the living rooms of their mobile homes. Those are *our* books."

"Well, that is absolutely wonderful," I told her. "Those are *their* books, and one of the great things we want to have happen is to see books in those houses. I've been in those hogans, I've been in those trailers. They don't have books; they don't have newspapers; they don't have magazines. They have the TV on, and the only English the kids learn is by mimicking the McDonald's commercials." Every five year-old on the reservation could sing the McDonald's song.

So I said, "Let's go ahead and buy some more books; let's encourage the kids to take the books home; and let's give the books to the parents.

And when a kid can read a little bit, have them to read to the parents."

She gave me a lot of push-back and said she couldn't go along with me on this, and I fired her. Books were cheap in those days. If you remember what college textbooks cost when we went to school, a good textbook was four bucks or something like that. Now that same book is like $170. I thought that was an interesting incident.

Lisa: Where did you find the teachers?

John: We advertised and had an agency that identified teacher candidates for us. They came from a number of different places. The person I appointed as principal of the school, Steven Hansen, was married to a Nigerian, a stunningly beautiful tall woman who had attended fancy English schools. She was probably the best educated person on the reservation. He was from Cortez, Colorado, a good guy. He didn't like to fire people, so I always had to do the firing. But he was very good at collecting data and managing the campus.

We had a lot of rigidity in our program. This was not a "show up and have a good day, we got a lot of toys here, play until you're tired and take a nap, we'll give you a free lunch, and then we'll put you on the bus home" kind of school. Kids had to work every morning from 8 a.m. until noon. And this was first graders. To be in the classroom, they had to be working on their materials. They had to be doing their times tables, and we put the best faculty at the lowest level.

Pauline Rindone, for example. Dr. Rindone was in charge of the elementary school. She was a gal from Mora that I went to school with at Highlands. She became a prominent educator in Santa Fe many years later. She would tour the classrooms, and I would follow her around. She insisted that the students had to be doing the work. I always liked that. We had test scores that were quite impressive.

Lisa: After the first year?

John: We used a program called CET, Curriculum Embedded Tests, coupled with an individualized instruction process. All publishers of school materials sell you their programs, their books, their booklets, whatever they are, and they always have tests with them—end of a chapter, end of a unit, halfway through to the final exam. And the scores that you get on those tests are correlated with reading comprehension levels, reading vocabulary levels, grade levels in math, arithmetic, etc. So, you could see what a kid scored after he'd been working in a couple of units of math for the first week. You could see if he'd gone up or down. We had enormous amounts of data there for decisions on progress or branching. I always thought data was ultimately an important defense against the onslaughts from the BIA and the public school people in Santa Fe.

Lisa: Did you ever use regular, nationwide standardized tests?

John: We didn't use those on anybody down at the first, second or third-grade levels, but we did have a testing program. But we didn't have grades or classrooms that were based on age. We based them on their initial testing that evaluated their strengths and weaknesses. So, we would have a classroom with students at different grade levels and ages, depending on what skills they brought in. It was age-free and not time based. You progressed based on what you had learned and could demonstrate.

Andi: No bilingual education?

John: No, the bilingual education was: You can speak Navajo on the playground, with your parents or anybody else. But in the classroom, we want you to be able to read and write English. And we got no pushback on that. I think the general reason is that the people of Alamo knew that they were right at the edge of being able to survive and live any kind of a reasonable life. Most of them lived in trailers, not hogans. Their teeth were falling out, they knew their kids had cavities. Their cars often wouldn't start in the cold weather because they were junk cars, and the batteries would die. They didn't have enough money to go shopping for school clothes and things like that. So, there wasn't much pushback from the community on this. They wanted the new economic opportunities, and they wanted their kids to be literate and numerate in English.

Mike: What did they eat? I mean, how did they get money?

John: They mostly ate mutton and beans. BIA didn't bring food to the reservation. There were food commodities they picked up in Magdalena. And when you went to eat dinner at the dormitories in Magdalena, as I did on a couple of occasions, you had tough sheep meat and cabbage and potatoes. Mutton stew was the biggest meal out there. I happen to like mutton, so that was not a problem for me. We had some teachers from places like Chicago and Seattle who thought mutton was something you put around your neck in the cold weather.

Lisa: How many years were you there?

John: Three and a half. I left in 1981.

Lisa: So at the time, it looked like the school was a success?

John: The enrollment was highest ever, and it declined substantially after I left. We were aggressive about enrollment. We had teachers going out in the evenings to trailers and hogans and recruiting kids. I remember standing in the line at the grocery store in Magdalena, about five feet from the cash register. And one of my teachers was just getting ready to go through the checkout. The checker was a Navajo woman from Alamo. I listened to a recruitment speech from my teacher to try to get this checker's kid to enroll at Alamo, and by God, if that kid didn't show up the next week. So, they understood the game—the money follows the kids, and we were doing a good job with the kids. We were doing better than they were doing in Magdalena.

Lisa: Do you know how some of your old students are doing or did?

John: I have heard from time to time about them, and I know that the majority of those I had as students actually graduated and got their degrees and became certified teachers. A lot of them went to other places on the reservation. Some of them went into the public schools. I don't know what the situation is down there now. I wanted a cadre of trained, college-graduate locals who could take over the school, but I wasn't there long enough to make that happen. In a sense, that was my failure. I was insensitive to some of the nuances in the community and on the school board. I probably was not a sufficiently servile school superintendent. My friends and family would not dispute that assessment.

Lisa: The money?

John: We got enormous amounts of money down there. We ended up in a lawsuit with the federal government. Mike was our lawyer, and I was the principal witness. I was on the stand for four days, and we ended up getting $10-plus million to build a completely new campus and social programs center for the Alamo community.

Lisa: What did you have before that, just portables?

John: We had portable buildings, paid for by the U.S. government, and we had an architect coming down from Denver to do our planning. It was very difficult to get all of that together because there was no infrastructure at Alamo. There were no sewers, water or electricity. They had only a radio telephone.

Lisa: So, you got money not just from the bank?

John: The bank was the early start-up money and a relatively small amount, the first little kick. We went from $10,000 to a $100,000, and then a $250,000 loan from the bank. Then we got the $10.5 million from the federal government from the lawsuit, *Alamo Navajo School Board v. U.S.* It was a bare-fisted lawsuit in federal court, and we won it, big.

We sued because we wanted them to make good on the treaty obligations and provide a campus and indirect costs and everything else that we needed to run a community school on the Navajo reservation. We spent a lot of time on it. It was the beginning of the first school year, and we almost ran out of money. Mike, you filed suit in Albuquerque, in federal court.

We got the $10.5 million, which covered all construction costs for the school. We got the indirect costs later. Operating money came after I left. But we were in a position where we went from no money to a little more money, then a whole lot more money. I got a raise from $35,000 a year to $50,000, good pay for a Superintendent of Education in those days, anywhere.

You could, in fact, read the Treaty of Guadalupe Hidalgo and draw the same inferences in terms of the education of Spanish Americans in New Mexico, because the principles are exactly the same. They were vanquished people, and we promised to educate their children, period.

Lisa: So, the school seemed to be doing well.

John: In terms of enrollment, the school was doing well. The first test scores that came in showed progress. We had a lot of data that showed they were advancing one full grade level in reading comprehension after one month of instruction consisting of 25 hours of classroom work.

Now, how much did that mean to people? Oh, it didn't mean much to some people. It sure meant something to the parents who were reporting back saying, 'Hey, you know what? He actually can read things. He's at home, and he can say words. He knows how to sound them out.' I said, 'You know, maybe we ought to just push your kid a little bit harder, huh?'.

Lisa: And you had teachers from around the country?

John: Yes, all over the place. They wanted to stay. We paid a little bit more than the public schools paid. We didn't care whether they were certified or not. In New Mexico, we cared whether they had the right kind of training. I always looked at their transcripts carefully, including their elementary school transcripts, to see what their training had been for their reading and math programs, and if they had any familiarity with the kinds of curriculum materials we were using in the school. We found good teachers.

Andi: Where did they live?

John: Most of them lived on the reservation. Some of them lived in Magdalena.

Lisa: So, the Alamo school was a success, and it continues to get funding because of the lawsuit that was won by you.

John: I don't know what the current funding is at Alamo. I don't even know whether the dormitories are still closed or not. But I know that there was a closure of most of the dormitories within the first two years after we got the school going.

Mike: My experiences taught me that these schools will sometimes flourish for two or three years because they have a good leader. After a while, there's lack of interest in the schooling, the kids have to come home, work and earn a living, and that's it.

John: Well, there is some of that for sure. Of course, there's the old adage that anything that works will eventually be stopped. There is a lot to talk about in terms of them going home. I know that for my students, they were admittedly a select group because they'd been admitted to the University of New Mexico. They were quite ambitious, and they knew a little bit about the world. A couple of them had served in the army. They'd been to San Francisco and to boot camp in Monterey and places like that.

Andi: Wasn't it rare for them to go back to the reservation and help their people?

John: I don't think it was rare in those days. I think there were some who didn't, but there were certainly a substantial number who did go back. But the kids that were in my class, they were all back already. So that might have been a fairly select group. I don't know.

Andi: You said the infrastructure—the water and everything was so bad. Did that all get fixed?

John: Yes, it got fixed eventually with money. Money brings in heavy equipment, lays pipelines, paves roads. Money brings electricity, machinery and institutional wherewithal.

Lisa: Money from education?

John: The money that was given by the U.S. government as a consequence of the lawsuit requiring them to comply with the treaty and U.S. laws.

Lisa: So, it helped beyond education.

John: There were many creations at Alamo beyond just the school itself. A health clinic—that happened after I was gone—a permanent building for basic adult education, a new community hall and other changes in the infrastructure.

The lawsuit encompassed all of the indirect costs that were relevant at that time when the main item on the reservation was the school itself. All the subsequent social and health programs came later, after I was there. My job was Superintendent of Education, and I focused on the school, and that's where we spent most of the money. But there were other people who came to join the effort whose focus was not the school itself. Bill Berlin, who was a good friend of Mike's and kind of a legendary character down there, was into the health programs and old-age programs. He did a very good job on those things. But the big one in the beginning was the school itself.

Lisa: So, it was all hearkening back to the ISDA, the PL 638 contracts.

John: That's the intellectual and political genesis of it.

Lisa: What is your opinion looking back now on having Indian-controlled schools? Was it a good effort? Was it not successful in the end?

John: I think it was one of the toughest things I ever did in my life, but I think we succeeded, certainly in establishing the school and the education program.

Meg: But what about the concept itself?

John: I think the concept itself is sound. Indigenous people have not really been helped much by "the haves" at Alamo, so they might as well take a shot at helping themselves. You've got to be careful. If what you want is all the kids wearing feathers and dancing in Gallup for a week every summer, and if that's where you're going to put all your effort, don't be surprised that the non-literacy/non-numeracy demon comes through the back window and devours you. Because we know what's mostly required in the modern world. We know that if you're not literate and you're not numerate, you're not likely to be going very far, no matter what your race or ethnicity.

I've never considered Alamo a major success in my life. I think I gave it high marks in terms of the diversity of effort that was required. I saw nice scenery and met interesting people. I've since then had what I consider to be some successes that were greater than Alamo. But the experiences I had there really taught me a lot and in the final analysis, I'm glad I tried to make Alamo succeed.

When I was called in to overhaul the London Underground after 29 people were burned in the King's Cross fire, I knew what to do. When I worked for British Airways and was told that they were going bankrupt and they needed my help, I knew what to do. So, I've had experiences that I was able to build on. But at Alamo, I'm not convinced I ever succeeded there to the extent that I probably should have.

Lisa: Well, if you had been able to stay longer…

John: It was a very close call. I mean, the school board meeting was five days away when they made the decision that they weren't going to offer me the contract. The contract had already been prepared, and I had already read it and signed it. I was the second highest paid school superintendent in the state of New Mexico at the time. The Albuquerque school superintendent was making $48,500 or something like that.

Andi: Then you completely changed course after that. You got out of the education field.

John: Yes, I did. I got out of the United States too. I worked primarily in London, Paris and Geneva for ten years. Would I do Alamo again? Yes, I would do it again, but I would be a little more careful with some things. I wouldn't be any less aggressive, but I think I would be smarter. Of course, many of us would say that about our lives.

EAST OF LA AND A UNIVERSE AWAY: AN INTERVIEW WITH JOHN AMARANT

On September 4th, 2022, Michael and his daughter Lisa interviewed John Amarant, an early figure in Indian education during the Indian education self-determination movement. His wife Betty was also present. This interview has been edited for brevity and clarity.

Mike: Please start by telling us your name.

John: John Amarant. I'm originally from California. My grandfather immigrated from the Azores Islands in the early 1900s when it was hard to make a living—either as a fisherman or a farmer, pulling up food from the volcanic ash. He landed at what was the port of entry on the West Coast at that time, Angel Island.

Mike: Where did they settle when they got here?

John: Contra Costa County, in the San Francisco Bay Area.

Mike: Let's fast-forward to when you were born.

John: 1948.

Mike: And when did you graduate from college?

John: In 1970. I received a BA from St. Mary's College of California.

Mike: And did you go straight to law school?

John: No, I took a year to earn my Master's in Public Administration from San Jose State. I started law studies at Santa Clara University in the fall of 1971.

Mike: So, you got two degrees.

John: Yes, I graduated from law school in 1974. I took a job with the district attorney in San Joaquin County, California, about 50 miles from my hometown. I was sitting at the DA's office, where I felt very discouraged and bored, prosecuting drunk drivers. The phone rings and it's Paul Scott. He introduces himself, "Hey, you don't know me, but a good friend of ours, George Caravalho, gave me your name and said you might be suitable for a job that I need to fill." George had been one of my mentors.

I said, "Oh, what's that about?" He had my full attention.

Paul asked, "Do you know anything about the Environmental Protection Act [EPA]?"

"It just so happens that I do," I said.

"We've got contracts to work with several cities to sort out the obligations to enforce select federal policies like EPA if they accept Community Development Block Grants."

CD Block Grants were a Nixon initiative to streamline the administration of federal grants to cities to be managed locally. By consolidating the federal grants into a single "block," the President sought to clarify which Congressional mandates (e.g. EPA, Historic Preservation, Civil Rights) would need to be observed by cities.

On President's Day, 1975, shortly after I'd been admitted to the California bar, I flew to Los Angeles and visited with Paul Scott and his folks. Chuck Johnson was a senior member of Paul's firm and would train me in development and delivery of services to our clients. Three weeks after my visit, I joined Paul's firm and immediately traveled to New Bedford, Massachusetts, to implement a CD block grant. Twelve weeks later, I returned to southern California to share my knowledge with Paul's team of consultants and to assist training their clients.

In 1975, the Indian Self-Determination and Education Assistance Act [ISDEAA or ISDA] passed. Paul was working a great deal in Washington, D.C., with the Bureau of Indian Affairs. He was conducting trainings at various Indian centers around the country about the ISDA, and its PL 638 self-determination contract regulations. I studied the act and helped Paul to summarize the highlights to be shared with tribal and bureau employees.

Almost immediately, Paul had two client prospects who expressed interest in learning more about self-determination: The Cheyenne & Arapaho Tribes of Oklahoma and the Ramah Navajo School Board. Chuck Johnson followed up with the "C&As." The Executive Director at

Ramah Navajo School, Larry Manuelito, introduced himself to Paul at the Phoenix conference. Larry brought Paul directly from the conference to Pine Hill—the name of Ramah's school campus. He was amazed at what he saw. Paul had a small blood quantum of Indian blood. He was from Oklahoma, so he had an immediate empathy for the Ramah Navajo response, and he was really impressed.

Paul came back to L.A. and asked me, "You got a sleeping bag?"

I said, "Yeah."

"Well, I want you to get on a plane early next week and fly out to Albuquerque, New Mexico. And then I want you to rent a car and drive west. When you get out there, talk with Larry. Hear what the problems are. Get a feel for the place. Come back and help us write a proposal so that we can help them."

So, I flew to Albuquerque on a Sunday night. Predawn the next morning, I started my journey in the dark heading west on I-40 to Ramah, which appeared to be at the end of the Earth. As I approached the foot of Mount Taylor, I turned south toward Zuni. There were no buildings, not even shoulders along the road. Arriving at the new Ramah Navajo School Pine Hill campus, tall, modern, cement walls with blue tin roofs snuggled between the piñon and ponderosa came into view. My eyes were drawn to the clear blue New Mexico sky. At an elevation of 7,000 feet near the Continental Divide, the vast view still inspires me.

I spent a week there. Chuck Johnson and I prepared grant proposals for both the C&A tribes and the Ramah Navajo School Board, and once they were funded, we began the process of identifying and proposing ways to meet their needs. We helped them with their financials and the property procurement. They wanted somebody to quickly look at their financial records. Paul's personal accountant took a look and said, "This is a mess." I looked at the guidelines for the personnel handbooks to see what was in and out of bounds.

They talked about some education for the board, so that maybe they could get some modest health benefits for non-Indians. When we negotiated the contract with Larry, we learned the board had approved it, and they wanted to add our services to help them prepare for and support their next contract negotiation.

I continued to do work with PL 638 contractors including the Ramah Navajo School Board as well as the Cheyenne and Arapaho tribes and the Yakima in Washington state. Chuck and I also worked with some of Paul's clients in Colorado and Texas. We began to explore moving to a city closer to our clients and decided on Albuquerque. In early 1976, Chuck moved with his family to Albuquerque, and Betty and I followed in early 1977. Eventually, the School for the Deaf hired Betty to work in Santa Fe.

We worked with Larry at Ramah about two years before he moved on to bigger things. We got quite a bit of work done there. I continued to work with Chuck Bleskan, the grantsman for the Ramah school, to expand school funding by contracting other BIA activities and negotiating a contract with Indian Health Services to fund a clinic at Pine Hill.

Paul Scott announced that he was restructuring his firm so as to reduce his managerial responsibilities, so we consultants became subcontractors, free to take our own clients. We agreed to maintain a tight network and advise one another.

It was 1977 when you and I bumped into one another at the Ramah School, Mike, and you teased me: "Are you the lawyer that's been running around here helping my client?" You invited me to come see you in Santa Fe, and I met you at your office at Sena Plaza, right behind the exterior stairway. There were two desks inside pushed up toward the windows. I thought, wow, this is delightful.

In addition to my joining you, there were two trial lawyers, Joel Roth and Ron Van Amberg, who you wanted to join your practice. You thought the two of us could bring in a set of clients that didn't conflict with their clients. I was willing to explore such a venture.

You introduced me to John Loehr in a roundabout way. "I've got this school that's coming up, and some other things going on, and I'd really like some help." You asked me to assist the Alamo Navajo Chapter to gain a self-determination contract where John Loehr was the contact.

I met John at his kitchen-less house on the west side of Albuquerque. He spent some time talking about the challenges of constructing a temporary campus and establishing an education program on that reservation. He estimated we would need a year and a half to do this work—to obtain the contract and build the school. I told him we needed permission from the Chapter to set up Alamo as a contract school, and that you recommended the school be a separate entity focused on education and not be part of the politics of the Chapter. I asked John to arrange for me to meet with the Chapter President, Dennis Apachito, to discuss his views about a self-determination school in Alamo. John already knew the Chapter President was upset with the current education arrangement. It was the same scene that was going on at Ramah. All the kids would show up at the Magdalena public school on the "count day" so all the desks were filled with children. Shortly after the count was recorded, the Navajo attendance began to "melt." Navajo students stopped attending classes at the public school. Despite the absence of Navajo students, the school district continued to receive federal aid based on the number of Navajo heads counted on "head-count days."

Lisa: Can you explain why? Would they just not bus them in?

John: At Alamo there were buses. The bus ride from the Alamo community in the center of the reservation to the Magdalena public school took a full hour. A two-hour roundtrip everyday was thought to be too much for even the high school students. As to why there was a melt in attendance, I speculate there was a bit of prejudice in the classroom—the curriculum was delivered in English or Spanish. There were no Navajo-speaking teachers, conflicting with students' interaction with their parents. There are many studies that note how Navajo children are raised differently than children in English- or Spanish-speaking homes. Navajo parents are known for respecting the observations, feelings and opinions of children. Children can actually own property, like a horse.

It's important for people to appreciate the challenges facing the Alamo Navajos. This particular community is so distant from the main Navajo reservation that they were (and still are) ignored. Their use of the Navajo language has atrophied so much that few people are speaking their native tongue, Navajo. Anthropologists and paleontologists argue that these people were, in fact, an Apache spin-off, hence all the Apachitos in the group. A further illustration of the confusion of cultures is the mix of Apache language with Spanish.

Some children were going away to the BIA dormitory because the government housing was better, but they would return home from school to their mostly Navajo-speaking families and were barely able to communicate. Some older people only learned Spanish! The current generation is widely believed to speak mainly English with a little Navajo between family members. One of the goals of the Alamo founders was to restore some Navajo traditions, believing that if they accepted that they are Navajo, they might learn to live as Navajos.

My first meeting working on behalf of Alamo was an incident that remains amusing but representative of the challenge we faced. I walked into the BIA office in Socorro and said, "I have a meeting today with the Chapter President. My name is John Amarant."

The receptionist said they were waiting for him to arrive and briskly walked me back to a good-sized meeting room, maybe for 20 people. I noticed the crowded magazine racks and thought, look at that! I mean, I'm not a fan of pornography, but, um, there were things up there that I didn't even know were printed. After maybe five or ten minutes, the door opened. Dennis Apachito arrived with a nephew to act as his interpreter. We exchanged formalities as they are done on the reservation. I explained why I was there.

Mr. Apachito paused, and at that moment the door swung open again. In rushed the PL 638 contract specialist, a BIA official. He was mumbling as he walked directly to the magazine racks and burst out, "I don't know *who* does this, but this is atrocious." As he gathered all the magazines into his arms, he said, "Forgive me for interfering, for interrupting your meeting." And he rushed out the door.

Mr. Apachito, who was looking back over his shoulder, turned to me, then looked down at the table and said, "You know, sometimes I think the only thing the Bureau is really good for is drinking coffee."

I replied, "I think you have a good point. Shall we talk about a contract school at Alamo?" And with that, he began to explain why he thought the Alamo community contracting and adopting the model of an Indian-controlled school was a really good idea. Mr. Apachito concluded his remarks saying, "I think we know more about what our children need than the Bureau does." I shared that we would soon approach some people who had volunteered to set up a school board. We needed to have had an election to fill the positions on the School Board.

After that initial meeting with Dennis Apachito, I worked with you, Mike, and John to outline the major steps to gain a PL 638 contract and included them in an application for a planning grant. We also drafted a proposed resolution to be endorsed by the Chapter President and affirmed by a vote at the Chapter meeting. Walter Apachito was one of those identified as a vocal supporter of the school and as a respected speaker in Alamo circles. He also knew Alamo couldn't make this change by themselves and welcomed the offer of outsiders—particularly the executive director and board members of the Ramah Navajo School Board. You, John Loehr and I would bring expertise from time to time to work with them in the future. Once the planning grant funds were in hand, we quickened our pace to secure approval of the contract and to speed the construction of the temporary campus.

To qualify for a contract, there were many straightforward administrative requirements (regarding accounting, sub-contracting, human resources, construction, record-keeping for students, purchasing, etc.) that we had expertise to address. Development of the education plan and curriculum for the Alamo school, however, would need to meet a different standard—perhaps unique to Alamo. I knew Bill Berlin because he worked with the Cheyenne and Arapahoe for many years and was reputed to be of one of the best people in the country to help with curriculum development. He was a retired professor at Purdue University and had a PhD from Indiana State University. John agreed, and Bill joined the team.

John Loehr moved to a house in Albuquerque near the university campus. John, Bill Berlin and I huddled there to draft the application for the school's contract. Each member of the team drafted a portion of the application. Rocky Todea, Ramah's accountant, joined us to describe the finance processes or controls to be developed and adopted by the school board. Bill and John went to work describing the elements of the education plan to be developed before the faculty arrived in late summer to familiarize themselves with it. Abe Plummer, from Ramah, as a former contract school executive, advised us on cultural issues to be integrated into the curriculum, the school board's involvement in key decisions, and the operation of the school. These three topics would contribute to the foundation of the Alamo School Board's learning, as well as broader education to prepare the community and the staff for the opening of the school in the fall of 1979.

My assignment was to lay out the key steps to deliver enough portable classrooms and an onsite cafeteria for 400 elementary school children. Plus, I had to explain the requirements for getting utilities installed. Remember, there was no water, sewer or electricity on the reservation. Electric power would first need to be brought onto the reservation, and then to the proposed campus. Alamo parents wanted the school in the heart of their community so kids could walk to it. It was a big challenge, and was done on time with the help of architects from Colorado, Cliff Pallison and his partner Norm Hodge.

Once the contract was approved, we drew an advance on the contract funds in order to make initial monetary commitments to the architects, power company and construction contractors who started to prepare the site for laying out the school's utilities and foundations. This is where the architects were great tutors. The Ramah finance and purchasing employees coached me and Abe Plummer (who became the first executive director of the school) on how to negotiate the lease payment and the delivery schedule for the facilities with a classroom manufacturer. Once the construction was complete, the school leaders shifted their purchases to furnishings, textbooks, curriculum development, hiring staff and paying their consultants and advisors.

Mike: The Indian Self-Determination Act had been passed, and the Indian-controlled school movement was launched.

John: Yes, there was still a high level of resistance, but eventually that was overcome and the contract was issued. To be fair, the BIA employees, many of whom were themselves tribal members, appreciated that managing a school required literacy, skills and experience that were largely lacking in communities such as Alamo. However, instead of recognizing that Alamo people were tired of waiting for the federal government to build a school promised in the mid-19th century, Bureau officials in Gallup staged a series of delay tactics during the negotiations for the PL 638 contract and later as part of the wrestling over the payment of the Alamo school's request for indirect cost funds. Mike, you will recall the fuss made about John's six-passenger plane. He could accommodate two or three board members, himself, a lawyer and maybe an expert. John was frequently ferrying us from Alamo to the negotiations with the BIA in Gallup, a five-hour journey by car but just 45 minutes by plane. He maintained the plane and filled it with fuel, and he charged the school exactly the same rate approved by the University of New Mexico when he was flying to reservation schools to deliver teacher training. It was actually cheaper than driving to those remote locations. In the course of our negotiations with the BIA, they began to refer to John as "the activist." John was eventually audited by the BIA, and they found no irregularities. Had it not been for John Loehr and his plane, this contract would not have moved along as quickly as it did.

The Indian Self-Determination Act is the last major policy statement by the federal government regarding American Indians. The initiative for change now rests with Native people to tell the federal government what is needed and how it should be delivered. Personally, I was too close to the problems to grasp the potential scope of the Act when it was adopted.

After having had 50 years to meditate on the issues, perhaps tribes are ready to ask: "What do our people need now, and how will it meet our needs?"

Such reflection is necessary. Self-determination is about empowerment to govern the community. To make decisions on the local level is an opportunity to build a future that will serve not only the children, but hopefully preserve and advance the community as a whole. Hence, the celebration of the opening of the Alamo School. It was really a landmark event, but only a first step.

My first actual step onto the proposed Alamo campus site was when I stepped from the floor of a pickup truck onto a bed dust that rose up well above my ankle.

"This is where we want the campus, right here in the center of the Chapter!" chuckled my host.

"Oh, man, this is the moon. To build anything here will be a challenge," I thought.

The road to the site was poor, but my hosts were so excited to have the school campus at the heart of the Alamo community that they were blind to the need for a better road. Trucks and equipment would need a road to deliver food and other supplies. The teachers would have to commute because there was no housing for them in Alamo. To develop some limited self-sufficiency to support the school, a road and a communications system would be necessary.

An important characteristic of PL 638 contracts is the unique grant of indirect costs. I had a face-to-face conversation with members of the Office of Inspector General in late 1977 and continued to dialogue with them until early 1979. Within the regulations describing the rules guiding the implementation of PL 93-638, there was a standard government document, OASC-10, describing what qualifies as an indirect cost and stipulating that such costs are allowed in addition to the contract amount. The two men who appended indirect costs to the PL 638 regulations said, "This is something we inserted because the federal government has a lot of money to support all of these [regional] offices. Tribes should have a share of that because that's what provides the overhead for what they [as contractors] need to do. It supports their lawyers, their accountants and all those kinds of things." I learned about it in an addendum to the PL 638 regulations that were published following the adoption of the [ISDEAA] Act.

I came back from my sabbatical to study for the bar exam and said, okay, let's try to educate the clients. This was one of our activities for both Ramah and Alamo during those years. In the early days of my PL 638 counseling, Ramah was going to the BIA Albuquerque area office and Alamo was going to the Gallup office. The two offices were not consistent in how they implemented the regulation.

The BIA failed to set aside monies for the indirect costs for these contract schools. The Bureau actually published a guideline in April 1977 refuting the direction from OIG [U.S. Office of the Inspector General] and directing PL 638 contractors to fund their indirect costs from the amount of their contract. In the absence of funding or direction from the Assistant Secretary's Office for BIA [that was consistent with the regulations], regional officials were challenged to fund PL 638 contract indirect support costs. In a few instances, BIA offices pared down their existing administrative units in a good faith effort to meet the regulatory mandate to fund indirect costs. But the initial responses from a majority of the regions was to simply say, "Well, there is no funding for that."

Unaware of this widespread subterfuge, we put together a proposal for indirect costs for the fiscal year beginning the fall of 1979 because the Alamo School was going to need it. The leadership of the school was caught completely flatfooted by the refusal of the PL 638 Specialist to fund the request for indirect costs. I had a really good relationship with the PL 638 contract administrator for the Alamo School, and I asked, "What's up with this? We're getting a lot of resistance, non-responses to our requests."

She said they were having trouble locating the money. They weren't willing to reach into their administrative budget to fund it, but they were looking for a special allocation. So, we kept putting our pressure on the PL 638 Specialist to solve the problem.

Eventually, Mike joined the negotiations to review the BIA's offer to settle Alamo School's request for indirect costs. A Chapter officer as well as school board members were invited to this meeting. Of course, the executive director and new finance officer from Alamo School were present to hear the BIA's offer regarding indirect costs. After waiting for nearly an hour for the BIA to join the meeting, the PL 638 Specialist appeared and presented a written offer.

Mike, you picked up the single copy of the offer, read it and stood up. Then you looked around the table and said, "This is completely unacceptable!" And you tore the written offer in half and dropped it on the table.

John Loehr was present, and I checked the facts with him. He chuckled and said, "He was right, you know." With that bit of theater, everybody from Alamo also stood up and left the meeting. You concluded the meeting by saying "Let me know when you guys are ready to talk." Everyone filed out the door.

Shortly after that meeting, I withdrew from the Alamo team for a few months to prepare for the 1980 winter New Mexico bar exam, which I passed. I was not part of the Alamo School Board's quest to recover its claim for indirect costs.

Mike: Our big battle over indirect costs wound up with two U.S. Supreme Court cases, which Bryant Rogers and I won. And that was what put the ISDA on the even keel. They needed to get enough money for these programs—under mandated contracts to be signed with Indian tribes or their sanctioned entities under the ISDA—to run their own programs *at parity* with those the government would have had to run. That is in legislative history. This is a huge component of what makes the ISDA the success it has become.

John: Alamo and Ramah were wonderful experiments. I was your partner from 1978 to 1988. I resigned from our law firm because I had an epiphany during my 15-month sabbatical that as a lawyer I couldn't effect the kind of change that was necessary for people to be successful. In representing our clients, we represented people struggling to get a foothold to enable the delivery of decent service.

In the late 1980's, I handled an incident concerning a Navajo PL 638-contract school south of Shiprock. It was a wonderful school staffed with people motivated to help about 100 Navajo children with disabilities. It should be noted that this school was led by a compassionate, smart woman who was professionally appalled that such a tragedy could occur at the school she supervised.

As it was explained to me, in the Navajo culture, if a person is disabled and can't work, then that person's role is ill-defined. If the disability occurs at birth, its seriousness grows as the child ages. What is the value of such an adult who can't earn a living or care for others?

The facts of the case concerned a child who fell out of a rowboat. A staff member at the school, acting without authority, took the young student out in a rowboat on a pond, acting on the belief that this ride would be a learning experience for the student, because impaired children frequently respond positively to motion. The child did not know how to swim and was without a life jacket. Once underway, the boat began to rock as the child got excited, and the child fell into the water and perished. The school had no financial reserves or insurance to draw upon.

I shared with the mother's attorney that we had very little to offer the mother for her loss. He simply said, "Let's figure this out."

I asked, "What does your client want?"

And he said, "It's simple. All she wants to know is what happened."

So, we arranged for a very solemn event to share what happened. The school arranged for a number of staff members to testify to the drowning event with the mother present. At the end, the mother heard it all and wept. That was closure. She thanked us and walked out of the meeting. I couldn't get my mind around what was going on—we'd made some offers, a settlement. But that's not what was wanted.

Lisa: And that was one of your last cases where you thought that you were not making a difference?

John: Yes. Bringing about successful change requires an understanding of the desired outcomes. How does one frame the purpose of community-controlled school boards on the performance of their teachers and pupils, and secure resources that will cover the costs for such services? Instead, board members currently are being accused of focusing on the benefits of the board's stipend, travel and hotel stays.

Mr. Chavez Coho [Ramah School Board President] shared a story with me about his first visit to Washington, D.C., and his "knowledge gap." When first elected as a Chapter official, the people who arranged visits to represent the Navajo Nation told him, "You've got to go to *Washing-done.* Show up here at the center, and you will travel there with everyone else to a meeting with the big officials from the Bureau of Indian Affairs."

He had no idea that he was traveling to Washington, D.C. He thought, "I've never heard of this place. I wonder where it is on the reservation."

Mike: He had never heard of Washington, D.C.?

John: He certainly didn't know that it wasn't on the Navajo reservation. He showed up with his bolo tie and his hat, all dressed up in his best cowboy boots. No bag, no overnight stuff. They put him on the airplane, they flew in there, and then they realized that he didn't have anything in baggage. And for three days, he traveled around Washington without any spare clothes.

THE TWO U.S. SUPREME COURT CASES: AN INTERVIEW WITH C. BRYANT ROGERS

In May 2021, my daughter Ashley interviewed my longtime partner C. Bryant Rogers, who was my co-counsel in two U.S. Supreme Court wins, Ramah Navajo School Board, Inc. v. Bureau of Revenue of New Mexico, 458 U.S. 832 (1982) and Salazar v. Ramah Navajo Chapter, 567 U.S. 182 (2012). This interview was edited for brevity and clarity.

Ashley: Bryant, when did you and my dad meet?

Bryant: We met at Pine Ridge, South Dakota in 1976.

I was an intern with Hobbs Straus for the summer after my second year in law school, working as a planner and grant writer. Bobo Dean was my supervising lawyer, and I had met Bobo when I worked at Choctaw because he was the tribe's attorney, which is really why I went to law school. He wrote me a letter of recommendation. The law firm needed somebody to work at Pine Ridge, and none of the attorneys wanted to go, so I went there to work with people who wanted to operate the Loneman Day School under the new Public Law 93-638, which at the time had been operated by the BIA. Ramah had already established their school, but this was one of the first formal uses for tribal contract schools after the law was passed in 1975. Mike agreed to come in and work with me to do that negotiation because I wasn't a licensed lawyer.

Ashley: And were you successful in getting that started?

Bryant: Yes, and we got something else that nobody ever got again. Not only did we get all the agency-level money for the school, but we also got a percentage of funding from BIA's area office to run the school, and nobody did that again until 1994. They set up their own school board, and Edwin Fills the Pipe was the first board chairman.

Ashley: Then you went back and finished your last year of law school at Harvard?

Bryant: Yes. All my papers and research topics at Harvard were on Indian law issues. While I was there, I met Laurence Tribe, who was my constitutional law professor and evidence professor. One day, we were in class talking about discrete and insular minorities and the Amish case, which is an important constitutional law case about allowing people to be different and not be forced to conform to uniform rules if they don't endanger other people. After I raised the issue of tribes—and Professor Tribe hadn't really thought about it—we had a long talk. He was writing a treatise on constitutional law, and I persuaded him he needed to have a section on Indians and tribes. He had all these law review people working with him on it, but they didn't know much about it, so they kept coming to me in the law library.

Finally, I was doing my third-year paper on the integration of basic Indian law principles into an introductory constitutional law course, but it was taking me forever. It was too long. I was writing a book instead of a paper, and I wasn't going to class because I didn't have time. I had exams approaching, so I went to Tribe and said, "I'm going to fail commercial transactions if I don't stop working on this paper. But let me write the Indian law section of your treatise, and let that be my third-year paper, but let me do it after finals instead of before (which was the rule)."

He agreed. I met with a Black attorney from Jackson, Mississippi. She had really good notes on commercial transactions, and she shared them with me. I passed, and then I stayed in the law library for two weeks and wrote that treatise section. Laurence Tribe literally did not change a word. It is still in its 1979 version, and then I did the update in 1988 for that. It's in the front of the book, *American Constitutional Law* by Laurence Tribe.

Ashley: That's amazing.

Bryant: Yeah, it was pretty cool. Later, the Native American Rights Fund and other groups collaborated to update something called the *Handbook of Federal Indian Law* by Felix Cohen that had been published in 1942 and then republished in 1945 and bastardized later after that, in 1958, when they were trying to eliminate tribes.[59] So, the federal government gutted

---

59. The most recent edition of the *Handbook of Federal Indian Law* by Felix S. Cohen was published in 2024, co-edited by Kevin Washburn.

it and then republished it. They had to reconstitute the 1942 version and then update it. And it's just a wonderful treatise. But there were no treatises in the handbook back then when I was in law school.

Ashley: Those law books are very important and seminal. Why did a white guy from Mississippi want to go into Indian law?

Bryant: I knew there were Indians around where I grew up because I saw them. There was a Choctaw fair, and I can remember distinctly when I was about six years old, a whole band of Choctaws, maybe 80 people, went by in front of our house in rural Forest, Mississippi, advertising for the Choctaw fair. They had walked ten miles at least to do that.

When I was in college at Mississippi State University, I was oblivious to most things. I was playing in a band while going to school. But there was a voter registration march that I decided to pay attention to. I went, and there was a person from the Southern Christian Leadership Conference named R. B. Cottonreader who had been leading these things since the 1950s. He had been beat up many times. I met him. I went down there with a camera and started taking pictures. As I was watching it and taking pictures, the cops were harassing them, and they told me I could not take pictures. I said, "Yeah, I can." So, they arrested everybody, including me.

Ashley: Were these all Black people?

Bryant: All Black people but me. So, we were a day in jail, spent the night, and then they dropped all the charges.

Ashley: What did that feel like?

Bryant: We were just in there, and I was able to throw my camera out that had the pictures, and I gave them to R.B. Cottonreader, so I don't have them anymore. That got me more focused on what was happening around the end of [the U.S. involvement in] Vietnam. Marches were happening. Creighton Abrams Jr., the U.S. Army general who commanded military operations in Vietnam, came to Mississippi State to speak, and six of us protested. We wore black armbands and stood outside the student union. We were surrounded literally by about a thousand people yelling and screaming, and I was debating this guy in the middle of that mob. And he had been in the army in Vietnam. He said, "You don't know what the hell you're talking about. You've never been to Vietnam."

And I said, "Well, I've never been to Paris either, but I know there's an Eiffel Tower."

I felt this hand on my shoulder, and I looked around, and there was this Marine in full dress with medals and everything. He stepped in front of me, pointed to me and said, "I agree with him." He had been in Da Nang. He started questioning this other guy, who had been a supply clerk in Saigon.

Watching this exchange was John Peterson, an anthropology professor at Mississippi State who had done his dissertation on the socioeconomic conditions of the Mississippi Choctaws.

Later, my wife at the time, Nell, taught English in Philadelphia, Mississippi, schools, where the 1964 civil rights murders were. She then started working as an adult education teacher at Choctaw, so I knew there was a tribal government out there.

When I finished college, I needed one more course in Spanish, so I did a correspondence course to get that last credit for my degree. I was working in my dad's furniture store, and I got a call from a woman with the U.S. Justice Department asking if I wanted to come interview for a job. I went to a hotel in Jackson, Mississippi, and interviewed.

Ashley: How did they know to contact you there?

Bryant: To this day, I have no idea. That was in 1970. I got my degree in 1971 because I forgot to apply for graduation when I finished my correspondence course. But in any event, this job was with the Community Relations Service (CRS) for the U.S. Department of Justice. They are mediators and monitors, and they would send a team to try to calm the situation down in communities that were in some kind of civil crises. They had a special project called Project 81 that was targeting the South when they had the final court-ordered school desegregation. There had been a deal between the Justice Department and Senator Eastland that they would not send in outside monitors [to marches and gatherings] because they didn't want anybody to know what was happening, so they got around it by hiring three people from each southern state and said they weren't outside monitors, a political deal. I was one of them from Mississippi, so I covered 30 counties in Mississippi. The other two monitors from Mississippi were Black, Bill Brown and Lloyd Davis, who died very young of sickle cell disease when he was about 35.

Ashley: And what, exactly, were you looking for?

Bryant: Riots, student walkouts, just harassment, because they fired all the Black teachers and moved all the students into the white schools, and then they were expelling Black students at a much higher rate. We were trying to prevent riots and walkouts and beatings.

In the course of that, I met John Peterson's wife, who was a teacher in Starkville, Mississippi, who was fired for being nice to the Black teachers that weren't fired. She was white. I got to know John and her a little bit from that.

Later, John wrote a grant proposal for the Choctaw Self-Determination Project, and this was five years before PL 638 was passed, and the goal of that project was to help the tribes take over Bureau of Indian Affairs (BIA) programs on the reservation. And they had a grant from the Office of Economic Opportunity for that. Phillip Martin was the Choctaw chief at that time.

By that point, I decided to quit the CRS. When we were going out into the Black community, the FBI was a hero after the 1964 murders in Mississippi. But that changed. The FBI started treating community activists as the enemy. I had been assured that when I had to write a contact report with everybody I talked to in the Black community that the information would not go to the FBI. Well, they lied. When I learned that, I quit.

When I was looking for a job, I learned about this grant writing position with the Choctaw. I applied, and John Peterson remembered me from those two prior interactions. I didn't know anything about tribes, but I knew how to write. I interviewed with the tribal council and they asked me, "Do you know what you're doing?"

I said, "I know how to write."

The chief told me what he needed me to write, so that's how I started. I did that for three years. It was an incredible experience. Chief Martin was a brilliant person and had no high school degree. He got a GED while he was in the Air Force in WWII, and he came back to Mississippi. He got a job as an electrician's helper. He was on the tribal council. He wrote all the resolutions, and was finally elected chairman. He told me my office was at a desk with a pencil in the BIA building. That was all they had.

The unemployment rate was at 75 percent, life expectancy was about 50 years of age. The average education was up to the third grade, there was no health care, really. They had a little hospital that had been built in the 1930s after half of them died from the flu in the 1918 influenza pandemic. They had nothing.

I just want to say that the difference working for the Choctaws in Mississippi and Pine Ridge in South Dakota compared to New Mexico was night and day in the sense that the anti-Indian brutality here in New Mexico is nothing like it was in those places. In Pine Ridge and in Mississippi, the brutality against Indians was evident and raw. It was just a different world.

Ashley: Where is the Choctaw reservation?

Bryant: These are people who did not go to Oklahoma when their tribe was forcibly removed in the 1830s. They hid in the swamps and wouldn't go, and so all their reservations are swamp areas now, so they didn't have an organized reservation. But then they acquired reservation land, but it was in little pieces, a checkerboard, not just in one place but over six counties in Mississippi. I learned a lot about Indian issues, like to be really thoughtful about what battles you take on.

Ashley: Please explain that.

Bryant: What I was trying to get at is that this explains my initial reaction to filing the Ramah case. I'm really conservative about asserting claims on behalf of my tribal clients. It isn't about me and what I think is right. What is the consequence for the people that I'm representing if I'm wrong and don't prevail in court?

Sometimes you have legal plans, and they blow up in your face. When Mike first decided to file a class action case with Ramah, he was a little surprised by my reaction. I was not enthusiastic about doing it as a class action because my experience with the Choctaw told me this could have been a disaster. Many tribes in Indian country had their rights stripped, and it was a big thing to take on. It could have gone bad. But it didn't.

Ashley: So, this was a big gamble.

Mike: Well, what I thought, and I think Bryant agreed at the time, was, OK, if we lose the class action, there's always Congress. The point is: you change the law. Now, this is grandiose thinking. I'm not denying that, and all the risks are there, and it could have gone south, but ultimately the march of social evolution—the increasing visibility of American Indians in the general polity of the country—was advancing in the right direction.

Indians were becoming visible all over. The Choctaws got recognized. The point was, a face was being put to these members of American society who had been discriminated against, be it genocide, stolen lands, forced marches to be required to live away from their homelands. All these atrocities were committed in the name of the great American destiny.

Destiny, right. And times were changing. So, yes, there were obviously risks in filing the Ramah class action, but it was important. I don't remember specific discussions, but there was that element that cases are lost. But if they're big enough and they get the attention of the Supreme Court or Congress, things can change.

Ashley: When did you come to New Mexico and why?

Bryant: After I graduated from Harvard, I got a Reginald Heber Smith Community Lawyer Fellowship that was awarded by Howard University. They chose one hundred people a year to receive what was called a "Reggie." I got Reggie and went to Zuni Pueblo to work for Zuni Legal Aid.

Ashley: How did you choose Zuni?

Bryant: When I was at Harvard, I worked for the Boston Indian Center on a volunteer basis. And I met Hayes Lewis, who was from Zuni and was at Harvard's School of Education. I got to know him, and his father was Governor of the Pueblo at Zuni. He asked me to be assigned there.

Ashley: Did you move to the reservation?

Bryant: I went back to law school and finished and then I went to Zuni in 1977. I worked on a lot of stuff, but at one point Mike was working with Zuni to try to get a separate school district and break away from Gallup-McKinley school district. I was involved because the All Indian Pueblo Council was trying to do the same thing without permission and was taking grant money that should have gone to Zuni. I was helping them get that money back and get control over it, so Mike and I overlapped somewhat on that project, but it was successful. They have their own school district now. After I left Zuni and Laguna in 1978, I went back to Mississippi and set up a legal aid office at Choctaw for two years.

Then I came back to New Mexico in August 1981 and worked with Mike at the Van Amberg law firm.

Ashley: Please tell us about the first U.S. Supreme Court case involving New Mexico gross receipts tax.

Bryant: The gross receipts case was a question of whether the New Mexico contractor's tax applies to a contractor who is building an Indian school on the reservation, and there had been a bunch of case law that went the other way on that. None of them had involved a federal regulatory scheme involving Indians and the Ramah legislation, which was unique. The way the case was presented was: We can either pay this tax, or we can have a cafeteria. The tax amounted to about three hundred thousand dollars.

Ashley: This was when they were building the new school at Pine Hill School?

Bryant: Yes. The Ramah Navajo School Board had X amount of money to build the school. Mike's primary approach was this is an Indian community and has federal preemption. I remember trying to persuade Mike by saying, "Let's call it not an Indian community but a tribal community. It's a reservation." And Mike went along with it. The bottom line is: We won.

Ashely: And you said basically that the tax couldn't apply to the Ramah Navajo's contractor—unlike charging on the receipts of Los Alamos National Laboratory contractors or whatever, that it was different from that.

Bryant: It was different from that because there was a federal regulatory scheme. There's a case called *White Mountain Apache Tribe v. Bracker*, 448 U.S. 136 (1980), and the state's lawyer was relying on that case to win.

Mike: The state won that case as regards its right to impose the contested taxes on state licensing issued to non-Indian contractors or fuel used by them to drive on state roads within the reservation, but lost where that activity occurred on BIA or tribal roads within the reservation.

We said, wait a minute, the facts are different but the adverse economic impact on the tribal entity is the same and the general principle applied in Bracker as regards its holding that the state could not impose its tax on non-Indian contractors hired by a tribal entity to do work on BIA and tribal roads, constructed per federal regulatory schemes for forestry and reservation roads, was equally applicable to support the school's tax exemption claim: Some portion of the money that was supposed to go to a school trying to educate Navajo kids under the Indian Self-Determination Act was going to go to the state of New Mexico for doing nothing. We said, wait, it had nothing to do with state education. You abandoned that, right? You closed the state-funded Ramah school. We argued that the Ramah School was constructed with a special Congressional appropriation carried out under a federal regulatory scheme regarding Indian education just as comprehensive as the Indian forestry and reservation road regulation at issue in Bracker. We prevailed on that argument.

Bryant: It was a key factor in winning that there was previously a state school to serve the Ramah Community, but the state closed that school.

Mike: Not only that, but the Ramah school helped start the Indian Self-Determination Act.

Ashley: So, did the state think, we closed that school, but we want a piece of this thing that you started that has nothing to do with the state?

Mike: They applied the state tax to an Air Force base, BIA school construction, to Los Alamos National Lab, other federally funded programs. We sought to carve out an exception for the Ramah school construction project.

Ashley: So, why did you win?

Bryant: Because there was a comprehensive federal regulatory scheme involving Indian education and in particular this Indian education because of the Ramah appropriations for the original school. And it was just a good argument about why the preemption was more powerful here.

Mike: We presented evidence that the amount of the tax would deprive them of a cafeteria, which was the closest approximation of how much the tax would be. Are you going to run a school without a cafeteria in the middle of nowhere? It was interfering with a special appropriation providing self-determination for Ramah's school program. Now this school had not existed before, but the government did have a responsibility to educate the Indians. So, we argued, are you going to educate these Indians without a cafeteria or a health department or buses to get them to school?

Ashley: Tell me about the moment in the arguments when Justice Thurgood Marshall asked about the *Central Machinery* case. Do you remember that?

Bryant: That's when I wrote a little note that said, "different regulations." I still have that little note. The regulations involved in *Central Machinery* were different than those applicable to Ramah.

Mike: It was during the state attorney, Jan Unna's, argument. He was second because we were the appellants, which meant we had given the opening argument. We had five or ten minutes at the end for rebuttal, so by then we had two bites of the apple. He only had one. But when I was arguing, I got interrupted every ten seconds by questions from the judges. I never could complete a sentence without getting asked another question. And then came Jan Unna for twenty-five minutes. He was not interrupted once until the very end. I don't know of another case where that ever happened. And I said to myself, as we're listening, "Oh, shit, they're buying all of this from him until the end."

I cannot say this without laughing and crying. Justice Thurgood Marshall was near the center of the panel there, distributed on the bench by seniority, so almost right in front of the podium. It's a very intimate situation. The justices are elevated, and they are surrounding you. You feel absolutely completely alone in the universe, nobody else but you and those nine people.

Justice Marshall leans over the podium, and he says in this gravelly, southern accent, "Oh, I see now, Councilor. That one was called *Central Machinery*." Everybody laughed.

Bryant: Marshall was basically saying to Jan Unna that the way you're distinguishing that case from this one is *the name*.

Ashley: So, did you feel good coming out of there? Did you think you had won?

Bryant: You never know. I thought the argument was well done, Mike did a good job. The final decision was six-three. Rehnquist voted against us. He asked, "Are you going to tell me if this contractor buys a bucket of nails in Albuquerque that the state can't tax that transaction because the nails are going to be used on this Indian school?"

Ashley: That's a good question.

Bryant: It was. I think Mike's answer would have been that if he had bought it for this project, yes, you can't tax it. That kind of exemption is now facilitated by a nontaxable transaction certificate.

One thing about the Ramah case—it's been expanded to other governmental projects like hospitals and housing. If the tribal governor says this is for the tribe, they don't tax the transaction. But we had to fight them about it for a while before the state caved. Other people have tried to use our Ramah case to win claims to exempt state taxation on the gross receipts of sales to non-Indians or non-tribal community businesses operating on their reservations. They've tried about ten times, and they've lost every time. It's never been expanded beyond governmental functions.

Mike: Before we won this case, it was not clear that there was a federally required tax exemption for monies tribes needed to spend for their own benefit, but where the taxable work was to be carried out by non-Indian contractors hired by the tribes and the legal incidence of the tax fell on the non-Indian contract. Our case led to nationwide recognition of the sanctity of federal monies used for the benefit of tribal services such as health care and schools, even if paid to non-Indian contractors and even where the legal incidence of the tax fell on those contractors where the funds involved were paid to the tribal entity in furtherance of a federal regulatory scheme established by Congress.

[Note from Ashley: The rest of the interview deals with their second Supreme Court case, Salazar v. Ramah Navajo Chapter. *It's a complicated case to understand, but SCOTUSblog does a good job boiling it down. According to SCOTUSblog, the Court decided in a 5-4 decision that "the federal government must pay in full each tribe's contract support costs incurred by a tribal contractor under the Indian Self-Determination and Education Assistance Act, 25 U.S.C. § 450, even if Congress has failed to appropriate sufficient funds to cover all of the contract support costs owed to all tribal contractors collectively." In plain English, SCOTUSblog said the case centers on the obligation of both parties in a contract to perform their part of the deal. Indian tribes were not paid all of the costs the government had promised to cover when tribes took on provision of education and other government services. "The Court ruled that a promise is a promise, even if the government doesn't have immediately available enough money to pay all of the contractors it had promised to pay for their services. Congress has to locate the money to cover such a promise, the Court said."]*

Ashley: When did you first become aware that indirect costs was an issue?

Bryant: In the early 1970s when I worked for Choctaw while working on that program to take over some of the BIA programs, we needed administrative costs. And we learned there was something called an indirect cost rate. The Choctaw were one of the first tribes in the country to get an indirect cost rate. That was in 1972. The rate does not pay extra money. All it does is identify how much of the contracted amount you can use for administrative costs, so if you have a hundred-dollar contract, and you got a 20% rate, you could charge twenty dollars for administrative costs and eighty dollars from the program.

One more thing: In 1988, when Mike was primarily embroiled in an unrelated case, I was working on amending the PL 638 statute.

Ashley: I wanted to ask you about that. Lobbying is not something you think about lawyers doing—having to lobby to change the law and then bringing a lawsuit based on the new law.

Bryant: Mike and I had done the two Busby cases. Busby is the Northern Cheyenne School in Montana. They had been promised in their contract that the BIA would keep the school to state standards, and then they didn't, and they had to shut it down. So, the kids had no school, similar to what happened at Ramah. They were bussed a hundred miles a day roundtrip to go to public school.

There are two reported cases on this, one of which was that these PL 638 contracts were not really contracts. They were socioeconomic arrangements, and so they couldn't be enforced under the Contract Disputes Act. We lost that. But the second point was that we sued as *parens patriae* on behalf of the students and survived a motion to dismiss on that and ultimately got a settlement of about 10 million dollars to fix the Busby school. So that was a success. But the other tribes were then stuck with the U.S. Court of Federal Claims ruling that said, these aren't really contracts.

At that time Nell, my ex who was working for Choctaw, was collaborating with a staffer for the Senate Indian Affairs Committee to look at revisions to PL 638. She talked to me about it, and I said, we really need to do this one. I was authorized to write that part of the committee report on this and to write the language of what became 25 U.S.C 450m-1: Contract disputes and claims. First, it said the contract dispute applies to these cases. And secondly, it allowed you to go into court and compel the government to pay the money owed on an ISDA contract by injunction or mandamus. No other federal contractor can get that. All you can do is incur the cost and sue for damages, which we were having to do before. You could sue, but not under the Contract Disputes Act, which had better terms. But if you didn't have any money to incur the cost, you couldn't recover. The government said, it's a cost reimbursable contract, so there's no cost to reimburse if you don't have the money to spend and didn't spend it.

So, I wrote that part of the legislative history that had Congress say, this is an unacceptable argument. And we actually used that in the Ramah case later in negotiations.

Ashley: Essentially, you went and changed the law, and then you were able to bring a lawsuit.

Bryant: Well, Mike started it.

Mike: The central idea is, the Indian Self-Determination Act gives tribes the right to run their own federally funded Indian programs at the same level that the government would have done it, and embedded in that notion was the fact that the government has indirect costs that are paid automatically by other federal agencies. All the functions that the indirect cost rate would be paid for in the private world, in a non-federal contract situation by private contractors.

Bryant: Before 1988, the BIA chose the indirect cost rate system which already existed, and they used it to calculate an add-on amount, which was unique to ISDA. No other federal grant or contract does that. The problem was: There was no remedy if they didn't honor it. There was no way to sue them to get it unless you could incur the cost and then go to the U.S. Claims Court in D.C. You couldn't go to your local district court because there was no statutory authorization.

Mike: You know, that's an interesting point, but I don't think it was the central part of the case.

Bryant: The origin of the second Supreme Court class action is this: Earla Begay was the finance person at Ramah. The facts of origin of this case were somewhat unique and not reproducible. So the arguments made sense with those facts, but not to Indian country in general.

Here's an example, essentially the example Mike used in the 10th Circuit:

> The BIA has a 20% indirect cost rate for the school. And the school gets a hundred dollars for their program, so the BIA is supposed to add 20 dollars to the funding because there's a 20% rate. Now, Ramah gets creative, and they get another 50 dollars from IHS (Indian Health Services) or somewhere else. BIA says, well, it's a 20% rate, but the 20% applies to the whole base. And so instead of paying you 20% of 100 dollars, it became 20 over 150. So, the rate went down to like 15 or 17%, whatever that would be because they weren't getting any indirect costs.

Mike: The BIA was trying to put the burden on other federal agencies to pay their share. That would have been administratively impossible.

Bryant: Right. In this case, it wasn't IHS money, it was Department of Justice money, which paid no indirect cost. So, the BIA said, "But we're only responsible for our share of the base based on the 20% rate. Since the rate went down, instead of paying you $20 we only have to pay you $17."

Mike argued that there was language in the statute that said the BIA is responsible for paying the indirect cost associated with the project you contracted. He argued that by choosing to use the indirect cost system, all the funding in the base was associated with this project, and therefore the BIA should be responsible for paying the whole pool. The reason why that argument worked is there was a big disproportion. The BIA was the dominant funder, and this thing was an add-on, so you can make that beautiful argument, right?

Well, the 10th Circuit accepted that on those narrow facts. Congress immediately passed a law negating that ruling, saying that was a flawed ruling because the BIA should never have been responsible for paying that other $3.

Then we came up with an alternative argument. It's not that the BIA is responsible for paying the indirect cost required to operate for the Department of Justice funded program. It's that they can't use the fact that Department of Justice money was brought in to reduce the amount the BIA would otherwise be statutorily obligated to pay to run their own program. It was a fallback argument that produced a lower amount of money, but it was still there as a claim. We commissioned a study with NCAI (National Congress of American Indians), and they confirmed our analysis.

After the 10th Circuit's ruling, even though Congress negated that ruling prospectively, it didn't change the fact that for those five years, 1989 to 1993, they still were liable for something. And that negotiation happened, and we ended up with that first settlement of $76 million after a lot of effort.

Ashley: Did that $76 million only apply to Ramah?

Bryant: No, that was a class action case, divided among all the class members. Keep in mind that we added a second class action claim in 2000. This was the swimming pool analogy that Judge Hanson hated, but it was a pretty good one. We told the judge that the BIA was supposed to pay $20 because of this indirect cost, and they claim they would only pay $17, so that's a three dollar difference. But they didn't even pay the $17! They paid $10 because they never asked for enough money in the appropriation, and so they never had enough money to fully fund their programs. Their argument was they only had to pay based on what we were appropriated.

Congress in 1994 passed a law that said the amount of indirect cost that is available to pay on these contracts is capped at the number appropriated in the statute. Government, you can't pay more than that amount to the tribes, even though that cap would only produce ten dollars.

Ashley: So, that was a big blow. Who pushed for that?

Bryant: The BIA. We then had two arguments. Even for that five years when we were negotiating over the other ten dollars too, the government wouldn't budge at all. They wouldn't pay one dollar for that issue because they were so confident they would win on the cap issue. That was in the Appropriations Act cap and later got codified in the statute itself.

There's something called the direct contract support cost, which was also added in 1994 amendments that basically said, in addition to indirect cost, there is a category of direct cost that is really administrative support that's not captured by the indirect cost rate. It's the cost to pay for workers comp and some kinds of unemployment insurance and costs that the government gets paid in the human resources offices of the government outside the agencies like the BIA.

Lloyd Miller had been pushing that. He had filed suit about that and got that in the state statute.

The bottom line is: Three different legal theories got merged together in about 2002 through amended complaints and a merger of the Zuni case with the Ramah case. We had the original modified theory that the rate system was unlawfully reducing the amount of money the BIA was going to pay to run their own programs, the indirect cost rate system, because if the base grows by four dollars, the pool grows by a dollar. Then there was the theory that we weren't getting any direct contract support costs, and the BIA was never paying the full indirect contract support costs due, so there were three different legal theories involved.

The 1994 amendment—the appropriation limited cap—only applied to indirect costs, not direct contract support costs. We were able to negotiate the second settlement covering 1994 and 1995 for direct contract support cost based on the modified original Ramah theory, though there was no cap for 1994. They didn't give us anything on the cap, even though it was part of our negotiation. So, we got the second settlement that was about $28 million in 2002.

Ashley: Could you briefly summarize the Indian Self-Determination Act and how you and my dad won *Salazar v. Ramah* in 2016?

Bryant: The ISDA was passed in 1975. It was a follow-up from Nixon's effort to secure approval of the Blue Lake being returned to Taos Pueblo. It got him focused on doing something for Indians, and the passage of the ISDA forced the government to allow the tribes to take over their programs, and provide the same money the BIA would have had to run them. The problem is that the Bureau of Indian Affairs has a whole federal apparatus to support that operation and not only the program money. Contract support cost was added in as a necessary element recognizing that you must have an audit. BIA does not have to pay that kind of cost with program money.

Later, the BIA recognized that there was something called indirect cost that could be used to add money to address this issue, a rate system based on the amount of program costs. There were many problems when they implemented it. In fact, a lot of tribes went in the hole because of the way that system worked for 13 years, and there were many twists and turns.

Mike and I disagree a lot on strategy, but we agree on a couple of things that are really critical. Throughout this case, we were absolutely convinced we were right, and the government was wrong and being wholly arbitrary and unreasonable the way they interpreted this statute. They're supposed to interpret these statutes in favor of the Indians and against the government when there was a reasonable alternative inter-pretation. Mike won that case in the first appeal based on that argument.

The court rejected Chevron deference[60] and said, if it's ambiguous and the Indians offer a reasonable interpretation, that's the one we're going to go with. But we were really angry, deep-seated angry at the govern-ment throughout this whole thing for being so pigheaded and arrogant and condescending and unreasonable. They didn't have to take this posi-tion. We had lots of other tribal clients besides Ramah. They needed this money; they needed it really bad, and the government was withholding it for no good reason that we could see, and it really pissed us off. I mean,

---

60. This was a Supreme Court ruling, *Chevron U.S.A., Inc. v. Natural Resources Defense Council, Inc.,* 467 U.S. 837 (1984), stating that judges must defer to federal agencies in interpreting parts of statutes if Congress passes a law that is unclear.

that's a real part of why we were able to press forward on the Ramah class action for 30 years.

We weren't getting paid for most of that time. We got some interim payments for some of the settlements but nothing like what it took to get this done. And we had a great team. Even after I got the 1988 amendments when Lloyd Miller came in, he was very instrumental in getting the 1994 amendments, which strengthened our claims. These amendments commanded the secretary to add the full amount of contract support costs needed to administer these programs. They commanded that.

Mike: And indirect contract support costs.

Bryant: Yes, and then added another category called direct contract support, which the government never honored and never paid a dime on. We did an equitable relief settlement after our second monetary settlement. It took eight years to negotiate that. We've reformed the indirect cost rate system, made them change the way they calculated the rates and adjusted them. We didn't solve everything, but we saved the tribes a lot of money with that equitable relief settlement, and for the first time, the government was ordered to pay direct contract support costs. They kept saying, but we don't have any money, we can't even pay full indirect costs, much less this new category of direct contract support costs.

We said, you do have the money. It's in the Judgment Fund [within the Bureau of the Fiscal Service]; the Treasury Department administers permanent and indefinite appropriation. It's available to pay judgments. Reach agreement with it, and you can pay it.

They paid the first settlement and the second settlement out of it, and they said, but those didn't have a cap. The Congress has said we can't spend this money.

Well, we thought that argument was frankly wrong, absurd. Why would they stick to this position? Mike thought it's primarily turf. The government did not want to release the reins of power and money because if you pay more money out of a limited appropriation to tribes, you will have to reduce your federal bureaucracy. And that's the central thing that was our obstacle.

I think there were two other elements. I don't think all the federal employees were malevolent. I think many of them never re-examined their position after they won the first go-round on their "cap" defense in 1995 or so. They were unwilling to take another look at it, no matter what we would throw at them, and every time we would find a little way to get over their argument, they went back to Congress, and after three or four times, they got the law amended to defeat us. And we found a way to overcome it every time, and it was not easy.

Bureaucrats don't like to make decisions that have big-money consequences. I think a lot of them just said: 'You know what, we're not going to change our mind. The courts are going to have to make us do it.' And the court did.

Lloyd Miller came up with a strategy of trying to get the Chamber of Commerce and the National Defense Contractors Association to file an amicus brief on our behalf. And they did that because the arguments the government was making against the tribes were making them very uncomfortable, that these are really contracts, and they really are enforceable as contracts. And they got concerned about it. We got him on our side, and it got us Scalia's and Thomas's votes.

Mike: We managed to slip it into the brief that was written by a firm in Washington, D.C., that had assisted in the Cherokee case that Lloyd had handled. And they had a brilliant lawyer who argued about 85 cases in the Supreme Court, winning half of them, which is an amazing track record. And we gave him the argument because he had a track record with the court.

The strategy was to argue the case strictly on contract law, federal contract law that applies to Lockheed Martin or the plumbing firm that comes in to fix the BIA facility plumbing, for example. They're all under this Contract Disputes Act. And he persuaded Bryant and me that that should be the lead argument.

Bryant: But it wasn't the only argument. We still used the Indian Trust Doctrine and the Ambiguity Doctrine.

Mike: Yes, but there were references in a brief to a statute where the contrast in wording worked to our favor, and that was cited in the Supreme Court decision as 25 U.S.C. § 2008D at the time. That was the codification, and basically it applied a different rule to contracts with schools than applied to the basic Title I PL 638 Indian Self-Determination contracts we were litigating under. That contrast in the wording of the statute was used by Justice Sotomayor in her decision. And that was a big, big play.

Bryant: We found 51 statutes where if you wrote the statute a certain way, the contract liability was clearly curtailed by the lack of appropriations, especially when Congress says: 'Out of this you shall not spend more than this for that to meet that obligation.' We didn't have any language like that. We made that contrast and it really helped to overcome the government's "cap" defense.

At the end, when we were desperately trying to negotiate the settlement for three and a half years, I will tell you, there were about 20 material, serious differences in our positions on law and fact, some of which were never resolved in the negotiation—an unbelievable amount of detail and crap we had to work through such as statisticians, government contract lawyers and procurement people and all—to try to get to a number.

The *Albuquerque Journal* front page headline, September 18, 2015.

NAVAJO CODE TALKERS:
A JOURNEY THROUGH
CULTURE AND WAR

One evening in the fall of 1985, Sam Billison and I were enjoying a beer in the Holiday Inn lounge in Farmington, New Mexico. We had just finished a meeting with the Navajo Academy board of directors, of which Sam was president. I had been its counsel, advising on some problems arising from the Academy's location, sharing the grounds with the Navajo Methodist Mission School, whose name bespoke its aim to convert Navajos to the only true religion—theirs. Sharing the campus with the Mission School was getting complicated.

Sam had gotten me involved when their school only needed minor legal assistance. As co-occupant of the deteriorating 100-acre campus in Farmington, the Academy was a "guest," invited to occupy much of the campus, including dormitories, classrooms and support buildings rent-free. At the time the arrangement was made, the Mission School's administrator was a laid-back fellow, and he and Sam got along well. All it took was a handshake, and the Academy moved in. They helped take care of the grounds and rebuilt several walkways which benefited both schools. But there was no written contract, let alone a lease. At first things went smoothly, but little by little, the Navajo students began migrating across the campus from the Mission School to the Academy. In the 1978-79 school year, the Academy had only 25 students. But by the 1986-87 school year, enrollment had grown to 250. During that time, a new, much sterner headmaster of the Mission School had taken over. Things went downhill from there. The home office of the Women's Division of the Methodist Church, located on the Hudson River in Washington Heights, New York, began to notice this enrollment change and became concerned. For a while HQ tolerated the arrangement, perhaps thinking the influx of new Navajo students could be drawn to join the church. But the opposite occurred. The Mission School's primary purpose, after all, was conversion. Ever since Christian zeal had found its way to North America, all Christian denominations (except perhaps the Mennonites) thought they were doing Indian kids a favor by converting them to Christianity. Some denominations did so by force and still try to do so, although much less successfully. The damage they did to Indian children lingers.

At the Mission School the means used were instructional. Teaching Indian kids English and Christianity was the program. Under the former Methodist administration, which had invited Sam's school to the campus, the missionizing had been less visible.

It was not the Navajo Academy's aim to absorb students from the Mission School—the exodus happened naturally. Mission School students were voting with their feet because of the quality of the Academy's curriculum and the fact that they charged no tuition, whereas the Mission School did. This sparked Sam's vision of a reservation-wide academy for gifted Navajo teenagers, which eventually became a reality.

An eviction notice emanated from the banks of the Hudson River ordering the Academy to vacate the premises. With no written agreement to use the campus, Sam came to me for legal help. I filed a lawsuit against the Mission School, but my arguments for the Academy were slender. Navajos had always based agreements on the spoken word. The English phrase "a man's word is his bond" comes to mind to describe Navajo culture. But that doesn't work in modern white man's courts, at least not often. In this case, the court in San Juan County, and eventually the New Mexico Court of Appeals, realized that the kids' welfare came first. In January 1990, the courts ruled that Navajo Academy could remain three years on the property until their informal lease ran out. The following year, it was established as Navajo Preparatory School, a member of the International Baccalaureate® (IB) World Schools, and in 1995, the Navajo Nation purchased the permanent 82-acre campus in Farmington from the Women's Division of the General Board of Global Ministries of the United Methodist Church.

An educator with a doctorate degree, Sam Billison was a born leader and a former Navajo Code Talker. After returning from the Pacific theater, a World War II battleground between the Allies and Japan, Sam went to Arizona State University's School of Education and was certified as a school administrator. He had served on the tribal council and was friends with Annie Wauneka and virtually every other Navajo politician from the late 1940s throughout his life. He was inquisitive, friendly and interested in all things related to Navajo education and the tribe's survival. We became buddies.

Our conversation that evening at the Holiday Inn Lounge soon turned to the Code Talkers. He told me how he had been trained as an underwater spy. At Iwo Jima, as one of the few Navajos who learned how to swim at the time, his job was to snorkel underwater as close to shore as possible to scout the coast where the Marines planned to swarm ashore. He was leading up to something. He began talking about the newly formed Navajo Code Talkers Association. They were revered by everyone in the Navajo world and elsewhere for their heroic service in World War II. He was their president, and they needed a lawyer, he said. Would I be interested in serving as their unpaid attorney? "You betcha," I replied. My representation of their legal problems was nothing big. I got them incorporated as a tax-exempt nonprofit under state law, so they became eligible for charitable donations. I later helped them raise funds.

Thus began a twenty-five-year association with a remarkable group of delightful though sometimes cantankerous veterans who conducted monthly meetings beside the same railroad tracks that I first encountered while waiting for a mechanic to fix my Volvo in late July 1968, soon after arriving in Window Rock. Meetings were held on Saturday mornings. The Friday before the meeting, I would drive from Santa Fe to Gallup, a three-hour trip, spend the night at the Holiday Inn, and show up at the meeting at nine the next morning. Sometimes I would have dinner the night before with Sam to discuss upcoming issues. The meetings were conducted in the Gallup Chamber of Commerce, a one-story brick edifice of uncertain vintage divided into two halves, one side serving as the headquarters for the Gallup Chamber of Commerce, whose business seemed to consist primarily as a tourist information center. The other half was reserved for the Code Talkers. Every half hour or so, a huge freight train would come thundering past, drowning out our conversation. It became a standing joke about how the trains would know exactly when to try to cut somebody off.

In the front was a small stage on which the head table for the officers and their legal counsel was situated. The fifteen rows of folding chairs created the auditorium with seats for perhaps 80 people. Along the southern wall was a glass case that housed Navajo Code Talker memorabilia. Framed photographs taken in the Pacific as well as during training at Camp Pendleton sat upon its shelves. Documents describing a typical code table were displayed along with commendations, news clippings and combat photographs. A list of more than 400 Code Talkers stood prominently in the center of one of the display cabinets. Eventually, they wanted to buy and build a museum of their own, and that was at the tail end of my representation of them.

I was pleased to learn that in 2020, the Navajo Code Talkers Museum became the nonprofit successor to the Navajo Code Talkers Association and their mission to build a museum is in the works.

They did amazing things to help end World War II. All of them were Marines, and they only fought in the Pacific, not in Europe. And they were in every major battle, starting with Guadalcanal. Everybody knows how horrific those battles were. Miraculously, only two of them were killed, and there were few serious injuries because they had teams of Marines surrounding them to protect them. And what made them so invaluable was that they developed a virtually unbreakable code out of their native language.

The wartime Navajo code wasn't just a straight translation of English words into Navajo, which they would transmit by radio. The code would be changed periodically. I don't know what the word for shark is in Navajo, but a submarine would be, let's say, the Navajo equivalent of the word shark; an aircraft carrier might be the whale; and the code words might be switched in other ways every two or three months so that it was always changing.

The final settlement of our Supreme Court class action case, *Salazar v. Ramah Navajo Chapter*, which together with two previous settlements over ISDA contract support added up to $1.44 billion dollars distributed to all North American Native tribes, made it possible for me to work pro bono for the Navajo Code Talkers and other nonprofits that I represented over the years, beginning with the first settlement. But the Code Talkers work was the most sustained, most vibrant and the most meaningful to me. My wife and I were able to donate toward the making of a documentary about their history: "Navajo Code Talkers: A Journey of Remembrance." For this purpose, we accompanied the Code Talkers still living and in stable health back to their battlefields. The money we gave was not enough to do the whole project, but it was enough to sustain some planning of this trip. Sam Billison and I, for example, went to Hollywood several times to talk with producers. At that point, we had heard that MGM was preparing a fictional motion picture about the Navajo Code Talkers, which came out as "Windtalkers," and we wanted to persuade them to give money to the Code Talkers Association for this project to take their local fighters back to the battlefields and film it. We actually managed to persuade them to give $100,000, which was great. Then we began planning the expedition.

A person in New Mexico who worked for the New Mexico Film Board was the father of a good friend of my second daughter, Lisa. I consulted him about getting New Mexico to underwrite the film project. The state didn't have the money, but through this person and his connections, we got in touch with a filmmaker from Michigan, George Colburn. He had a lot of experience doing documentaries, and we asked for his help in arranging all the logistics and then taking five or six Code Talkers back to the battlefields.

We wanted to go to every major battlefield that the Marine Code Talkers had fought in, starting with Guadalcanal. The MGM money basically funded the first trip in 2005. Tragically, Sam Billison had died before that could take place, and he was given a Marine Corps flyover ceremonial service at his home in the middle of the Navajo reservation 40 miles or so west of Window Rock. I distinctly remember that November day, when we went to a fairly barren cemetery, and there were lots of people there. The Code Talkers wore their colorful yellow uniforms with red trim. In the middle of it, the Marine Corps had arranged for a flyover. They call it the Missing Man Formation, in which three aircraft would fly in a V formation low enough over the cemetery to be seen, then one abruptly flies out, representing the fallen soldier. The other jets continue at level flight until they are out of view.

In December 2004, *The Guardian* included in their obituary for Billison: "Were it not for the Navajos," said Billison's commander Major Howard Connor, signal officer of the 5th Marine Division, "the Marines would never have taken Iwo Jima. Billison liked to remind Americans that the code was devised by 'a bunch of 16-year-old kids who were sheep herders.'"

In November of 2005, we took a first expedition to Guam as a staging base. My wife Andi and daughter Katy came along. Katy is a photographer. We went to Tinian, which is the small island next to Saipan where the Enola Gay, the B-29 bomber that dropped the first atomic bomb, took off. We stayed in Saipan, which is the largest of the Northern Mariana Islands. We had to fly back and forth in short hops, but we had a fantastic tour guide. He took us everywhere that the Marines had fought in the second World War, after the invasion of Cyprus and before the invasion of Saipan and Tinian.

I remember one episode when we were not too far from our hotel, which was on the beach, and we walked to a place that was still not developed. It was forested with pine trees and palms. As we were walking along, one of the Code Talkers, Keith Little, turned to me and said, in so many words: "Well, right over there is where my platoon was fighting and on either side of me were buddies of mine. They got killed, and I didn't get a scrape."

And he was so overtaken by that remembrance. It was a very soul-stirring moment.

On that first trip to Guam, we also toured the battlefields at Saipan. We went to that infamous cliff at one end of the island from which many of the civilians jumped to their deaths, thinking that the Americans were going to torture them, which was not true.

Then we went to Tinian, the small island next to Saipan. The airfield there where the Enola Gay took off is still government property. You can see the curvature of the earth when you're looking down the five-mile-long runway. We stayed in the luxurious gambling casino hotel on Tinian, which was so gaudy and out of place in these surroundings, a low-key island scene with one-story homes and lots of jungle and school kids singing in their native languages for the Marines who came along. That was very heartwarming.

At one point, we got to the airfield, and at one end there's an outdoor museum that shows where the pits were that housed the bombs, that the planes would be dragged over. The bomb base would be opened, and the atomic bombs would be loaded from these pits into the belly of the planes. We saw that, and then we had rented two cars, two big vans. In a light-hearted moment somebody said, let's drive down the runways. I think it was an east-west runway following the prevailing winds. We hopped in and barreled down the full length of the runway at about 100 miles an hour, pretending we were planes. And then the president of the school board association got mad at everybody. He was a kind of a moralist, sort of a severe man. He was not a jokester, not a hail-fellow-well-met. And he got mad at everybody for endangering our lives. I would be that person because I cannot stand amusement parks with roller coasters.

Then another incident happened on Tinian. The Japanese had had gun placements in the caves that opened up from a bluff overlooking the Pacific, and they put their artillery in there. As we were walking in the jungle up a slope to get to the caves, at one point I tried to take a step, and my foot wouldn't hit solid ground. I grabbed onto a tree and paused to examine the situation. I had almost fallen into an unmarked booby trap still left from World War II. The Japanese had dug these holes above the caves, and they put sharp spears at the bottom to try to kill U.S. soldiers who were marching to get them. And so, I nearly fell into this trap. I don't think there were any pointed spears at the bottom anymore, but if I had fallen, I would have plunged 20 to 30 feet and probably at least broken something if not killed myself.

The government of Saipan held a ceremony for the Code Talkers in front of their capital. It was very moving.

The second trip took place at the end of March in 2006. It was impressive and exciting. We went to Guam again to meet the governor. We had a ceremony with some schoolchildren, which was filmed. There were reporters everywhere when we went to Guam.

Then we left Guam, leaving at 5 a.m. on a jet with the goal of going to Iwo Jima. Once a year they open the Japanese military base, which has been there since World War II, for visitors, including almost every year for a contingent of former soldiers who fought there, along with their families. It's a two-hour flight from Guam. George Colburn had arranged for us to be at the beginning of the parade program for the tour of the island, and due to a mix-up we wound up at the end of the column, which meant that we couldn't tour the Japanese caves underground, where they hid during the terrible battle. But we toured the island on the surface.

We first went to the famous black beach where the Marines landed. It was too bad that Sam Billison wasn't with us, but that was the beach that he was talking about when he said he was diving to reconnoiter the beach and see what was going on before the invasion. We walked around that beach for a good hour. Mount Suribachi dominates the whole area. And then we spent a couple of hours at a ceremony at which retired military officials and diplomats from both sides gave speeches, which were fairly perfunctory. I can't remember what they said. There was translation from Japanese to English and English to Japanese. You could tell that the American soldiers who were there, former generals and former officers and enlisted men, were still angry, still very emotional. It was a horrendous battle.

We went to Okinawa, and we had a tour of the battlefields there—the last, horrific battle of World War II in June of 1945.

My daughter Ashley, who was with us this time, had spent two years in Japan as a teacher and speaks Japanese. She was talking to a guard who spoke Japanese while we were filming. Then suddenly one of the Code Talkers walked by, and the guard of this military historical site just stopped talking and went over and hugged the Code Talker, a former Marine, who was in uniform. There were moments like that throughout this trip.

In the summer of 2001, two months before the 9/11 disaster in New York when the Twin Towers were destroyed, there was a very emotional ceremony in the rotunda of the national Capitol, in which George W. Bush honored the Navajo Code Talkers. It was a congressional resolution sponsored by the senior U.S. Senator from New Mexico, Jeff Bingaman. The impressive rotunda is just underneath the prominent dome of the Capitol. It is a huge space with portraits of all the U.S. presidents, and the press were there. The whole place was packed with senators, congressmen, guests, relatives of the honorees, and several Navajo Code Talkers, who were to be celebrated that day with the Congressional Gold Medal. Families of the original 29 Navajo Code Talkers who had died would also receive medals. The Navajo Code Talkers wore colorful, orange military-style uniforms, which made them stand out from everyone else.

As we were sitting there, I started chatting with the woman next to me, who was a reporter from Agence France-Presse. The Code Talkers stood scattered close by. She asked me at one point, "Why doesn't anybody know about this story of the Navajo Code Talkers?" And, in an ordinary tone of voice I immediately answered, "Because Navajos don't brag."

The Code Talkers who were nearest to us heard me. As I spoke, I glanced their way and saw them give a quick nod of the head. So subtle. Just the head. They didn't turn around. They didn't say anything. They just nodded their heads.

Mike with Nelly (Code Talker Keith Little's wife) and Code Talkers Sam Sandoval and Sam Tso. Photo by Katy Gross

MY VISIT TO THE NATIONAL CIVIL RIGHTS MUSEUM

In October 2004, I took a late afternoon flight to Memphis to see an eye specialist the following day. At 10:00 a.m. I went to his office in a suburb and was out in half an hour. I was told to come back later that afternoon for a final procedure. What to do in the meantime? I remembered there was a civil rights museum in downtown Memphis and decided to visit it. I caught a cab just outside the doctor's office and asked to be taken to the museum. The cabbie gave me a quizzical look, but didn't say anything. Off we went into the rain.

Soon the spiffy suburb was no more. Split-level houses and manicured lawns gave way to urban grime and seediness. Honking cars and big trucks, traffic lights on every corner and constant noise replaced the eye doctor's prim neighborhood. We were surrounded by multi-storied factories and warehouses whose windows had not been washed in decades, along with billboards hawking everything from peep shows to lighting fixtures. A few minutes later, we pulled into a deserted parking lot and stopped near a sign heralding the National Civil Rights Museum.

No one, not even a car, was in sight. The urban decay had given way to a small island of quiet tranquility. I paid, and the taxi driver quickly took off. In the lifeless parking lot, I stood right below the terrace in front of room 306, where Martin Luther King Jr., age 39, had been assassinated by James Earl Ray. I was alone with Martin's ghost. From a shabby hotel visible 300 yards across the other side of the parking lot, now part of the museum, James Earl Ray[61] had fired the single bullet

61. There was controversy over whether Ray was the assassin. He was tried, convicted and sent to jail for the rest of this life. Throughout, he

that killed Martin Luther King while he had stood on the landing just above where I was standing.

I had memories of Rev. King in sharp focus, as I had seen and heard him at Brown University in my senior year in the fall of 1963, and again during the Meredith March in Mississippi in 1966 when, with several other Brown students, I had been a tutor of incoming freshmen at Tougaloo College. We had been provided with dormitory rooms and food, but nothing else. None of us got paid.

On June 26 that year in Jackson, Mississippi, a short drive south of Tougaloo College, James Meredith spoke at the culminating rally of the Meredith March. On June 6, he started out on a solitary, 220-mile march in Memphis, describing it as a "march against fear," after having been denied admission to law school at the University of Mississippi. He wanted to call attention to racism and voter discrimination in the South. Just two days in, he was hit with birdshot fired from a rifle by Aubrey Norvell, a white man. Shortly after he was struck in the head, neck, back and legs, an image of Meredith lying on the dusty highway was taken by an AP cub photographer and published nationwide. Meredith's wounds required time recuperating at a hospital. Norvell was apprehended at the scene, pleaded guilty and spent 18 months of a five-year sentence in prison.

Civil rights leaders including Martin Luther King, Stokely Carmichael and Floyd McKissick came to see Meredith at the hospital and decided to carry on the Meredith March. Eventually, James Meredith was released and managed to rejoin the demonstration. What had grown to dozens of marchers eventually swelled to thousands, and at the June 26 rally in Jackson, Mississippi, an estimated 15,000 people gathered.

Meanwhile, a team of Brown University students, including me and Joel Pasternak, had arrived on the Tougaloo College campus just a few days before the march ended. Meredith, along with other civil rights and Black Power leaders and the growing flock of co-marchers, rested on the lush, rural Tougaloo campus, an island of tranquility alongside Highway 55. For a couple of days, Tougaloo became the civil rights center of the country. Leaders huddled on the campus debating each other over Black Power versus less confrontational approaches to making the white world

---

maintained that he was innocent. Most who have looked at the evidence and tracked other possible assassins have concluded that Ray was the murderer of Martin Luther King.

respect Black people. Martin Luther King was, of course, a main figure. He was relaxed and joyful throughout the week and into the finale at the Mississippi State Capitol. We "Brunonians," a corps of mostly pale-faces, got caught up in the enthusiasm. Other major figures like Claude Brown, Stokely Carmichael, Whitney Young and Ralph Abernathy were there, along with many entertainers including Sammy Davis Junior, Dick Gregory and a slew of other famous folks who gathered to support Meredith's final march into Jackson. Meredith enjoyed the goodwill and harmony—a welcome contrast to his previous journey along the Mississippi highway.

The march from Tougaloo to the Mississippi Capitol that Sunday took five or more hours. All the Brown summer volunteers joined thousands of other marchers, trekking 14 miles in the hot sun to Jackson—except for Joel Pasternack and me. The two of us cheated. We were lazy and drove my car to the State Capitol hours before the marchers arrived to get a good place near the stage where a rally was to take place. When the activities began in front of the State Capitol, we stood just a few feet from the podium from where Meredith and other dignitaries would speak. The marchers and attendees filled the entire space behind us.

Now, 38 years after the Meredith March, I couldn't bring myself to climb the steps to the landing right above me at the Lorraine Motel, where Dr. King had been shot to death on April 4, 1968, which was now integrated into the museum. In the drizzle I stood frozen. Memories of hearing him at Brown University in the fall of 1963 speaking to a large crowd in Sayles Hall, the University's main auditorium, echoed in my head. Martin was vibrant, often funny, his booming voice with a southern cadence talking about bringing us all together. He gave a stirring speech to the packed crowd, at times loud and strong and other times soft and gentle, almost whispering. His relaxed and approachable presence had loomed large for me ever since that summer of 1966 when the Meredith March swarmed onto the Tougaloo campus.

Now, standing in the drizzle at the spot where Martin was assassinated, I was alone with his ghost, as the parking lot in Memphis was deathly quiet. At first, I thought I was in the wrong place or that the museum was closed. The stark scene was ominously ordinary. It was hard to believe that a world-shaking tragedy had taken place right here. It seemed that something more should be here to commemorate that event.

I went to the entrance at the end of the parking lot. It was open. I paid a nominal fee and checked my brief case and coat. As I did so, I could still hear Martin's voice echoing in my head: "I may not get there with you. But I want you to know tonight that we, as a people, will get to the Promised Land...."

As I entered the museum, I was fascinated. But I didn't have much time before my next eye appointment. The exhibits were divided into epochs of Black history in the United States. On the self-guided tour, each memorable event had its own display and was organized into a life-sized diorama or an interactive exhibit, beginning with the slave ships. They told the story of the multiple centuries of atrocities visited on Black Africans who were treated no better than pack animals by their white plantation overseers.

The display of the African slave ships depicted the cargo hold in which the abducted men and women endured a months-long voyage with no escape. The slaves often drowned when seas were rough. It took one to six months to cross the Atlantic. There was no hygiene. As many as half did not survive the journey across the Atlantic. Survivors arrived emaciated, sick and woefully underweight. In ports from New England to the South they and their offspring were sold into slavery. Small children were ripped from the breasts of feeding mothers; fathers and mothers were separated from their children never to see each other again. All would spend their lives in forced labor. The stages of Black persecution were graphically depicted.

Centuries later the Nazis invented gas chambers to exterminate Jews in assembly line fashion. Such efficiency did not exist in the centuries of Black slavery. Nor was commerce in slavery confined to the South. Providence, Rhode Island, with its fine harbor and its Ivy League college, my alma mater Brown University, grew wealthy from slavery and played a central role in the slave trade. In the 1700s half of all American slaving voyages sailed from Rhode Island.[62] Indeed slavery became the economic foundation of the United States. Upon arrival in slave markets such as the ones in Charleston, South Carolina, and Providence, Rhode Island, slaves were fattened up a bit and then, chained to auction blocks, sold to the highest bidder.

---

62. *See,* Brown University's study of slavery in Rhode Island, *Slavery and Justice Report,* 2d *edition,* copyright 2022. That study was initiated by the first woman and only Black president of Brown U., Ruth J. Simmons.

Perhaps no group of human beings in recorded history has been subjected to such systematic, sustained persecution, hatred, indifference and maltreatment as the enslaved Africans brought to this continent. I say this as the child of Holocaust survivors from Austria. Systematic murder of Jews may have killed more people than slavery of Blacks did. But measuring degrees of depravity is pointless. Ultimately all forms of racial, sexual and ethnic discrimination are abominable.

> "The portrait that emerged, shared in the first section of the Slavery and Justice Report, was not of a few evil men enriching themselves on slavery, but of an entire economy organized around enslavement. As one historian hosted by the Committee put it, slavery in New England was literally the business of 'the butcher, the baker, and the candlestick maker.'"
>
> – Rachel Chernos Lin (2002) *The Rhode Island Slave-Traders: Butchers, Bakers and Candlestick-Makers, Slavery & Abolition*, 23:3, 21-38.

After touring the main museum, I went over to the motel. I saw the room Ray occupied and the window through which he had pointed his rifle at King and dispatched the magnetic, world-famous Civil Rights Movement leader. The room startled me. It was deplorably ordinary. I reflected that prejudice, brutality and hatred have dogged human beings since time immemorial. Ridding the world of such cruelty is a never-ending task.

It was now time to leave for my final eye procedure. The same uniformed Black guard who had taken my belongings two hours earlier was still there. I gave him my ticket stub, and he handed me my belongings. As I took them, I could not contain myself. I said, "You know I'm in a picture out there." And I told him about the last display which I had just seen—a large blow-up of the crowd gathered at the finale of the Meredith March in front of the Mississippi State Capitol. The caption read something like: "Largest gathering of Blacks in the history of Mississippi." Except, in the left front only a few feet away from Meredith at the podium were two clearly identifiable white people—Joel and me. Joel was sitting cross-legged on the grass facing the camera, and I was standing next to him with our colleagues' cameras draped around my neck.

At that, the guard's mouth dropped. Without a word he sprang out of his chair, opened the door to the cubicle, came around to the front, and hugged me. And I cried.

ACKNOWLEDGMENTS

would like to thank C. Bryant Rogers, my co-counsel, for his professional collaboration and guidance throughout most of my career and for his ongoing friendship. I extend my sincere appreciation to Alfred Mathewson and Kevin Washburn for generously sharing their perspectives for this book. Sincere thanks to Anita Pfeiffer, Bessie Randolph and Beverly Coho, Mary Cohoe, Betty Gress, John Loehr and John Amarant whose voices and visionary leadership in the early days of self-determination education made a lasting difference for all Native Americans. Deep gratitude goes to my brilliant daughters, Ashley and Lisa, for conducting insightful interviews; to Katy for creating beautiful photographs for this book; and to my wife Andi and my three daughters who reviewed my drafts and straightened out some of my wild stories. My brother Tom has been my longest friend and confidant throughout this journey.

Special thanks to Beverly Wooldridge, my office assistant and friend who masterfully organized all aspects of my professional life for 24 years. My sincere gratitude to Ivonne DeWolf and Nyima Phoenix who continue to provide indispensable assistance in my office as well as friendship and support. Marita Prandoni has been my ever cheerful editor throughout this project, providing fact-checking, research, and keeping me up-to-date on pertinent developments in the wider world. Our conversations in German stimulate my childhood memories. I have also benefited regularly from her scrumptious, home-baked treats. My heartfelt appreciation to my publisher, Jennifer Browdy, for her patient assistance and expertise in disseminating my story, and to Rick K. Theis for the final polish.

I could not have completed this years-long project without the help of these and other wonderful people.

ABOUT THE AUTHOR

Michael P. Gross, a retired attorney who resides in Santa Fe, New Mexico, spent more than five decades collaborating with Native Americans to find a path to self-determination, greatly affecting a new relationship between tribes and the federal government. Fresh out of Yale Law School in 1968, Gross became a legal warrior in the War on Poverty. His first case was to represent a small Navajo community in Ramah, New Mexico, to re-open their school, which had been closed against their will.

Gross's initiative to raise seed money and incorporate an all-Navajo school board in Ramah resulted in the first grassroots self-determination school in the U.S., ushering in an end to centuries-long forced assimilation. The Ramah model was named in the executive draft that became federal policy, codifying tribal authority to administer funds and control their own educational activities and culminating in the far-reaching Indian Self-Determination and Education Assistance Act of 1975 (PL 93-638).

Later in his career, Gross won two major lawsuits in the U.S. Supreme Court, the second, a class action case on behalf of almost every tribe in the United States. His persistence in achieving justice for Native Americans instigated a giant leap forward for Indian self-determination, which continues to protect their languages, cultural heritage and basic human rights.

www.Ingramcontent.com/pod-product-compliance
Lightning Source LLC
Chambersburg PA
CBHW032221050726
47591CB00001B/207